*Stunning Males
and Powerful Females*

NEW PERSPECTIVES ON GENDER IN MUSIC

Editorial Advisors
Susan C. Cook
Beverley Diamond

*A list of books in the series appears
at the end of this book.*

Stunning Males and Powerful Females

Gender and Tradition in East Javanese Dance

CHRISTINA SUNARDI

University of Illinois Press
URBANA, CHICAGO, AND SPRINGFIELD

This book contains material that was:

First published as the article "Pushing at the Boundaries of the Body: Cultural Politics and Cross-Gender Dance in East Java," by Christina Sunardi, from *Bijdragen tot de Taal-, Land- en Volkenkunde* Volume 165 Number 4, pp. 459–492. Copyright © 2009 Koninklijk Instituut voor Taal-, Land- en Volkenkunde. Reproduced with permission from Koninklijke Brill NV.

First published as the article "Making Sense and Senses of Locale through Perceptions of Music and Dance in Malang, East Java," by Christina Sunardi, from *Asian Music* Volume 41 Issue 1, pp. 89–126. Copyright © 2010 by the University of Texas Press. All rights reserved. Reproduced with permission from the University of Texas Press.

First published as the article "Negotiating Authority and Articulating Gender: Performer Interaction in Malang, East Java," by Christina Sunardi, from *Ethnomusicology* Volume 55 Number 1 (Winter 2011), pp. 31–54. Copyright © 2011 by the Society for Ethnomusicology. Reproduced with permission from the Society for Ethnomusicology.

First published as Sunardi, Christina (author) and Timothy P. Daniels (editor), "Complicating Senses of Masculinity, Femininity, and Islam through the Performing Arts in Malang, East Java," in *Performance, Popular Culture, and Piety in Muslim Southeast Asia*, pp. 135–160, 2013. Copyright © Timothy P. Daniels, 2013. All rights reserved. Published by PALGRAVE MACMILLAN®. Reproduced with permission of Palgrave Macmillan. The full published version of this publication is available from http://us.macmillan.com/performancepopularcultureandpietyinmuslimsoutheastasia/TimothyPDaniels and http://www.palgraveconnect.com/pc/doifinder/10.1057/9781137318398.

© 2015 by the Board of Trustees
of the University of Illinois
All rights reserved
Manufactured in the United States of America
1 2 3 4 5 C P 5 4 3 2 1
♾ This book is printed on acid-free paper.

Library of Congress Cataloging-in-Publication Data
Sunardi, Christina.
Stunning males and powerful females: gender and
tradition in East Javanese dance / Christina Sunardi.
pages   cm. — (New perspectives on gender in music)
Includes bibliographical references and index.
ISBN 978-0-252-03895-2 (cloth: alk. paper)
ISBN 978-0-252-08059-3 (pbk.: alk. paper)
ISBN 978-0-252-09691-4 (ebook)
1. Folk dancing, Javanese—Indonesia—Java.
2. Dance—Indonesia—Java.
3. Dance—Social aspects—Indonesia—Java.
4. Dance—Sex differences. 5. Java (Indonesia)—Social
life and customs.
I. Title.
GV1703.I532J389   2015
793.3'195982—dc23   2014037012

To my mother,
Lois Roland,
in memory of my father,
Charles Roland,
and to my husband,
Sunardi

Contents

Note on Conventions   ix
Preface: Inspiration   xiii
Acknowledgments   xxxi

1. Aims and Approaches   1
2. Maintaining Female Power through Male Style Dance   33
3. Negotiating Pressures in Terms of Gender:
   Male Dancers and Female Style Dance   63
4. Constructing Gender and Tradition
   through Senses of History   94
5. Maintaining the Representation of Female Power
   through *Beskalan Putri*   127
6. Where Tradition, Power, and Gender Intersect:
   Performer Interactions   158

Afterword   183
Notes   185
Glossary   193
Works Cited   195
Index   211

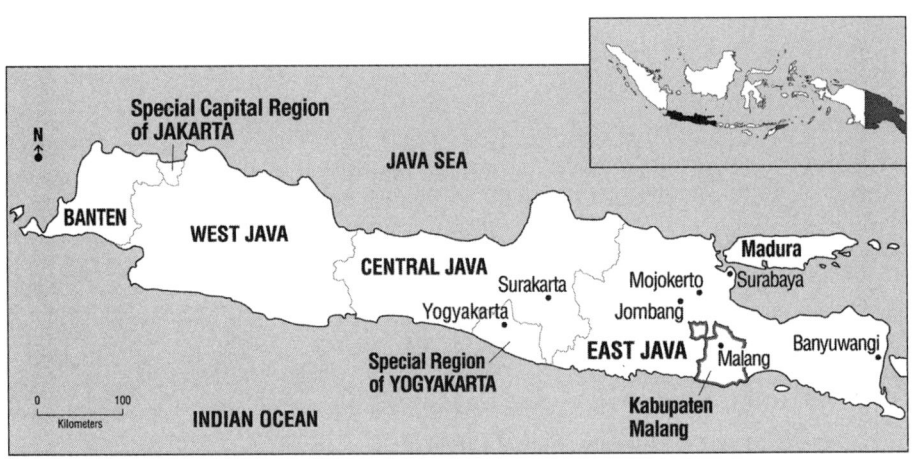

Map 0.1: Map of Java showing provinces, special regions, selected cities (including the city of Malang), and the regency (*kabupaten*) of Malang. Map drawn by David Wolbrecht. Copyright © 2013 University of Washington.

Note on Conventions

Malang, "east Java," and "East Java"

Malang is both a regency (*kabupaten*)[1] and a city that lie within the cultural region of east Java, one of several cultural areas within the province of East Java, Indonesia (Map 0.1). Unless I specify "the city of Malang," my references to Malang are references to the regency. As R. Anderson Sutton demonstrated in his study of regional gamelan traditions in Java, national political divisions (including the names of provinces) and cultural regions do not always neatly correlate (1991). Following Sutton's approach, I use lowercase letters to refer to cultural regions (i.e., east Java, central Java) and uppercase letters to refer to names of Indonesian provinces (i.e., East Java, Central Java) (Sunardi 2010a: 120 n3). The traditions of music, dance, and theater that musicians and dancers in Malang I consulted referred to as east Javanese are from the central part of the province of East Java, including the areas of Malang, Mojokerto, and Surabaya, corroborating Sutton's outlining of this cultural region as "the triangular area marked by Surabaya, Mojokerto (or Jombang), and the coast south of Malang" (1991: 121; see also Sunardi 2010a: 89).

The dances around which this book revolves—*Beskalan Putri, Beskalan Lanang, Ngremo Putri, Ngremo Lanang, Ngremo Tayub,* and masked dance—are east Javanese (*Jawa timuran*), meaning that these dances are from the cultural region of east Java and associated primarily with ethnic Javanese culture of this region. This is not to suggest, however, that these arts are practiced and supported exclusively by ethnic Javanese of east Java or that these arts have not been influenced by other regional traditions. Performing arts that are related to but distinct from those of east Java are linked to other cultural regions in East Java, such as Banyuwangi at the eastern end of Java and the island of Madura to the north (Sutton 1991: 121; Crawford 2001: 329). When performers in Malang spoke about "central Javanese" arts, they were usually referring to the arts of Surakarta (a court city in the province of Central Java) and sometimes to the arts of Yogyakarta (a court city and special administrative area in south central Java). My use of "central Javanese" follows suit and includes the arts of the Surakarta and Yogyakarta areas (see also Sunardi 2010a: 89). It is important to note also that the connections performers drew between styles of arts and particular regions did not mean that these regional forms were exclusively practiced in the region with which they were associated.

Spelling and Names

I have spelled Indonesian and Javanese words according to standard conventions used in Indonesia. In older spellings, which some individuals used for their names, "oe" is used instead of "u," "tj" is used instead of "c," "dj" is used instead of "j," and "j" is used instead of "y." Because I encountered many ways of spelling the dance *Ngremo* in Javanese (including different ways to accent the "e"), I have followed my principal gamelan teacher's advice and used the Indonesian spelling—*Ngremo*.

I capitalize the names of dances, such as *Ngremo*. Lowercase letters are used to refer to types of music, dance, or theater, whether in Indonesian, Javanese, or an English translation. I also capitalize styles associated with the name of a place that is capitalized, such as Malangan (in the style of Malang) (see also Sunardi 2011: 52 n8).

While using terms of address appropriately is critical in speaking Indonesian and Javanese politely in Java, I have chosen mostly not to use honorifics in this book mainly because their usage is not fixed. The appropriate term of address a person uses when speaking to another is determined by a number of factors, including the relationship of a speaker to an addressee, the context, and their social and cultural status at a particular moment. For example, a person I may address as "father" or "mother," another person may address as "brother" or "sister." I mean no disrespect to the people I consulted by not using honorifics. When referring to a publication for which the author used an honorific as part of his or her name, however, I do include the honorific when referencing the author's name.

Notation

I have notated musical examples primarily, but not entirely, in the *kepatihan* system, a standard system used in Java in which numbers are used to represent pitches, a period is used to designate a rest, and the symbols indicated in Figure 0.a are used to indicate colotomic instruments. For basic drum patterns, however, I depart from *kepatihan* notation to write the syllables of the strokes as I learned them from my principal teacher Kusnadi. These syllables closely resemble the sound made on the drum. My hope is that this is easier to read for nonspecialists than the symbols typically used to notate drum patterns in *kepatihan* notation. George Ruckert's (2004) use of syllables to notate patterns played on the North Indian *tabla* (a set of two drums) inspired my usage of east Javanese syllables.

Returning to *kepatihan* notation, a horizontal line above a number, rest, or drum syllable indicates a rhythmic subdivision. Underlined numbers for vocal melodies indicate that a syllable of a word is sung over more than one note. There is no one standard tuning of pitches in Java; however, one way to approximately equate Western pitches to the Javanese pitches used in the two tuning systems of *sléndro* and *pélog* is as follows: for *sléndro*, 1 = d-flat, 2 = e-flat, 3 = g-flat, 5 = a-flat, 6 = b-flat; and for *pélog*, 1 = d, 2 = e, 3 = f, 4 = a-flat, 5 = a, 6 = b-flat, and 7 = c. Pitches without dots indicate the middle register. A dot above the number indicates the upper register while a dot below the note indicates the lower register.

Colotomic instruments are indicated by placing the symbols in Figure 0.a above a particular beat.

⌣   =   *Kempul* – set of smaller hanging gongs

⌢   =   *Kenong* – set of horizontal gongs

◯   =   Gong – large gong or gongs

Figure 0.a: Symbols for colotomic instruments.

The drum patterns and vocal melodies that are notated are basic patterns and melodies as I learned them from my teachers and would typically be performed with more elaboration or ornamentation. For the vocal melodies, the rhythm is somewhat free and thus only loosely indicated. There is some flexibility as to exactly when a singer may begin and end particular phrases within the structure of the piece, although the singer ideally should sing the last note of a phrase going to the gong tone shortly before or on the gong stroke and typically sustains the last note past the gong.

Preface
Inspiration

I did not expect that my derrière would be the subject of discussion between a former dancer in his eighties, a loud, energetic middle-aged woman, a young man who was one of my masked dance teachers, and a middle-aged male dressed like a woman selling tofu in an east Javanese village in the Malang area. And yet, there I was. Or rather, there my derrière was.

Muliono, a strong but quiet young dancer had driven me through treacherous, hilly, rural roads to interview the old man, Supeno, about the east Javanese female style dance Beskalan Putri *"in past times" (as performers often put it). One of Supeno's daughters, who was either visiting or lived with him, took the rather unusual opportunity to meet a visitor from America. Noticing the activity while making rounds, the tofu seller, who also had been a dancer, stopped in and joined the conversation. Before long we were talking about spiritual knowledge and costuming tricks males used when they performed female style dance. Knowing that I was studying* Beskalan Putri, *Supeno's daughter imagined me in costume with a bit of padding to enhance my buttocks.*

"If Auntie America were like that, she would look better, she is tall. She is tall, her butt, yes, like that for real!" she exclaimed, talking about me in the third person to be polite, as is typical in Java. "And it would be really good, I'm telling you! Oh Dad, she's got the body!"

"She's got the body," the tofu seller added. The woman continued to cluck away about my figure as the tofu seller considered how she or Supeno might look tall.

"Yes, like those Arabs," Supeno observed.

"For sure!" agreed the tofu seller.

"For sure!" agreed the woman. "Her butt would be better with that!"

Picturing myself with a bit more flesh (I was self-conscious about looking a bit stringy in Javanese dance costumes), I laughed, "So that it would be better, yes?"

"Yes, well yes!" the tofu seller declared as though any other possibility were idiotic.

"Sexier," Mul softly stated.

"Sexier, yes," I echoed. Muliono's shyness hindered him from speaking much to me most of the time even though he was one of my masked dance teachers. Under the circumstances at Supeno's house that day, I appreciated Mul's comment as a sincere but innocent compliment and lesson in performing female style dance. My moment with Mul quickly passed, however, as the woman said over us, "You must, Auntie! You must!"

Supeno instructed happily, "You can make it yourself. Find sponging first." Although Supeno had stopped performing Beskalan Putri decades ago and had become a *modin*, a village Islamic religious official, he had clearly not forgotten how to look like a beautiful woman.

"Ah-huh, ah-huh," I nodded.

"Add a bra, you can do that," he continued.

"Ah-huh," I said repeatedly to indicate my interest.

The woman said softly, day-dreamily, "I like it."

The tofu seller and Supeno's daughter dominated the continuing chatter about costuming and my figure. They arrived on the availability of fake eyelashes nowadays. In the middle of it all, Supeno sang a little drumming, leading the tofu seller to demonstrate how to move one's hips to that particular pattern.

Supeno rather suddenly ended the foray by announcing that these other details could be given after the steps and movements had been learned.

* * *

The power of femaleness as expressed and embodied through presentational dance performance was indeed no light matter. In encouraging me to sway my hips, pad my rear, or don fake eyelashes, the people at Supeno's house that day were communicating the importance of embodying femininity, not just for the visual impact, but for everything that the power of femaleness and dance performance contributed to their senses of tradition, history, and identity. My captivation with the ways musicians and dancers have approached this power has led to *Stunning Males and Powerful Females*, a book that explores how performers—males and females—have expressed, embodied, accessed, and continuously reproduced female power through east Javanese dance and its accompanying gamelan music (played on an ensemble comprised mostly of gongs, keyed percussion instruments, and drum[s]) in Malang. This book has grown out of and develops my earlier work on performance in this fascinating place (Sunardi 2007, 2009, 2010a, 2010b, 2011, 2012, 2013).

I found Malang to be a complex and vibrant locale. Known in Java (and beyond) for its breathtaking mountains, cool climate, and apple orchards, Malang is home to people of diverse ethnicities, including those of ethnic Javanese, Madurese, Chinese, and Arab backgrounds. Ethnic diversity is characteristic of other places in East Java as well, sometimes contributing to complex senses of ethnic identity, as in the case of people of mixed Madurese and Javanese heritage in Probolinggo explored by Konstantinos Retsikas (2007a, 2007b). Religious diversity has also characterized Malang, despite the large Muslim majority. One of my teachers was Catholic. Hinduism is also practiced, particularly in the Tengger mountain communities that span the regencies of Malang, Pasuruan, Probolinggo, and Lumajang (Hefner 1985: 44). Local Javanese spiritual beliefs and practices are also quite present. And certainly no less important, as I explore in this book, is the diversity of gender identities and sexual orientations. I was so entranced with Malang, its people, and its arts that after a year of fieldwork from September 2005 to August 2006, I returned, writing parts of my dissertation and conducting more fieldwork there from mid-January to early September 2007, and have made multiple trips to visit my teachers since then.

During my fieldwork and ensuing visits I resided in the village of Tulusbesar (or Tulus Besar) in the subdistrict of Tumpang. I lived near the Mangun Dharma Art Center (Padepokan Seni Mangun Dharma, or PSMD), which was about twenty-three kilometers east of the city of Malang. While I studied primarily with artists who lived in Tumpang and in Poncokusumo, a neighboring subdistrict, I also consulted and observed artists in other parts of the regency and in the city of Malang (Map 0.2).

Living in Tulusbesar, which is fairly close to the hub of Tumpang, felt much like living in a town. Tumpang's market (bustling with people at certain times of the day), stores, shops, banks, minivans used as minibuses, horse-drawn carts, pedicabs (*becak*), motorcycles used as public transportation (*ojek*), post

Map 0.2: Map of the regency of Malang showing the village of Tulusbesar, the subdistricts of Tumpang and Poncokusumo, and the city of Malang. Map drawn by David Wolbrecht. Copyright © 2013 University of Washington.

office, medical facilities, salons, mosques, mushollas, schools, police station, military office, centuries-old ruins, food stalls, traveling vendors, and more made for a lively community. At the same time, I also had the strong sense that I was living in a rural area. Rice fields and fields of other agricultural products including sugar cane, corn, tomatoes, and chili peppers—to name a few—were ubiquitous. It was not unusual to see a man walking a bull or guiding a multitude of ducks down the road with a long bamboo rod. The caws of roosters, clucks of hens, and chirps of chicks were a normal part of the sonic atmosphere. Poncokusumo, where I also had many lessons, was a bit more rural and stunningly beautiful with its agricultural fields worked into the mountainous terrain. The importance of the land and animals was hard to miss.

Most of the artists—musicians, dancers, puppeteers—I came to know best in Tumpang and Poncokusumo worked jobs in addition to performing in order to make ends meet. One of my dance teachers made costumes and masks. Another, when I first met him, worked as a gardener at PSMD, a job he ending up leaving to eventually become a meatball soup (*bakso*) vendor. One musician was a woodworker. Some artists collected rocks or sand out of rivers. Others worked in farming or in construction. Some were teachers. The situation was similar to Gillian Roberts's observation that "[m]ost of the musicians, dancers and craftspeople who contribute to the work of PSMD . . . have other jobs as well, some as teachers, others as civil servants, others as farmers or labourers" (2001: 5). In general, the artists I met worked hard to make a living and to support their families in difficult economic circumstances.

Although Tumpang and Poncokusumo had a rural vibe, many of its residents were quite cosmopolitan. Through television, newspapers, and word of mouth people were generally fairly up to date on current national and world events. Young people in particular were up to date on fashion trends and celebrity gossip. People regularly went to the city of Malang for various reasons, such as to work, to shop, to go to school, and for recreation. For various reasons, many people I came to know had traveled to other parts of Java, other places in Indonesia, and/or abroad—or had family members who had done so, such as my dance teacher who had a son working in Malaysia at the time of my fieldwork. I also met or heard about a few people who had made the *haj*, the pilgrimage to Mecca. Technologically, too, people were "plugged in" to the extent that they could afford. Cell phones and texting were a regular part of life. Indeed, the people I met made Malang a fascinating, beautiful, and inspirational place in which to study the complexities of music, dance, and gender.

Situating This Book as a Product of Fieldwork: Interacting with Individuals

This book stems from a deep investment in ethnographic methodologies, in the agency of the people consulted, and in a commitment "to take them on their own terms as best you can" (Wong 2004: 21). At the same time, doing fieldwork is complicated. It involves perceiving as well as being perceived within complex webs of power relations informed by hundreds of years of history that shape the specific moments of interaction between "subject" and "researcher" (Seeger 2004: 20; Gupta and Ferguson 1997; Barz and Cooley 1997). I could not agree more with Timothy Cooley, who observes that, "[a]s individual fieldworkers, our shadows join with others, past and present, in a web of histories: personal histories, the histories of our academic field, and the histories of those we study" (1997: 5), and with Deborah Wong, who writes that "[t]he artifact that the ethnographer creates may be a text, but it emerges from relationships with real people and an accountability that is potentially life changing" (2004: 22). My own relationships with performers and my own feelings of accountability toward them have been among the strongest factors pushing me to see this book through to completion. Moreover, as Michael Bakan (1999) and Michelle Kisliuk (2000) highlight by reflecting on their own experiences, analysis of the researcher's relationships with the people who are the subjects of study recognizes the roles that researchers and subjects play in generating the instances, and often unexpected results, that lead to new insights during fieldwork (see also Sunardi 2011: 37).

Interactions with artists, and with my dance and music teachers in particular, have made this book very much a product of collaboration, albeit mediated through my voice, understandings, and aims. While conducting fieldwork, I spent most of my time in private lessons, practicing (alone or with another artist), observing and/or participating in rehearsals or group practice sessions, observing and/or documenting performances, and conducting interviews. Much of what I learned was gained through conversations that occurred during my private lessons, at practice sessions or rehearsals, and at performances, in some of which I played a gamelan instrument or danced. My studies of performance practice—particularly dancing, drumming, and singing—and experiences performing have been critical to my understanding of ways in which musicians and dancers made sense of gender. At the same time, chitchat with taxi drivers, with minivan/minibus drivers, with audience members or guests at performances, with performers backstage, and with others as I was out and about or as people (including artists) dropped in to visit my husband and me at the home we were renting was also important to my understandings of east Javanese arts, senses of gender, and a range of individuals' perspectives.

My private lessons were particularly rich moments of interaction. In the course of hours-long lessons, my teachers imparted their memories of past performance practices, their own learning processes, and the secrets of performing well, at times entrusting me with knowledge that to them was special, personal, and spiritual. They insisted on my ability to learn dance movements, drumming patterns, melodic elaborations on other gamelan instruments, and vocal melodies, even when I—exhausted, frustrated, insecure about what exactly I was doing "in the field," sometimes on the brink of tears (and, on a few occasions, in tears)—was ready to give up. By pausing for us to drink some coffee, tea, or water together, offering a snack, or telling a story, they encouraged me with sensitivity and care.

My teachers were actively involved in other aspects of the research process. They facilitated my entry into arts communities by introducing me to other performers who then introduced me to others. My teachers helped me to organize recording and video sessions, took me to performances, and provided me opportunities to play or dance. No less crucial were their insights as we analyzed audio and video recordings, including my field recordings, and thought through issues together. Because these moments of interaction were also affected by who the agents—both the "subject" and the "researcher"— were at a particular time in their lives when the encounter occurred, and what the agents were feeling at a particular moment—curious about a new acquaintance, nervous in front of a new teacher, mad at a spouse, worried about finances, still sleepy from an afternoon nap, newly comfortable with their foreign student, remembering deceased loved ones—I have chosen to write much of this book in the past tense.

My relationships with my teachers, particular individuals with particular takes on the arts, have shaped the ways I have framed my analyses as well as the ways that I have come to understand and write about the performing arts in Malang. Kusnadi, a highly respected senior musician in Malang, was my primary gamelan teacher (Photograph 0.1). Born in 1944 in the village of Tulusbesar, he grew up in a family of performers that included an uncle who was a puppeteer and two brothers, one of whom, Djanam, is a musician and another of whom, Asbari, is a puppeteer and musician. Kusnadi began to play gamelan as a boy in the 1950s, mastering east Javanese and central Javanese styles of gamelan music and dance drumming over the course of his long career. At the time of my fieldwork, he was the director of the men's gamelan group at PSMD where he had worked since the center's founding in the 1980s (p.c., November 17, 2005; February 4, 2006). In addition to his musical activities, he and his wife ran a food stall (*warung*) at the market in Tumpang. Their daughter helped out, too. Teaching me several instruments several times a week, Kusnadi quickly became like a father. The musicians in his group, including the two aforementioned brothers, became like uncles. I have continued to study with him and practice with the musicians in his group during subsequent visits to Malang following my fieldwork and still regard him as an important teacher and mentor.

I might not have had this relationship with Kusnadi had it not been for M. Soleh Adi Pramono (b. 1951) and the American artist Karen Elizabeth Sekararum (b. 1964, Karen Elizabeth Schrieber), who at the time of my fieldwork were running PSMD as a husband-wife team.[1] Importantly, PSMD has provided a space for artists, students, scholars, and arts aficionados interested in performing, researching, studying, and sponsoring performances of a variety of Malangan music and dance practices, and has accomplished much in promoting and developing Malangan arts locally and nationally. Soleh, an artist who came from a family of performers and is a graduate of the college level dance academy in Yogyakarta, founded PSMD in the 1980s.[2] He was active there as a choreographer, puppet master, masked dance narrator, musician, and teacher. Karen Elizabeth, who had spent part of her childhood living and studying dance in Java, came to Malang in 1990 as a

Photograph 0.1. Kusnadi plays the principal drum (*kendhang*) used for the east Javanese dances discussed in this book, 2006.

graduate student in anthropology to pursue a language program, and moved to Tumpang after her language program ended to study dance with Soleh for her MA thesis (p.c., November 29, 2005). They eventually married and ran PSMD together. In addition to managing PSMD and performing as a PSMD artist, Karen Elizabeth had a successful career as an independent vocalist and dancer, performing in many parts of Java with some of the most sought-after puppeteers and frequently appearing on television (see also Roberts 2001: 5).

Soleh and Karen Elizabeth played instrumental roles in my fieldwork. Soleh helped me during the initial stages by inviting me to study at PSMD, sponsoring my research with the local immigration office, teaching me a masked dance, and introducing me to other arts organizations in Malang. He and Karen Elizabeth also helped my husband and me get settled in Tumpang and they introduced me to other performers as potential teachers and interviewees. Such contacts included the aforementioned Kusnadi as well as a number of other individuals who also became my teachers, including Budi Utomo (b. 1963; Photograph 0.2)—whose arts studio Sanggar Seni Setyotomo was also in Tumpang—Djupri (b. 1939; Photograph 0.3), B. Supriono Hadi Prasetya (b. 1976), Muliono (b. ca. 1976?),[3] and Stefanus Yacobus Suryantono (b. 1955). These contacts led me to others. For example, I met my other principal teacher Sumi'anah (b. 1955),

Photograph 0.2. Budi Utomo demonstrates a movement and position from the male style masked dance *Bapang*, 2006.

Photograph 0.3. Djupri with the author, 2006. (Photograph taken by Mr. Sunardi.)

through Kusnadi and Budi Utomo. Soleh and Karen Elizabeth also provided critical information and perspectives about the arts as accomplished artists and arts managers in their own rights.

Conversations and experiences performing with the central Javanese artist Didik Nini Thowok (b. 1954, Didik Hadiprayitno) have been no less important. I have come to know Didik and his work since the late 1990s over the course of my studying abroad and subsequent stints in Yogyakarta where he is based, and through his visits to and performances on the West Coast of the United States in 2003, 2004, and 2011. Didik, an internationally renowned artist, specializes in female style dances from Java, Bali, and other parts of Asia (see also Janarto 2005; Ross 2005; Mrázek 2005; Hatley 2008: 161–163, 167, 268; Hughes-Freeland 2008a, 2008b: 161–162). He has dedicated much of his artistic and scholarly life to raising awareness about cross-gender traditions in Indonesia and other parts of Asia.[4] He has also been contributing to the preservation and transformation of Javanese regional arts, including the Malangan dance *Beskalan Putri*. It was his hauntingly beautiful performance of this dance in San Francisco in 2003 that captivated my interest in Malangan arts in the first place, and it was he who first led me to PSMD and M. Soleh Adi Pramono in 2004 when he helped my husband and me make a preliminary visit to Malang to scout potential research sites.

Because most of my teachers and most of the other artists I consulted were male, male voices are at the core of this book. Of my principal teachers, Sumi'anah was the only woman. I have attempted, however, to somewhat balance male perspectives with the voices, perspectives, and experiences of the women I consulted, as well as my own perspectives as a female. Through analysis of the experiences of both males and females, I hope that this book balances a focus on women that has predominated in studies of gender in Southeast Asian studies (Andaya 2007: 127; Peletz 2006: 309).

As I worked with my teachers and other performers in Malang, I entered a complex and delicate network of professional and personal (including familial) relationships between the people I consulted. Each individual had particular relationships with other artists and particular positions within interrelated circles of other performers, sponsors, and institutions (see Brinner 2009: 163–212). Critical for me to consider as a researcher is that performers made decisions about what information to share with me in the context of their position(s) within these complex webs of professional and personal relationships. Moreover, each of these individuals had unique takes and, in some cases, worked to assert the cultural authority of his or her particular perspectives on and interpretations of dance and music.

The flexibility of dance and music in Malang further complicated matters. There were often different ways of performing the same dances and particular musical compositions in different areas of the regency (e.g., what performers identified as "east" vs. "south" Malang) and in different villages or hamlets of the same area (see Sunardi 2007: 38–50; 2010a: 89–91, 117–118). Different individuals, too, sometimes had their own approaches, and sometimes the same person performed or taught a dance differently on different occasions, as Gillian Roberts found (2001: 8). While the flexibility of dance and music certainly enriches the arts in Malang, it also meant that what was communicated or performed at a particular moment depended on who was consulted, how she or he interpreted the dance or music at that time, what he or she remembered, and what he or she decided to share with me as a foreign student.

Studying the Arts in Malang as a Tall-Broad-Shouldered-Foreign-But-Brown Female Researcher

Learning to dance and play music as a research strategy has heightened my awareness of the ways in which my own body—my sex, my color, my stature, and other aspects—affected how people interacted with me as I conducted fieldwork. The impact of my body as a researcher is critical to consider because "as a means of access to information" (Buckland 2006: 13), the researcher's body affects conclusions that are drawn from her or his particular experiences conducting fieldwork. Helen Thomas and Jamilah Ahmed productively highlight that "[t]he researcher's body is immersed in the field and is simultaneously outside the research (by means of its strangeness and lack of knowledge) and in the research (by the fact of its physical presence)" (2004: 3). My body was certainly strange and undeniably present. At the risk of self-indulgence, I take further cues from Nicole Beaudry (1997: 81–82) and Carol Babiracki (1997), who consider the impact their gender may have had on their fieldwork; from Eileen Hayes who creatively positions herself as a "mad black woman festigoer" (2010: 9–31);[5] from Tomie Hahn and the reflexive writing approach she takes in her study of Japanese dance (2007: 9–14); and from James Clifford to emphasize that I, as a heterosexual female American researcher of mixed race who was married to a Javanese man, was neither "an ungendered, unraced, sexually inactive subject interact[ing] . . . with interlocutors" (Clifford 1997: 202), nor was I perceived to be.

Attitudes toward me were complex. In some ways, many Javanese did not always seriously evaluate the quality of my dancing, singing, or drumming. More appealing for some performers and some in the general population was that I was a foreign woman. Like Sean Williams, who regularly performed a type of West Javanese aristocratic singing called *tembang Sunda* during the course of her fieldwork, I was in many ways "regarded locally as a novelty act" (2001: 13). When I expressed reservations about performing because I was not very good, I was reassured enthusiastically, "It is not necessary for you to worry. You are a foreigner. People will already like it. It does not have to be good." Doing my best to ignore the sting I sometimes felt (as I would have preferred to not perform at all than to perform prematurely and look completely foolish in front of an audience, even as a foreigner—especially in front of the usually rather large audiences that tended to amass to see a foreigner perform Javanese dance), I did my best to use these opportunities to participate, to observe, and to learn. In many cases, my foreignness gave me opportunities not offered to Javanese performers of equivalent or significantly higher ability. I thought, too, that if my participation benefited my teachers or others in the community in any way—from drawing audiences who wished to see a foreign dancer to enhancing a teacher's reputation for having a foreign student—at least that would be one way I could give something back to those who had given me so much by letting me hang out in their communities and tag along with them to their gigs.

The question of how to compensate research consultants is not always easily answered. Anne Rasmussen sensitively captures the dilemma, writing, "As ethnographers whose 'deep hanging out' is enabled by the hospitality and tolerance of our consultants, we are always challenged by what to give in return. Money? Gifts? An enthusiastic smile, perhaps?" (2010: 32). Anthony Seeger states that, "[i]ncreasingly, part of our time and energies will have to be devoted to meeting the desires of the communities we study" (2004: 23). One way that I could give back to my teachers and meet the desires of some people in the community was through an enthusiastic and sincere shot at performing. I must also admit that, with a couple of exceptions, I came to enjoy my moments on stage and, briefly, on television. For the most part, people in the audience received my mistakes and clumsiness with gracious compliments and the type of encouragement often given to beginning foreigners and small children: "Oh, very good!" "You can already do it!" "So clever!"

In spite of the spectacle of my foreignness, however, many musicians and dancers did work very hard to instruct me, sometimes entrusting me with very special forms of knowledge, as indicated earlier. Sometimes they beamed with pride when I did do something well (or as well as could be expected from their foreign student), and I have felt a special, unspeakable bond when performing with them, in effect embodying their traditions, their histories, their senses of gender, and their knowledge in my own ways. I continue to feel their presence and continue to develop my understandings of what they were imparting to me as I teach and perform gamelan and dance in the United States—all the while still learning.

Some individuals were proud and inspired that I, as someone from the United States, the world's most powerful nation, had decided to come to Malang to study east Javanese arts. They were particularly proud that I chose to conduct my research in east Java rather than in central Java or Bali, places they knew to be more prestigious and better known in both Indonesian and foreign academic and artistic circles. A friend revealed that my studying singing in the course of performing the female style dance *Ngremo Putri* motivated her to learn to sing: since I, a foreigner could learn, she believed that she, a Javanese, should be able to as well. Many performers were also impressed that I dedicated so much time and money to studying what they identified as traditional arts, especially given that many young Javanese were not interested in these forms of music and dance. This, too, was not unique to my experience. The American historian Laurie Sears, discussing her experiences attending shadow puppet plays in central Java, writes that puppeteers often commented on her presence, "[taking] the opportunity to praise this effort at cross-cultural understanding, to chide the Javanese for not taking a greater interest in their own performance traditions, and to express a bit of surprise that the most powerful country in the world would send people to Java to learn its language and arts" (1996b: 297).

One disturbing psychological effect of Dutch colonialism also affected my relationships with performers. Many Javanese talked about themselves as members of a nation that was not as advanced as a western country such as the United States. Many had internalized beliefs about the superiority of westerners' intellects and used attention from westerners to legitimize the cultural prestige of something or someone in Java. Sumarsam (1995) has traced the historical impact of such assumptions, showing that the status given to court styles of central Javanese gamelan music as "high art" resulted, in part, from the interaction between Dutch scholars and Javanese elites in the late nineteenth and early twentieth centuries. Profoundly affected psychologically and intellectually, Javanese scholars absorbed western attitudes, which have persisted into the present and have been reinforced with continuing western ethnomusicological interest in gamelan styles associated with the central Javanese courts (Sumarsam 1995: 10, 102–160). In the context of this history, my association with an individual in Malang had the potential to increase his or her prestige as well as that of the music and/or dance he or she practiced—a potential that may have motivated performers to work with me.

Interactions with me as a foreign researcher were further complicated by several other factors that ultimately shaped the knowledge that I acquired while conducting fieldwork and have used to produce this book. Oddly enough, my foreignness was tempered by a dab of central Javaneseness. Before starting my research in Malang, I had spent a number of years studying central Javanese gamelan music and dance in Yogyakarta and in California, had married a Javanese man, and had spent time living with his family in a village just south of the city of Yogyakarta. Not completely new to Javanese arts and culture, fairly fluent in Indonesian, and having had previous study in the basics of the Javanese language, I was able to learn east Javanese gamelan playing techniques and dance movements more quickly than foreign students without previous experience. Yet my prior exposure to central Javanese arts contributed to several mistaken assumptions I made about east Javanese arts and a certain feel in my playing and movement that performers recognized as central Javanese. Moments of my confusion and physical awkwardness sparked commentary from my teachers and generated questions I asked, thereby affecting answers I received (Sunardi 2010a: 118–119).

My marriage to a central Javanese man also affected my relationships with performers and members of the community in which we resided. My husband garnered respect and a bit of awe partly because he was from the culturally prestigious area of Yogyakarta (which was prestigious partly for the courts in the city of Yogyakarta). In addition, he had married an American, he had lived in America, he appeared to have an endless supply of money without having to work, he was generous with cigarettes, and he helped his neighbors. His jokes and chitchat at lessons, rehearsals, performances, and when out and about put people at ease and made them more comfortable with me. Most seemed to believe that since I had married a Javanese man, I must have truly adored, admired, and appreciated Javanese culture and Javanese people. In some cases, my marital status (and the perceived sexual experience and activity that came with that status) put people at ease in talking about matters of sex more openly and frankly with me. One of my teachers said that since I was already married he could talk about adult matters with me, including relations between a husband and wife as a "biological necessity" ("*keperluan biologis*").

My difference was further mitigated because I did not look as foreign as those with fair skin. Of black and white heritage, few in Malang guessed I was American or even western when they first saw me. My experiences fielding inquiries about my identity were similar to the experiences of the African American anthropologist Timothy Daniels, who was also met with confusion because he was not white and thus was different from what most Javanese imagine when they think of a generic American. Daniels found that "[m]any local Javanese perceive 'Negroes' and 'Africans,' much like they do dark-skinned Indonesian ethnic groups such as the 'Papuans' of Irian Jaya, to be backwards and uncivilized" (2009: 11). There were, however, certain advantages in being perceived as a dark-skinned person whose complexion happened to be similar to that of many Javanese people's. I was dark enough to not be "white," but light enough to not be "black" either. For many Javanese, my brown skin distanced me from the Dutch who were involved in a complicated history of colonialism in what is now Indonesia. I was also perceived as different from the Americans (i.e., white Americans) who have had so much influence in world politics and economics since the mid–twentieth century.

Instead, for those who thought I was from South Asia, my color linked me to the celebrities of the Indian films popular in Java. For those who mistook me for an Arab, I was associated with the respected Muslims of the Middle East. In a Muslim-majority society where Arab cultural models and the Arabic language hold a great amount of prestige for many (Rasmussen 2010: 64), the significance of being taken for an Arab cannot be underestimated. For the Javanese and other Indonesians who thought I was from one of the eastern Indonesian islands, I was believed to share their national identity. Surprised to learn that I was from the United States, new acquaintances often held their arms next to mine, making comments such as, "Your skin is the same," "you are like an Indonesian," "we are the same, aren't we?" For better or for worse, I brought the benefits of westernness without the cultural, political, and economic baggage of whiteness. Such perceptions of African Americans, including persons of mixed race, may change with the increasing presence of African American figures in international politics such as former Secretary of State Condoleezza Rice, President Barack Obama, and First Lady Michelle Obama.

Some performers, however, perceived me to be a means to insert their unheard (or under-heard) voices into the prestigious space of academic literature (see also Sunardi 2010a: 94, 118; 2011: 37). As a brown person, I was assumed to be sensitive and sympathetic to the perspectives of historically unempowered groups, whether such groups be performers with little formal education in relation to those with degrees from college-level arts institutions, east Javanese performers in relation to central Javanese performers, or those who understood their perspectives as coming from marginalized, disadvantaged, and/or subaltern positions in other ways. As an American doctoral student, I was also assumed to have wealth and powerful contacts.

Aware of the prestige that foreign scholarship carries in Java, performers took seriously their roles as sources for my research and strove to convey what they believed was true and correct. One individual, dissatisfied with existing publications, asked that I fix incorrect information.

I write this not to imply that I am "correcting" the literature. I am uncomfortably well aware of my own flaws, weaknesses, inevitable errors, and potential misunderstandings. Furthermore, given the flexibility of dance and music in Malang, what some artists might have perceived as errors or incorrect information may have been a matter of differing interpretations, approaches, or versions. I do, however, wish to underscore that for all of their generosity, performers sought to make me and my fieldwork beneficial to them, a realization that has also been influenced by Anthony Seeger's discussion of his fieldwork among the Suyá people of Brazil. His point that he and Judy Seeger became the Suyá's "'Whitemen' who studied them and could be counted on to bring gifts and sometimes act as intermediaries with the rest of Brazilian society" (Seeger 2004: 24), has helped me to understand that, similarly, in Malang I became a foreign ethnomusicologist who would sponsor rehearsals and performances, bring gifts, share over-the-counter medicines like Advil, and represent the perspectives and musical traditions of the artists I consulted—thereby putting their traditions on equal par with the more prestigious (and more researched) traditions from central Java and Bali. By inserting their knowledge about east Javanese performing arts (and those of Malang in particular) into the prestigious cultural spaces of U.S. academia, they hoped that I would bring them international recognition, which in turn would bring them economic benefits in the form of increased employment opportunities (Sunardi 2010a: 94).

Although I was foreign-but-not-so foreign, I was no less ambiguous in other ways. Many in the general population believed that I was a *waria*, a male who dressed and lived as female. At about five feet, eight inches, I was noticeably taller than every Indonesian female I met in Malang (at least, as far as I can recall), and for that matter, most Indonesian males. My relatively broad shoulders and slender, sinewy athletic build reinforced the maleness people perceived in me, as did my studies and performances of *Ngremo Putri*, a female style dance that was usually performed by males as a cross-gender dance. My association with male dancers who lived as *waria* in their daily lives—waves and smiles to the *waria* who had seen me hanging out backstage at performances or sitting with the gamelan musicians at performances, sometimes playing, sometimes taking photos, sometimes videotaping—was further evidence that I was a *waria*, too. My personal experiences of the fascination for *waria*—who many said were more beautiful, and ravishingly so, than "real women"—has provided critical insight into the cultural need for the power of femaleness as embodied by people who simultaneously pushed at and reinforced dominant boundaries of gender in contemporary Malang, no doubt affecting the analysis that follows. Viewing both on- and offstage realms of artists' lives and experiences as complementary and overlapping sites of cultural production, I have been captivated by dance and music not just as performing arts, but also as strategies that individuals use to negotiate cultural norms.

Acknowledgments

Researching and writing this book have allowed me to travel, to work with many gifted individuals, to play music, to dance, to read, and to indulge in thinking. It has also been hard, testing my endurance, confidence, and motivation. I could not have made it through this process without support. I express tremendous gratitude to my parents Lois Roland and the late Charles Roland for bringing me into the world, raising me in a loving home, teaching me important values, supporting me in my endeavors, and allowing me to go my own way. I am thankful for the encouragement of my siblings, C. Brian Roland and Charla Fischer; brother-in-law, Eric Fischer; and extended family, in particular my late grandmother Esther Hansen and my aunt/godmother Martha Hansen; my in-laws in Java, especially Bu Siswanto and Yuwanti; and my dear friends Laura Emery and Kristin Calcagno. I am so grateful to my husband Sunardi, who has been my cameraman, chauffeur, go-between, translator, confidante, cook, spiritual supervisor, companion, friend, stylist, and through it all, the love of my life.

I am grateful to the institutions and individuals that made my fieldwork in Indonesia possible. My research was funded at various stages by a Fulbright-Hays Doctoral Dissertation Research Abroad Program Fellowship; a University of California Office of the President Pacific Rim Mini Grant; University of California, Berkeley Center for Southeast Asia Studies Grant-In-Aid Scholarships; and a University of California, Berkeley Graduate Division Travel Award. Didik Nini Thowok and LPK Tari Natya Lakshita in Yogyakarta as well as M. Soleh Adi Pramono and Padepokan Seni Mangun Dharma (PSMD) in Malang sponsored my research. Lembaga Ilmu Pengetahun Indonesia (LIPI), Nelly Paliama and the rest of the staff at the AMINEF office in Jakarta, and the staff at the Consulate of the Republic of Indonesia in San Francisco facilitated the clearance of my research with the Indonesian government.

I deeply thank all of the individuals in Java who participated in and helped me with my research. For including me in the activities at their arts organizations and introducing me to other performers, I thank M. Soleh Adi Pramono, Karen Elizabeth Sekararum, and those who worked or studied at PSMD; H. Mohamad Amin Sahara and the members of Sanggar Taruna Budaya; and Suryo Pranoto, Didik K., and the members of Ludruk Mitra Budaya. I thank Warananingtyas Palupi and Tjundomanik Tjatur Pawestri, who were conducting fieldwork at the same time I was, for sharing contacts and other information as well as for fascinating discussions that motivated me in the field. I also thank Gillian Roberts for her friendship in Malang and for graciously allowing me to perform with her when I was quite the frustrated novice. For allowing me to use their facilities and gamelan instruments, I thank PSMD, Sanggar Seni Setyotomo, Gedung PGRI Poncokusumo, the village office of Tulusbesar, the *jaranan* (hobbyhorse) group of Tulusbesar, and Sanggar Taruna Budaya. Many thanks, too, to Setyo Adi, the village head of Tulusbesar at the time of my fieldwork, as well as to the other village officials for warmly welcoming my husband and me into their community and for supporting my interest in the arts.

Opportunities to discuss my work have been critical to the development of the ideas presented in this book. Many thanks go to Sonja Lynn Downing and Lawrence University; Jeffrey Hadler and the University of California, Berkeley Southeast Asia Center; Odai Johnson and the University of Washington School of Drama and Center for Performance Studies; Celia Lowe; Laurie Sears and the University of Washington Southeast Asia Center; Laurel Sercombe and the Pacific Northwest Chapter of the Music Library Association; and Sara Weiss and Yale University Council on Southeast Asia Studies for inviting me to present and/or discuss my research. Participating on conference panels with Shalini Ayyagari, Kiko Benitez, Rachel Devitt, Sonja Lynn Downing, Denise Elif Gill, Pattie Hsu, Tim Fuson, Anne K. Rasmussen, and Francesca Rivera have also been formative experiences, and I thank my co-panelists for their productive feedback on my research.

Comments from mentors, colleagues, reviewers, and editors on my prior work have also helped me to develop my analysis in this book. I would like to thank Benjamin Brinner, Patricia Shehan Campbell, Timothy Daniels, Shannon Dudley, Jocelyne Guilbault, Jeffrey Hadler, Patricia Hardwick, René Lysloff, Midiyanto, Lois Roland, Laurie Margot Ross, Eric Sasono, Philip Schuyler, Laurie Sears, Tikka Sears, Stephen Slawek, Keith Snodgrass, Tom van den

Berge, Bonnie Wade, Sean Williams, J. Lawrence Witzleben, and anonymous reviewers for *Asian Music; Bijdragen tot de Taal-, Land- en Volkenkunde; Ethnomusicology;* and Palgrave Macmillan Press for their close and careful reading of my work, for helping me to clarify my points, for teaching me more about how to write, for introducing me to sources and ideas, and for encouraging and supporting my efforts to make a scholarly contribution. I am also grateful to Koninklijke Brill NV, the University of Texas Press, the Society for Ethnomusicology, and Palgrave Macmillan for giving me permission to use material from my previously published work in this book (see the copyright page for more complete credit lines).

I express my gratitude to the University of Washington Simpson Center for the Humanities for awarding me a 2012–2013 Faculty Research Fellowship, which allowed me teaching relief and to participate in the interdisciplinary Society of Scholars discussion group. I thank Kathleen Woodward, Director of the Simpson Center, for leading such dynamic, productive, and interesting meetings. The motivation, energy, insights and just plain brilliance of the other participants—George Behlmer, Stephanie Camp, Anne Dwyer, Benjamin Gardner, Gillian Harkins, Celia Lowe, Louisa Mackenzie, Suhanthie Motha, LeiLani Nishime, Maria Quintana, Anjali Vats, and Patrick Zambianchi—renewed my own enthusiasm for this book. I thank them all for their comments on my work and for making the Society of Scholars an incredibly rich space of intellectual exchange.

The University of Washington, Seattle, has been a stimulating and encouraging environment in which to work. In addition to those already named, I thank my many other supportive colleagues, including Rick Bonus, Ter Ellingson, Áine Heneghan, Richard Karpen, Robin McCabe, Ileana Rodriguez-Silva, Donna Shin, Larry Starr, JoAnn Taricani, Judy Tsou, Sara Van Fleet, and Anand Yang. I thank the University of Washington School of Music and the University of Washington Southeast Asia Center for emotional and financial support. I also acknowledge the contributions of the many undergraduate and graduate students who have taken my classes. I tested some of my ideas, arguments, and approaches on them, and they pushed me in productive ways through their responses and reactions to my work. I would like to especially thank Kimberly Cannady, Julia Day, Maren Haynes, Kait LaPorte, Emma Zylstra Lux, Bonnie McConnell, Aaron Malver, Leah Pogwizd, Michiko Urita, and the students not already named who were in my fall 2013 graduate seminar on gender: David Aarons, Claire Anderson, Rebecca Cweibel, Lauren Halsey, Joseph Kinzer, Jocelyn Moon, and Subhash Prajapati.

I am grateful to other friends and colleagues (including those who have been, and still are my teachers) who share a love of Indonesian arts and culture and have mentored and supported me scholastically, artistically, and/or emotionally during the time that I have written this book. Among the many who have done so are Benjamin Brinner, Stephen Fandrich, I. M. Harjito, Ramona Holmes, Mindy Johnston, Jessika Kenney, Florence and James Peacock, Marc Perlman, Jarrad Powell, Heri Purwanto, Stephanie Shadbolt, Jesse Snyder, Henry Spiller, Anne Stebinger, Sumarsam, R. Anderson Sutton, Takim, Andrew Weintraub, Sean Williams, and my dear friends Boymin, Koir, and their two daughters. I hope that those whose names I have not been able to include in this book or in these acknowledgments due to considerations of space will know that I am grateful to them and recognize the impact that they have had on my work and on me.

For their close and careful reading of earlier drafts of this book or parts of it I thank Laurie Matheson, Midiyanto, Laurie Sears, Laurel Sercombe, Didik Nini Thowok, Bonnie Wade, and two reviewers for the University of Illinois Press. I thank Laurie Matheson and Bonnie Wade for believing in this project for several years, mentoring me with productive feedback, and reading multiple drafts of the entire manuscript. On matters of translation, I thank Midiyanto, Heri Purwanto, and Sunardi. For helping me to translate the titles of their publications in the works cited list, I thank Robby Hidajat and Henri Supriyanto. I also thank Desiana Pauli Sandjaja for helping me to translate University of Illinois Press release forms and to Boymin, Danu, Sunardi, and Teguh Priantohadi for their tremendous help in requesting signatures on Press consent forms. I would like to thank David Wolbrecht for drawing the beautiful maps, James B. Morford for his help in checking and refining the notated examples, and Katherine Jensen for preparing the index. Many thanks go to Dawn Durante at the University of Illinois Press for her endless patience in helping me through the publication process as well as to other members of the Press staff for seeing this book through production.

I take full responsibility for any errors or misunderstandings; I hope that responses to such imperfections will result in future projects that will further our knowledge and appreciation of the performing arts, senses of gender, and Indonesia.

1. Aims and Approaches

This Book in a Nutshell

Stunning Males and Powerful Females is about gender, power, and tradition—topics that are all the more fascinating in the regency of Malang in east Java, Indonesia, a place where the majority of people are Muslim and where cross-gender dance performance is quite common. Drawing on ethnographic fieldwork spanning the years 2005 to 2007, this book focuses on ways male and female performers have accessed and embodied femaleness through east Javanese presentational dance and its music in the twentieth and twenty-first centuries, examining the perseverance of "female power" in the face of a variety of cultural pressures that work to contain, control, and suppress it. This exploration, informed by what musicians and dancers emphasized to me as I studied music and dance with them, attended and participated in performances, formally interviewed them, and chatted more casually with them, has led to the main argument of this book: Through the continuous transformations performers have made to tradition, they have been negotiating culturally constructed boundaries of gender and sex—sometimes reinforcing these boundaries, sometimes transgressing them, sometimes doing both simultaneously.

I develop this argument through six chapters. This chapter introduces my main aims and analytical approaches. Chapter two contextualizes a cultural ambivalence toward female power, exploring how female dancers and the (mostly) male musicians who accompany them contend with this ambivalence through male style dance. Chapter three considers the cultural ambivalence that has surrounded the expression of female power by males, examining ways male dancers have nonetheless accessed and embodied this power through female style dance. Chapter four demonstrates how performers constructed boundaries of gender through their senses of the past. Of particular importance was the strong connection they made between the female style dance *Beskalan Putri*, Malangan tradition, and female power, leading me to explore the representation of female power through *Beskalan Putri* in more detail in chapter five. Through analysis of performer interaction, chapter six brings together the main themes that link the book—power, the negotiation of conceptual and physical boundaries of gender, concern with tradition and preservation, and performers' senses of history—as a means to understand how even the briefest moments of interaction between performers contributed to ongoing cultural processes by and through which tradition and gender are produced. Having benefited from an educational environment in which boundaries between disciplines are sometimes questioned and sometimes ignored, I draw theoretical and methodological approaches from ethnomusicology (my "home" discipline), anthropology, gender studies, dance studies, Southeast Asian studies, and other disciplines—combining interpretive ethnography, textual analysis, and analysis of performance.

Approaching Power

One of my aims is to contribute some new ways of thinking about spiritual power and the ways it is manifested in Java. Benedict Anderson captured many aspects of spiritual power (*kasektèn*) in his influential essay "The Idea of Power in Javanese Culture," defining it as "that intangible, mysterious, and divine energy which animates the universe" (1990a: 22) and referring to it as "Power" with a capital "p" (ibid.: 23, 19–20 n8). Other translations of this sense of spiritual power in Java include "magical energy" (Koentjaraningrat 1980: 135), "potency" (Keeler 1987: 38–39; Errington 1990: 42), and "spiritual potency" (Errington 1990: 42). The more of this divine energy that a person or object has, the more spiritually powerful a person or an object is (Anderson 1990a: 22–27). Spiritual power is acquired in a number of ways, such as through ascetic practices and/or through the possession of spiritually powerful objects (Anderson 1990a: 23–27; Keeler 1987: 41–48). This power affects others in a number of ways, but seemingly without effort on the part of the spiritually potent person (Anderson 1990a: 54). A sign of a person's potency is refined speech, behavior, and disposition (ibid.: 50–51). The idea is that others are drawn to spiritually potent people, as though "magnetically attracted" (ibid.: 53). Others will seem to simply follow a spiritually potent person's lead. Spiritually potent people thus do not need to make overt commands or force others into compliance; a "request" should suffice (ibid.: 54; see also Sunardi 2011: 45–46). Economically speaking, wealth seems to flow to a spiritually powerful person without that person's pursuing it (ibid.: 53). Others seem to want to give the person money in various forms, including cash, gifts, and employment opportunities.

Anderson developed his analysis of power in Java based on the ways males express and embody it, in effect outlining a dominant, male-centered, aristocratic ideology of spiritual power (Djajadiningrat-Nieuwenhuis 1987: 46; Brenner 1995: 28–29; 1998: 148; Weiss 2006: 55–56; Sears 2007: 54–58). Anderson's essay, however, was not about the issue of gender per se, but about the notion of charisma (Anderson 1990a: 19, 72–77; 1990b: 78; Brenner 1995: 28; 1998: 148; Sears 2007: 54–55; Hughes-Freeland 2007). While I recognize that Anderson was presenting a male-centric, elite masculine sense of spiritual power, I found that the verbal discourse and behavior of performers I consulted (many of whom admittedly were male) did often support many of his ideas, and I thus do draw on his work.

At the same time, other analysts have enriched understandings of spiritual power in Java and different ways it is expressed, embodied, negotiated, and connected to social status by focusing on issues of gender and examining women's roles and experiences (e.g., Errington 1990; Keeler 1990; Brenner 1995, 1998; Cooper 2000; Weiss 2006). Nancy Cooper productively distinguishes the "pure state" of power, which may be accessed by males and females, and "the gendered uses of power" (2000: 613). She uses the term *centripetality* to specify a type of "attracting power" that she associates with women (2000: 613). As I build upon this fascinating body of literature I, too, am interested in the manifestation of spiritual power as it is gendered female.

There is a historical precedent for spiritual power gendered female in Java in *shakti*, a centuries-old "Indic metaphor of female power" (Becker 1988: 385).[1] *Shakti*, as well as the importance of the unification of female and male forces, was an important component of Tantric philosophy, which, imported from India, was known in Java in medieval times (eighth through sixteenth centuries) (Becker 1993: 3, 8).[2] The modern Javanese concepts of *sekti* and *kasektèn* (*sakti*, *kesaktian* in Indonesian), are derived from the Indic concept but no longer necessarily gendered female (Becker 1988: 388; Hughes-Freeland 1995: 198). Indic senses of *shakti* as female energy and its importance to male potency, however, do survive, as Judith Becker and Felicia Hughes-Freeland have shown in their analyses of central Javanese female style court dance (Becker 1991: 116; 1993: 128; Hughes-Freeland 1995: 201). My analysis in this book suggests that Indic senses of *shakti* survive in east Javanese dance as well.

Using Anderson's (1990a: 33, 53) and Cooper's (2000: 614) metaphor of a magnet to describe the attracting force of spiritually powerful people, I write about spiritual power gendered female as "the magnetic power of femaleness" or "magnetic female power." I am expanding Cooper's notion of centripetality (which she associates with women [2000: 613]) to refer to spiritual power associated with femaleness more broadly—that is, femaleness connected to female bodies and/or to behavior or demeanor commonly accepted as feminine in Javanese society. Viewing the magnetic power of femaleness in this way facilitates my exploration of ways it has been accessed and embodied by women, men, and *waria* (males who dress and live as female). In some cases I abbreviate my references to the magnetic power of femaleness to "the power of femaleness" or "female power." Critical to a person's ability to access spiritual power, both in its "pure state" and as gendered, is the possession of knowledge (Anderson 1990a: 54–58; see also Sunardi 2011: 46), including a type of knowledge that is itself spiritual in nature.

Ilmu *(Spiritual Knowledge)*

Ilmu (Indonesian), or *èlmu/ngèlmu* (Javanese), is a complicated term in Java with different shades of meaning. An Arabic-derived word (Daniels 2009: 41), it has broader meanings as "knowledge" or "science." It also has particular shadings that are more closely connected to mystical beliefs and practices in Java. Other scholars have translated, defined, or described *ilmu/ngèlmu* as "science" and "a kind of abstract knowledge or supernormal skill" (Geertz 1960: 88); "esoteric knowledge/science" (Mulder 2005: 165); and "mystical knowledge" (Keeler 1987: 235; Daniels 2009: 41). Like Clifford Geertz, who conducted fieldwork in Java in the 1950s, I also found that some individuals talked about *ilmu* "as a kind of substantive magical power" (1960: 88), suggesting a continuity of some ideas about *ilmu*. While I recognize that *ilmu* as it relates to mystical beliefs and practices may mean different things to different people, I have come to understand *ilmu* as a substantive "packet" of knowledge, often of a secret and esoteric nature that can lead to a remarkable ability to do something by helping a person to access and embody spiritual power, and it is this sense of *ilmu* that is the focus of this book.

Ilmu exists for many different kinds of abilities, such as to disappear; to fly; to be invincible; to be present in more than one place simultaneously; to win the love of another; and to perform music, dance, and theater (see also Geertz 1960: 88–89). In writing about *ilmu* and forms of *ilmu*, I have done my best to be clear in my explanations, examples, and analyses while also respecting the wishes of some performers to keep some aspects confidential. In the context of performance, *ilmu* is knowledge that enables artists—including musicians, dancers, and puppeteers—to enrapture, mesmerize, and in some cases, heal. This knowledge gives a performer a particular radiance that makes him or her appealing to viewers, even if he or she is not necessarily considered the best technically or, in the case of dancers, the most beautiful or handsome. As I understand it, this is similar to or the same as "the *téja* (radiance)" that Anderson writes "was thought to emanate softly from the face or person of the man of Power" (1990a: 31).

Using *ilmu*, male and female performers gain the power of presence to affect audiences emotionally—making them feel happy, enthralled, in love—physically—giving them the shivers, widening their eyes, freezing their expressions—and sometimes spiritually—healing their hearts and minds. Without *ilmu*, a performer may be very good, even excellent, but she or he will not be able to embody the spiritual power necessary to strongly affect those watching. Musicians and dancers implied that *ilmu* was a critical component of a performer's competence. After I had learned a dance well enough to perform it, several of my teachers encouraged me to obtain *ilmu*, indicating that this was necessary in order for me to reach the next level of proficiency—that is, the ability to truly captivate and affect the audience.

Ilmu in the performing arts is closely related to affect and effect, which many Javanese artists talk about in terms of *rasa*, a Sanskrit-derived term for feeling, mood, and/or taste that is closely tied to the artist's deep understanding of the art (such as the dance or a musical composition) (Walton 2007; Weiss 2003: 23; Benamou 2010: 244). Susan Walton writes, "[t]he *rasa* magnetizes the viewer, pulling her or him into the dramatic situation so that the viewer can relish the work in an almost gustatory way, experiencing it in mind and body" (2007: 32). Also emphasizing the element of affective power, Sarah Weiss explains that "[i]n performance, *rasa* is the force that reflects the unification of the performer with the performed" (2003: 38). The deep understanding of the art that is necessary to perform with *rasa*—to affect viewers—includes technical skill gained from experience, and also *ilmu* gained in diverse ways. In other words, for those artists who emphasize the importance of *ilmu*, the assumption is that one needs *ilmu* to truly perform with *rasa*; technical skill is not enough in itself.

Paradoxically, *ilmu* has no form and is invisible, but it does have substance, like an invisible gas, and is transferable (Geertz 1960: 88). Transmission often involves the movement of *ilmu* from one person's body to another's so that the recipient comes to have, hold, own, or incorporate it into his or her own body. In short, *ilmu* can be embodied and is "embodiable." Transferring *ilmu* may be a conceptual process. My teachers gave me *ilmu* in "bits" of knowledge about dance technique, the character portrayed, or the meanings of a movement or composition title conveyed verbally.

Ilmu may also be more tangibly transferred. Some performers identified objects—including parts of dance costumes and daggers (*keris*)—that contained *ilmu*. The implication is that an individual absorbed the *ilmu* contained in these objects by wearing them and thus became able to access the spiritual power necessary to perform efficaciously. A couple of performers transferred *ilmu* to me in the form of chants, spells, and prayers conveyed aurally or written on paper. I was assumed to gain *ilmu* as the words permeated my body in a variety of ways, including aurally, through the touch of the person giving them to me, and/or by possessing the words on a piece of paper and by committing the words to memory, whether or not I understood the meanings of the text. One of my dance teachers also instructed me to ingest the words—to tear up the paper on which the words were written, put the pieces into tea or water, and drink the infusion. Doing so, I would literally internalize the *ilmu* the words contained. The power and knowledge attributed to the possession of words in Java is also manifest through shadow puppet play stories in which "a piece of writing" is a "powerful weapon" (Anderson 1990a: 58).

Ilmu can also be transferred by osmosis. My teacher who instructed me to ingest the words on the paper encouraged me to come frequently to his house so that my abilities as a musician and dancer would improve by just being near him as his *ilmu* permeated into me. One important implication is that a person does not necessarily have to rationally grasp *ilmu* in order to gain it, be affected by it, or affect others with it. I was repeatedly told, however, that a person who does not have sufficient inner strength to receive, possess, and embody certain kinds or amounts of *ilmu* risks illness, insanity, and even death (see also Geertz 1960: 321; Keeler 1987: 253).

There are a number of ways an individual may gain the inner strength (and enough of it) necessary to productively possess *ilmu*. While a special few are endowed with enough inner strength from birth, most people need to gradually develop it, often by making some sort of sacrifice, often in the form of asceticism (Keeler 1987: 44–48). Many temporarily give up physical comforts as they engage in ascetic practices such as fasting, going without sleep, abstaining from sex, meditating, and soaking in rivers late at night (see also Geertz 1960: 311, 321–326; Keeler 1987: 41–48; Mulder 2005: 51). Other forms of sacrifice are material—such as the money I forfeited to fly to Java, to pay for lessons, and to sponsor recording sessions. Sometimes sacrifice was inadvertent, as when an individual fell ill, unintentionally sacrificing health and physical comfort as he or she received *ilmu*. In making a sacrifice, a person strengthens his or her mind and body to be a container that is strong enough to hold spiritual knowledge, a potent substance.

The power that performers connected to *ilmu* enriches understandings of spiritual power in Java. As has been suggested, *ilmu* and spiritual power are closely related (Anderson 1990a: 57), if not the same for some. Like spiritual power, *ilmu* has quantity. Similar to the ways in which a person may gain spiritual power, a person may obtain *ilmu* through asceticism and sacrifice, and/or having imbued objects in one's presence or keeping them on one's person.

One important aspect of spiritual power is that the amount of power in the universe is finite, thus the "concentration of power in one place or in one person requires a proportional diminution elsewhere" (Anderson 1990a: 23). To protect their own spiritual power, among other reasons, many performers tended to carefully guard their *ilmu*. The dancer Djupri related that his grandmother Muskayah often taught him when the house was quiet and the neighbors could not see them (p.c., February 1, 2006). In the course of my own private dance lessons with him, Djupri gave me some forms of *ilmu* only when we were alone, restricting how I could share the knowledge with others. Transferring *ilmu* willingly could still result in the giver's lessened ability.

Furthermore, performers tended to be selective about to whom to pass on their most potent *ilmu* and when they did so. It seems to me that most performers usually passed on their most potent *ilmu* after they retired and usually reserved it for their most trusted, dedicated, and/or gifted students, often (but not always) their "children"—either a biological or adopted child, or a more distantly related relative such as a nephew or grandchild. Illustrative of the selectivity master artists showed when passing on their *ilmu*, Marc Benamou gives the example of one master musician in central Java who believed that only one other musician could receive his *ngèlmu* before he passed away (2010: 116).[3] I also understand this selectivity as a response to a competitive world in which "better" performers garnered more employment opportunities. At the same time, having the *ilmu* of a particular master implies that that master selected someone to be the recipient and owner of something special, giving the recipient a certain responsibility to protect that knowledge.

Important, too, is that the possession of *ilmu* is not necessarily contingent upon an individual's biological sex. A performer does not need to be a female in order to gain *ilmu* for performing female style dance and vice versa. Simply put, *ilmu* may be transmitted across boundaries of gender and sex.

Approaching Gender and Sex: Conceptual and Physical Boundaries

This book develops the idea that performance and boundaries of gender and sex are integrally related—that is, that performance contributes to continuous cultural processes by and through which boundaries of gender and sex are negotiated, and that boundaries of gender and sex affect the ways in which femaleness and maleness are performed. Boundaries of gender and sex are conceptual—informed by ideologies that shape assumptions about how gendered individuals should look, sound, and behave—and also physical—experienced through bodies, objects such as clothing, and the physical spaces of performance and daily life. Albeit fluid, contested, and continuously redefined, these boundaries are being constantly reinforced and undermined in contexts of shifting cultural ideologies about womanhood and manhood, and constantly negotiated through performance conventions.

Inspired by Judith Butler (1990, 1993, 1999) and others, I approach sex and gender as unstable constructs that are continuously constituted by and through what people do, as well as through the ways people describe what they and others do—or should do—with their bodies. Bodies are sexed by people in terms of the biological sex that they ascribe to bodies and gendered in terms of the behaviors and social roles that they ascribe to sexed bodies (Butler 1990, 1993, 1999). The gendering of sexed bodies is a cultural process—shifting as individuals negotiate their identities in webs of local, national, and transnational ideologies (Wieringa and Blackwood 1999: 15, 17). Indeed, gendered constructs and identities are "fragile" (Sears 1996a: 4), "brittle structures" (Biddle and Jarman-Ivens 2007: 13)—delicate, easily "broken," and yet also able to be reassembled. It is the potential for such breakage and reassembly that allows space for gender constructs, identities, and in some instances, social norms, to change. At the same time, the fragility of maleness and femaleness contributes to a cultural ambivalence that surrounds these constructs because, on some level, many people recognize that femaleness is not located only in female bodies and maleness is not located only in male bodies, particularly when made visible through cross-gender performance. Thinking about sex and gender in these ways helps me to examine how individuals negotiate, claim, own, contest, and transform senses of maleness and femaleness historically through their own minds and bodies, and by what they say about what other people do—or should do—with their bodies.

My focus on boundaries in this book builds on Sean Williams's "examination of the ways in which physical and musical domains are divided along gender boundaries" (1998: 74) and Tomie Hahn's approach to "performance as a process where boundaries of identity (gender, ethnicity, age, social class, etc.) are negotiated metaphorically" (2004: 323). My thinking about performance and boundaries of gender and sex has also been inspired by Eileen Hayes's analysis of drag kinging, transgender identity, and "boundaries of community membership" (2010: 173). I show that in negotiating conceptual and physical boundaries of gender and sex through dance metaphorically—

and also physically—performers in Malang both reinforced and destabilized dominant ideologies of maleness and femaleness. Like Williams, I am also interested in "the tensions between the sexes and highlighting the areas in which men and women can meet and communicate both socially and musically" (1998: 74). While people produce and contend with conceptual and physical boundaries of gender and sex in many realms of culture, I focus on these boundaries as demarcated, blurred, and crossed through the body, gendered styles of dance, types of performance, and performance structure and roles.

The Body

To fully understand the complex role of the body, the conceptual and physical aspects of the body itself must be taken together. While bodies are sites of cultural production and signifiers of culturally and historically constructed meanings, they are also physical, material sites by and through which culture, cultural meanings, and cultural knowledge are lived, experienced, produced, and transmitted (Foster 1986, 1995; Cowan 1990: 4, 23; Errington 1990: 11–15, 36–37; Franko 1993; Hahn 2007: 1, 6–8; Hughes-Freeland 2008b: 20). Given that "the body is both marked by culture and 'speaks' of and to cultural practice, the self, and history" (Thomas and Ahmed 2004: 7–8), people may use their bodies strategically to align themselves with particular histories and senses of identity (Wong 2004: 161–193). I am interested in how dancers use their bodies strategically to align themselves with senses of femaleness and maleness as well as the roles that musicians play in making such alignments happen in performance.

To explore the production of maleness and femaleness through dance performance, I build on Judith Butler's explanation of gender as "an identity tenuously constituted in time, instituted in an exterior space through a *stylized repetition of acts*" (original emphasis, 1999: 179), and Henry Spiller's definition of gender identities as "the matrix of ideas, behaviors, and assumptions that result in the division of people into at least two distinct categories that we typically characterize as 'sex' or 'gender'" (2010: 22). I approach femaleness as a part of this "matrix of ideas, behaviors, and assumptions" that includes culturally constructed senses of femininity, assumptions about what makes a body female, and the stylized constitutive acts within a particular cultural context that are believed to signify womanhood. Maleness, also part of this matrix, includes culturally constructed senses of masculinity, assumptions about what makes a body male, and the stylized constitutive acts that signify manhood. Because femaleness and maleness are in large part produced through acts, a body does not need to be biologically male to produce maleness or biologically female to produce femaleness. My attention to the body develops Saskia Wieringa's and Evelyn Blackwood's positioning of "the female body [as] the source of identity among . . . [the] different categories of sexuality and gender" explored in their edited volume *Female Desires: Same-Sex Relations and Transgender Practices across Cultures* (1999: 25). Positioning the body as the source of identity, however, is not to suggest that sex determines any one specific gender identity, as Wieringa and Blackwood recognize (ibid.: 17). At the same time, thinking about bodies—both female and male—is a productive place to start. I thus focus on female-bodied dancers in chapter two and male-bodied dancers in chapter three.

Although I often write in terms of gender binaries—femaleness and maleness, female and male dancers, female and male styles of dance, femininity and masculinity—I am ultimately working to demonstrate the gender pluralism that performers in Malang were producing through performance, and in some cases, their offstage lives. As defined by Michael Peletz, "gender pluralism"

> includes pluralistic sensibilities and dispositions regarding bodily practices (adornment, attire, mannerisms) and embodied desires, as well as social roles, sexual relationships, and ways of being that bear on or are otherwise linked with local conceptions of femininity, masculinity, androgyny, etc. (2006: 310)

I approach gender pluralism through the gender binaries articulated in the verbal discourse of most Javanese with whom I spoke (see also Locher-Scholten and Niehof 1987: 7). I show that despite this dualism, performers were expressing pluralistic understandings of masculinity and femininity through performance, and in some cases, in their offstage lives, which sometimes included senses of gender and sexuality that were nonnormative in relation to dominant Indonesian ideologies. Such dominant ideologies—which separate femaleness from maleness, map femininity to female bodies, map masculinity to male bodies, as well as privilege and normalize heterosexuality—have been shaped by nineteenth- and twentieth-century Dutch colonial and Islamic discourses and have been promoted by the Indonesian government since the declaration of independence in 1945 (Blackwood 2005; 2007: 185–188).

My findings support two of the "nine preliminary theses" Tom Boellstorff offers regarding nonnormative genders and sexualities in Southeast Asia (2007: 208):

> *Thesis 4:* "Male" and "female" remain powerful structuring principles for nonnormative genders and sexualities, but in complex ways. (italics in the original, 2007: 211)

and

Thesis 8: Despite rumors of the demise of the sexuality/gender binarism, it remains analytically useful and experientially real. (italics in the original, ibid.: 215)

I show that the senses of gender that performers expressed with their bodies included complex, multifarious senses of masculinity and femininity. Such senses included female masculinity—masculinity that is expressed, embodied, and owned by females (Halberstam 1998: 1–2, 15; see also Blackwood 2010: 29; Blackwood and Wieringa 2007: 9, 14–15; Sunardi 2013: 141)—as well as male femininity—femininity that is expressed, embodied, and owned by males (Boellstorff 2004b; 2007: 82, 99, 108; see also 2005b: 169, 171, 175; Sunardi 2013: 141).

I am also interested in the importance of context to the expression of particular senses of gender, and in thinking about the expression of gender as "situational" (Oetomo 2000: 50; Boellstorff 2007: 100). I have been influenced in particular by Evelyn Blackwood, who uses the concept of "contingent masculinity" to draw attention to gender subjectivity as "conditioned by circumstances, a process rather than an entity" in her analysis of *tombois* (females who live as men) in West Sumatra (2010: 21). Emphasizing the importance of context in the shifting expression and production of gender, she analyzes how individuals may "take up and embody sometimes contrastive subject positions in different contexts" (ibid.: 177). I explore how performers expressed situational or contingent senses of gender as part of the processes by and through which they were negotiating conceptual and physical boundaries of gender and sex on- and offstage (see also Sunardi 2013: 141).

Gendered Styles of Dance

Performers in east Java, as in other parts of Indonesia, construct, express, and demarcate femaleness and maleness in part by classifying dance into gendered styles. Although there are a range of male and female Javanese dance styles depending on regional style, character portrayed, and type of dance, in general male styles feature wider, more open stances; higher arm positions; and larger movement volumes (Photograph 1.1). In general, female styles feature more narrow stances, lower arm positions, and smaller movement volumes (Photograph 1.2) (see also Sunardi 2013: 136–138).

Gendered styles can be further categorized—for example, there are "strong male" styles and "refined male" styles, and while female styles are predominantly refined, there are different degrees of refinement (Holt 1967: 159–160; Choy 1984: 52–53; Brakel 1993; Brakel-Papenhuyzen 1995; Hughes-Freeland

Photograph 1.1. Tri Wahyuningtyas (a female) poses in a position from *Beskalan Lanang* (a male style dance) in costume, 2006. (In performance, she would wear a set of bells around her right ankle.)

Photograph 1.2. Wahyu Winarti (a female) in costume for *Beskalan Putri* (a female style dance), 2006.

1995). Male and female comic characters also exist. There are, of course, exceptions to the generalizations I have outlined, and the ways performers undermine or push at conventions of performing gendered styles is a means by and through which they push at and reshape preexisting constructions of femaleness and maleness. This book focuses primarily on *Beskalan* and *Ngremo* as they are danced in female (*putri*) and male (*lanang*) styles—*Beskalan Putri, Beskalan Lanang, Ngremo Putri, Ngremo Lanang,* and *Ngremo Tayub,* a substyle of *Ngremo Lanang.* I also refer to Malangan (Malang-style) masked dance, albeit to a lesser extent.

For the most part, *Beskalan, Ngremo,* and masked dance are presentational, meaning that they are performed by trained dancers and accompanied by trained musicians for an audience (which may include guests at an event) that is distinct from the performers (Turino 2008: 26). Distinctions, however, between presentational and participatory performance—or performance "in which there are no artist-audience distinctions, only participants and potential participants performing different roles" (ibid.: 26)—may be blurred in Java. In certain contexts, boundaries between audience and performer can be flexible, as Henry Spiller has highlighted from his observations of dance events in West Java (2010: 37). In some performances of *Ngremo Tayub* I observed in Malang, viewers—usually male guests—entered into the dance space at a certain point in the dance, tipped the performers, requested a song, and danced with the professional dancers for the duration of that song. While I do consider the impact that audiences had on cultural constructions of gender, my focus in this book is on the professional dancers and musicians.

While gendered dance styles characterize east Javanese dance, most artists in Malang recognized that a person's ability to perform a particular gendered style did not necessarily map to his or her biological sex. Most recognized that male style dance was not necessarily best when performed by a male, and female style dance was not necessarily best when performed by a female. Most linked a dancer's competence in performing a particular gendered style to his or her personality and disposition. Many explained that one had to consider the character of the individual dancer and which dances best suited him or her. Recognizing that an individual's personality did not necessarily map to biology either, performers provided examples of certain males who were best suited for strong male style dances, those best suited for refined male style dances, and those best suited for female style dances. They also provided examples of females who were best suited for particular gendered styles. As in performance in Yogyakarta (among other places in Java and Bali), "[p]erformance is gender-ascribed, but available to both sexes" (Hughes-Freeland 1995: 201). To put it in Butlerian terms, performers in Malang recognized that because femaleness and maleness are in large part produced through acts (such as dancing), a body does not need to be biologically male to produce maleness or biologically female to produce femaleness (see also Sunardi 2013: 137). At the same time, although most performers recognized that a dancer's biological sex did not determine which gendered dances best suited him or her, biological sex was not without consequence. Performers recognized differences between female-bodied and male-bodied dancers, leading me to analyze, particularly in chapters two and three, the impact of the dancer's sexed body in the performance of gendered styles of dance and ways dancers chose to use their bodies.

Significantly, I did not hear musicians or dancers refer to a specific category of cross-gender dance. For them, the dances were the dances and, as gendered styles, portrayed female or male personas regardless of the dancer's sex. Nevertheless, the terms *cross-gender dance*—an individual dancing in a style that is the opposite of his or her biological sex—and *same-gender dance*—which I use to refer to an individual dancing in a style that is the same as his or her biological sex—are useful. Distinguishing cross-gender from same-gender dance helps me to explore the impact of the dancer's sexed body on musicians' and dancers' perceptions of gender in performance, performers' uses of their bodies to produce specific senses of gender, and ways male and female performers claimed specific senses of gender by embodying maleness and/or femaleness in particular ways. At the same time, as I show, through both cross-gender and same-gender dance, dancers and the musicians who accompany them have reinforced and subverted dominant norms.

Analysis of cross-gender performance in particular facilitates exploration into the ways performers were negotiating the mapping of gender to sex in dominant gender ideologies. When dances are performed as cross-gender dances—that is, when males embody femaleness and vice versa—performers' manipulations of their bodies are particularly exposed and conventions of enacting masculinity and femininity are particularly visible. Judith Butler writes in an analysis of drag (a form of cross-gender performance), "[i]n the place of the law of heterosexual coherence, we see sex and gender denaturalized by means of a performance which avows their distinctness and dramatizes the cultural mechanism of their fabricated unity" (1999: 175). The visible denaturalization of a one-to-one mapping of gender to sex makes many instances of transvestism particularly rich sites in which to investigate strategies that individuals use to push at preestablished boundaries of gender (Morris 1995: 580), as has been shown in Marjorie Garber's analysis of cross-dressing in Western popular culture, fashion, and arts (1992: 3), Siu Leung Li's study of cross-dressing in Chinese opera (2003), Charlotte Suthrell's investigation of transvestism in the U.K. and India (2004), and other studies. At the same time, cross-gender performance is not necessarily always subversive; gender reversals also may reinforce dominant gender ideologies even as such ideologies are challenged (Butler 1993: 125, 231, 237; Anderson 1996; Peacock 1987: 168–172; Shaw 2005: 16).

Types of Performance

Beskalan, *Ngremo*, and masked dance are performed in a variety of contexts in Malang. *Beskalan* and *Ngremo* usually function as opening or welcoming dances that precede various types of performance, including different types of theater, music, and/or dance. Usually an individual, group, or institution hosts such performances to celebrate particular events, including weddings, circumcisions, anniversaries, birthdays, village purification ceremonies, particular days on the Javanese calendar, Indonesian Independence Day celebrations, and inaugurations. Masked dances may be performed as independent dances—often as opening or welcoming dances—or they may be performed as part of a masked dance drama called *wayang topèng*, usually for the types of events listed above (see also Onghokham 1972: 113). *Beskalan*, *Ngremo*, and masked dance are also performed for other reasons. For example, I observed *Beskalan Putri* performed by two females and the masked dance *Bapang* performed by two males as entertainment during an agricultural meeting. I also saw *Bapang* performed by one man as a dance to welcome the head of the regency (*bupati*) as he visited a village. *Beskalan*, *Ngremo*, and masked dance are also performed in the contexts of competitions and festivals (see also Sunardi 2010a: 89–90; 2011: 52 n5; 2013: 136–137).

The looks of surprise and confusion that melted into chuckles, or gentle explanations when I asked about female dancers performing *Ngremo* or *Beskalan* as an opening dance for a certain type of performance or about male dancers performing for another, made it clear that the sex of the professional dancers was sometimes connected to and thus implied by the type of performance these dances opened. For example, it was expected that female dancers would perform *Ngremo Tayub*, a male style dance, for *tayub* (if an opening dance was featured). *Tayub* or *tayuban* are participatory performance events that feature professional female singer-dancers and gamelan musicians hired by a host to entertain the host's guests. At various points in the course of the performance, and following a protocol related to social status, guests may come into the performance space, tip the performers, request a song, and dance with the dancers (see also Hefner 1987b: 80–85; Hughes-Freeland 1993: 107; Widodo 1995: 11–12, 21).

In contrast to expectations that females would perform *Ngremo Tayub* for *tayub*, most performers usually expected that males would perform *Ngremo Lanang* and/or *Ngremo Putri* for a type of east Javanese theater called *ludruk*.

Photograph 1.3. Males perform as females in an opening act of *ludruk*, 2006.

Ludruk features a series of opening acts that include dancing, singing, and comedy; a play; and interludes between the acts of the play—and is generally known in Malang and other parts of east Java for featuring males in both male and female roles (Brandon 1967: 48–49; Hatley 1971; Peacock 1987) (Photograph 1.3). As James Peacock emphasizes, *ludruk* has long been associated with male performers and female impersonation: an 1822 account of a performance called *ludruk* described two male performers, a clown and a female impersonator (Pigeaud 1938: 322, cited in Peacock 1987: 29). As *ludruk* developed as a form of theater in the twentieth century, males continued to play female and male roles (Brandon 1967: 48–49; Peacock 1987: 29–31). According to several performers in Malang, since the 1960s females have also taken female roles, but this was more common in places outside of Malang, such as Surabaya. In the *ludruk* shows that I attended in Malang by groups from Malang, for the most part, males dominated the casts, although females sometimes did perform in the course of the opening acts as singers or dancers.

While the sex of dancers in particular contexts has been flexible and subject to change over time, performers' associations of particular types of performance with male or female dancers in particular historical moments provides

Aims and Approaches

a useful analytical frame for the analysis of ways changes made in one type of performance have affected performance practices in another, how males and females have affected each other in different ways, and ways in which dancers and musicians have negotiated conceptual and physical boundaries of gender through types of performance.

Performance Structure and Roles

Performers conformed to and/or pushed at cultural expectations about their gendered and sexed identities through their roles in a performance structure that usually featured male or female dancers, an authoritative male drummer, and predominantly male musicians (Sunardi 2011). Dancers interacted closely with the drummer, articulating in movement what the drummer articulated in sound through the patterns played on the drum. Dancers also wore a set of small spherical bells called the *gongsèng* on their right ankles (see Photograph 1.2) for *Beskalan*, *Ngremo*, and the male style masked dances *Gunung Sari*, *Klana*, and *Bapang*. Performers identified the *gongsèng* as a distinctive feature of east Javanese dance. Dancers used the *gongsèng* to accent the movements and particular beats and off-beats, adding another sonic dimension to the performance. Dancers could also use the *gongsèng* to cue the drummer in various ways or to signal to the drummer that he or she understood the drummer's cue.

Dancers played other roles in the performance structure as well. By performing in the appropriate character, dancers (ideally) inspired the drummer and musicians to play with the appropriate feeling. In some cases for some dances, dancers sang. Dancers often sang in the course of performing *Ngremo*, welcoming the audience and/or guests and presenting poetic texts with a variety of meanings.

Some of the terms performers used to refer to dancers had gendered implications. The use of "*tandhak*," or "female singer-dancer," was one way that gender was constructed through performer roles, allowing cultural and discursive space for both females and males to be associated with femaleness. "*Tandhak*" was associated with femaleness in two main ways. For one, it was used to refer to singer-dancers who were biologically female. Key in this usage was the biological sex of the singer-dancer: at the *tayub* events I attended, female *tandhak* performed as singer-dancers dressed as females and, if *Ngremo Tayub* was performed as an opening dance, male style dance. "*Tandhak*" was also used to refer to males who specialized in performing as female singer-dancers and to males who specialized in female roles in *ludruk*, the latter of whom were more specifically referred to as *tandhak ludruk*.

Strikingly, performers' use of the term *tandhak* to identify female or male performers contributed to the blurring of boundaries separating femaleness and maleness.[4]

With the exception of female vocalists, professional adult musicians were predominately male (Photographs 1.4 and 1.5).[5] Playing a number of roles, the drummer provided the sonic articulation of the dance movements through the drum patterns. In fact, some performers believed that the basis of the dance was in the drum patterns. Furthermore, by playing the drum, the drummer communicated to the rest of the musical ensemble as the group leader. By mediating the dancer's wishes, such as to adjust the tempo or go to a different section of the dance, the drummer was the liaison between the dancer and the rest of the musicians. The drummer also had a responsibility to energize the dance, which he often did by pushing and pulling the tempo. The drummer was frequently one of the most authoritative members, if not the most authoritative member, of a particular group. In the group in which I regularly played, my teacher Kusnadi was considered the most authoritative member and he usually played the drum. Sometimes, however, he would turn the instrument over to another drummer in the group, or allow a younger musician who was learning to play the drum an opportunity to gain some experience by playing for a rehearsal and/or performance. Usually the most authoritative member played the drum to lead the other gamelan musicians, as in other regional styles of gamelan, including central Javanese (Brinner 1995). The difficulty of playing the drum also necessitated a very high level of competence, usually gained through years of experience, also as in other regions, including central Java (Brinner 1995: 133–164).

Usually at the end of the chain of command, the rest of the gamelan musicians followed cues communicated by the drummer or dancer. They also followed the drummer's fluctuations of tempo, some of which were quite subtle while others were fairly dramatic. This is not always easy for those new to east Javanese gamelan music, but competent musicians seemed to not have too much trouble partly because from their experience, they already knew which movements to expect to be slower and which faster.

Following the drummer and dancer through aural and visual signals, the gamelan musicians contributed to the performance in many important ways. The musicians playing the colotomic instruments (*kenong*, *kempul*, and gong) helped to keep the dancer, drummer, and other musicians oriented in the structure of the composition. Of particular importance was the gong player marking the main cycle (see Becker 1979; Becker and Becker 1981). Those playing the skeletal melody on metallophones helped to keep all of the performers oriented. Sometimes this melody helped the dancer and drummer

Photographs 1.4 and 1.5. Musicians in a gamelan ensemble play for *ludruk*, 2006.

to remember dance movements and drumming patterns. The musicians also contributed to the appropriate mood and feeling of the dance through their use of dynamics and—depending on the instrument, composition, or section of the composition—melodic elaboration. As performers interacted within this structure—often featuring male or female dancers, an authoritative male drummer, and primarily male musicians—they negotiated senses of themselves as males and females and made decisions that affected the form and content of the dances, which I explore in particular in chapter six (see also Sunardi 2011).

Cross-Gender Dance in Perspective

It is important to keep in mind that in Malang, cross-gender dance was not unusual. The performers (and audience members) I consulted were quite used to dances performed as cross-gender dances, recalling the practice decades into the past. For example, one performer recalled seeing a woman perform *Ngremo Lanang* as an opening dance for shadow puppet theater in 1956 (p.c., Asbari, June 30, 2006). Another musician recalled that when he was playing for *tayub* in about 1963, the dancers (females) were still dancing *Beskalan Putri*. He pointed to the use of *Ngremo*, mostly *Ngremo Lanang*, starting in about 1965 (p.c., Achmad Suwarno, April 3, 2006). Growing up with *ludruk*, performers were quite accustomed to males performing female roles. Performers also recalled it being customary for males to play female roles in masked dance drama "in the past." When I was in Malang, I noticed many female dancers performing male as well as female roles.

A brief sampling of cross-gender traditions in Java puts cross-gender dance in Malang in a larger context, further showing it to be not unusual. Cross-gender performance has existed throughout what is now the Indonesian province of East Java since at least the nineteenth century (Pigeaud 1938: 277, 301, 321–323, 328). The 1822 account of female impersonation in a performance described as *ludruk* that Peacock cites from Pigeaud's book has already been mentioned (Pigeaud 1938: 322, cited in Peacock 1987: 29). In Banyuwangi, males dressed as females in the nineteenth century performed a type of ritual dance called *seblang* (Sutton 1993: 136; Wolbers 1989: 8) and a type of social dance called *gandrung* (Wolbers 1986: 79; 1989: 8; 1993: 35; Yampolsky 1991a; Sutton 1993: 136). In central Java, males have performed female roles in a variety of contexts—such as female style court dance in eighteenth-, nineteenth-, and twentieth-century courts (Sumarsam 1995: 276 n59; Raffles 1988: 342; Hughes-Freeland 1995: 184; 2006: 65–66; 2008b: 154–157; Ponder 1990: 134). Prior to Indonesian independence, males also played female roles in Yogyakarta court performances of *wayang wong* dance theater (Holt 1967: 160; Brakel-Papenhuyzen 1995: 49; Hughes-Freeland 1995: 185; 2008b: 157; 2008c: 144). The first time the female style dance called *golèk* was performed at the Yogyakarta court during the reign of Sultan Hamengku Buwana VIII (1921–1939), it was performed by a male dancer (Choy 1984: 55; see also Hughes-Freeland 2008b: 157; 2008c: 144).

Females, too, have performed male style dances as cross-gender dancers. In twentieth and twenty-first century Surakarta, females have played male roles in different forms of dance drama, including *langendriyan* as well as other forms of theater (Holt 1967: 160; Brakel-Papenhuyzen 1995: 49–50; Hughes-Freeland 1995: 183; 2008a: 28; 2008b: 157; 2008c: 163 n13). In Yogyakarta, females have cross-dressed in the folk dance traditions *reyog, jathilan,* and *angguk* since the 1990s (Hughes-Freeland 2008a: 28; 2008b: 157). In Banyumas, females perform the male style dance *Baladéwan*, a closing dance for a type of rural dance tradition called *lèngger* (Lysloff 2001/2002: 12–13). In West Java, refined male roles in Sundanese wayang dance are often danced by females (Spiller 2010: 22), and males or females perform male characters in Cirebonese masked dance (Hughes-Freeland 2008a: 28; Spiller 2010: 22–23; Ross 2011: 146; 2013).

Cross-dressing in performance has had complex, multifarious meanings in Java including symbolic and ritual significance influenced by centuries-old Hindu and indigenous logics in which androgyny or the combination of male and female elements represents cosmic power and fertility (Wolbers 1989: 8–11; Sutton 1993: 139; Hughes-Freeland 2008b: 155). Speaking to more worldly concerns, performers in Malang speculated that *ludruk* theater used to be all male in order to prevent problems that might be caused among the male members of the troupe by the presence of women, and because it would have been inappropriate for women to have been out traveling with men. Females taking male roles, on the one hand, can be understood as a strategy of female empowerment, as on the neighboring island of Bali (Diamond 2008; Hatley 2008: 263), and on the other hand, as performers explained to me, a matter of necessity because few boys at the time of my fieldwork were interested in studying dances like *Ngremo, Beskalan,* and masked dance because they felt that doing so would compromise the perception of their masculinity. From my observations, young males interested in the arts tended toward music or *jaranan* (hobbyhorse dance)—the latter often featuring trance and feats of strength that reinforced the masculinity of male dancers (see Kartomi 1973; Schrieber 1991; Clara van Groenendael 2008). Given such multivalent meanings of cross-gender performance in Java, it is no wonder that I encountered some rather complicated expectations about cross-gender representation in early-twenty-first century Malang, such as expectations for cross-gender dance to maintain tradition and senses of the past.

Approaching "Tradition"

Concerns with Preserving Regional Culture

My principal teachers expected *Ngremo, Beskalan*, and masked dance to reinforce constructions of femaleness and maleness that they had come to consider normal and to maintain the conventions of east Javanese dance performance, which they described in terms of "tradition" (*tradisi*) (see also Sunardi 2009). They were not bothered by the onstage transvestism per se when these dances were performed or were remembered being performed as cross-gender dances. They were, however, bothered by what they perceived as current performers' failures to perform gender convincingly, competently, and artistically. Both males' performance of female style dance and females' performance of male style dance at the time of my fieldwork frequently fell short of their expectations. Fundamentally, they were concerned that performers "nowadays"—since the 1990s, by their accounts—were departing too far from preestablished conventions of tradition. The sixty or so other artists I consulted consistently echoed such sentiments. For their parts, the musicians and dancers being critiqued were expressing masculinity and femininity in their own ways and in so doing, pushing at established conventions of performance and asserting their own prerogative to define tradition and gender in their own ways. The concern with east Javanese tradition (and Malangan tradition in particular) shows that "aspects of identity" other than gender are also "at stake in transgendering and cross-dressing" (Morris 1995: 583). Since the issues that were most pressing for most artists in their conversations with me were related to regional identity and the maintenance of tradition, these issues became a focus of my attention.

Underlying artists' concerns that Malangan traditions be maintained through what they deemed correct and convincing performances of male and female style dances was their fear that Malangan arts would eventually die out or disappear. Performers were also responding to the dominance of central Javanese and Surabayan arts in Malang (see also Onghokham 1972; Sutton 1991: 169–170; Sunardi 2010a). The dominance of these styles was nothing new. Drawing on observations made in Malang in 1963, Onghokham has noted the dominance of central Javanese and Surabayan styles at that time, attributing their dominance to "[t]he increase of travel between the different parts of Java and the influence of radio broadcasting from the urban centers [which] have caused centralizing tendencies in Javanese culture at the cost of local art traditions" (1972: 111). For example, for the opening dance of a *wayang topèng* (masked dance theater) performance he observed, he found that *Ngremo*—a dance associated with Surabaya—had replaced a "bapang dance"—a masked dance that had been part of "the Malang wayang topèng performance" (ibid.: 114). No less important to the popularity of styles associated with Surabaya and central Java, I believe, has been the cultural value given to particular regional styles.

The institutionalization of culture in Indonesia since the declaration of independence in 1945, among other factors, has contributed to the varying levels of prestige that most people in Java have given the performing arts associated with different places (see also Sunardi 2010a: 92–93).[6] There is a complex history, likely centuries long, of cultural interaction between people from different regions in Java as well as between people from court or urban centers and rural areas which effectively blurs the boundaries of these very categories (Sutton 1991: 170; Day 2002: 189–190; Weiss 2006: 92–94, 114–120; Sumarsam 2008). Nonetheless, higher prestige has been given to arts associated with court centers and urban areas (Perlman 1998: 57; Weiss 2002; 2006: 114–120). At the time of my fieldwork, the most prestigious music, dance, and theater traditions were those associated with the four central Javanese courts—the Susuhunan and the Mangkunegaran in the city of Surakarta, and the Kasultanan and the Paku Alaman in the city of Yogyakarta—which were established in the eighteenth and nineteenth centuries (Sumarsam 1995: 49; Ricklefs 2008: 120–121). Next in terms of prestige were the arts associated with the central Javanese court cities Surakarta and Yogyakarta but not necessarily of the courts. Arts associated with central or east Javanese non-court cities ranked lower still, and at the bottom were arts associated with towns and villages.

Disrupting this ranking order—and providing fodder for those who insisted on the cultural value of east Javanese arts—was the general knowledge in Java that kingdoms with courtly culture flourished in east Java prior to the establishment of the present-day courts of Surakarta and Yogyakarta. Such east Javanese kingdoms included Singosari (1222–1292) and Majapahit (1293 or 1294 until 1478 or c.1520), the latter of which was a great empire at the height of its power (Holt 1967: 66; Kinney 2003: 155–163; Ricklefs 2008: 20–21, 39). Like R. Anderson Sutton, I could not help but notice the ruins of temples that were "reminders of the courtly culture that once existed" and contributed to "the awareness that [east Java] was once a center of mighty court culture" (1991: 123). The thirteenth-century Kidal Temple and late-thirteenth to mid-fourteenth-century Jago Temple were located in Tumpang, where I was based, no doubt affecting performers' senses of the past and cultural heritage (Holt 1967: 68, 71; Kinney 2003: 89, 93, 95, 124). A subdistrict in Malang named Singosari, home to the thirteenth-fourteenth-century Singosari Temple (Holt 1967: 68; Kinney 2003: 137, 148), further reinforced local senses of a courtly past.

While many central and east Javanese performers and scholars recognize the greatness of the east Javanese courts and trace aspects of central and east Javanese arts to them, most generally do not think of present-day east Javanese arts as "court" arts per se because these courts fell hundreds of years ago, and prior to the establishment of the existing central Javanese courts. Rather, east Javanese arts are generally connected to city, town, and village cultures. Within this region, the arts from Surabaya, the capital city of the province of East Java, are generally given more institutionalized prestige than arts from Malang, which are often associated with villages.

The higher status given to central Javanese and Surabayan styles in conjunction with audiences' desires had material consequences for the performers I consulted. Due in part to government cultural policy that has promoted what it has defined as the most prestigious arts, the presence of central Javanese and Surabayan styles had been reinforced in Malang, contributing to the dominance of these styles in performed repertoires. Audiences in general had come to prefer central Javanese and Surabayan styles, and were thus more likely to hire artists who performed them. In addition, performers had to compete with popular music such as *dangdut*, a genre that features electric guitar(s), bass, keyboard(s), and drums at its core, often with flute, and has been influenced by *orkes Melayu*, Indian film music, Middle Eastern popular music, as well as American and British rock (Frederick 1982; Manuel 1988: 210–211; Yampolsky 1991b; Weintraub 2010). Another genre that was quite popular was *campur sari*, which combines gamelan instruments with electric keyboards, bass, and guitar, among other instruments depending on the group (Brinner 2008: 19; Supanggah 2003). Aware of these market factors, musicians and dancers consistently explained that they had to perform what audiences desired in order to be hired, and, like the artists Tony Day consulted in East Java in the early 1990s, were concerned about "the commercial viability of their art" (2002: 190).

To appeal to audiences, many performers in Malang believed that they had to learn central Javanese and Surabayan styles of gamelan and dance, and/or incorporate elements from *dangdut* and *campur sari* such as song repertoire, drum patterns, and instrumentation (e.g., keyboard). Sometimes learning these more popular styles came at the expense of learning, relearning, or deepening knowledge of "traditional" Malangan arts. A young singer-dancer declined several invitations I extended to practice pieces from older repertoires of Malangan gamelan music. She and her mother, a former performer herself, asked for my understanding. Explaining apologetically that they were not like me with lots of money, they implied that I had the time and luxury to study what I wished. Performers like them, they continued, have to think about what would sell.

Musicians' and dancers' reasons for performing specific styles, however, are complicated. In addition to economic necessity (real or perceived), the young woman and her mother just referenced may have preferred the more popular styles for aesthetic and personal reasons, including life experience and heritage. One of my teachers appreciated and performed east Javanese arts but also savored central Javanese music, dance, and theater. Identifying with his central Javanese heritage, he identified with and aspired to the refinement and eloquence associated with the culture of this region. Other performers, however, including most of the performers I consulted, were invested in maintaining Malangan music and dance.

Other factors contributed to performers' concerns with tradition, including national political ideologies stemming from the totalitarian New Order government under the reign of Soeharto (1966–1998) that promoted the notion of unchanging tradition (*tradisi*) and authentic (*asli*) Javanese culture to erase a history of social activism and thereby control its citizens by convincing them that the past and present do not and should not change (Pemberton 1994: 9). Philip Yampolsky (1995), Felicia Hughes-Freeland (1997), Ian Wilson (1999), and René Lysloff (2001/2002), among others, have examined the strategies this regime used to recontexualize performing arts traditions in different parts of Java in order to implement New Order notions of tradition and authenticity. Those strategies included instruction at national arts conservatories and academies, sponsorship of competitions and festivals, regulation of mass media through censorship, and implementation of training programs for performers, to name a few (see also Sunardi 2009: 471). Most of the performers I consulted lived through the New Order era and were exposed to these types of discourses about tradition and authentic culture. They were likely to have been influenced by such discourses, which contributed to their own concerns about the preservation of Malangan and east Javanese traditions as well as their investment in their senses of the past.

Memory and Senses of the Past

My dance and drum lessons and the recording sessions I organized were often months-long processes of remembering as my teachers repeatedly emphasized the necessity for me to learn the older, "complete" forms of dances—versions that had largely fallen out of performed practice. Their consistent reference to how "x" used to be performed, or how "x" was performed "in past times" or "in the past" (*dulu, biyèn/rumiyin*) led me to take a strong interest in these older forms and I worked to learn them. Often, after studying a movement or a drum pattern with one of my teachers, I returned for the next lesson only for him (almost all of my principal teachers were male) to realize that what he had previously taught me was not quite "correct" or "complete" and that the movement or music went a different way. In some cases, performers were recalling details of performance practices that they had seen or performed from many years prior to my fieldwork—ten, twenty, thirty, even forty or more years into the past. What I learned at any given lesson was what my teacher remembered at that moment, making my studies simultaneously fascinating and frustrating. In other cases, it seemed that performers were also continuing to develop and refine their own interpretations of the drumming, choreographies, and characters of the dances.

Other challenges arose as I strove to cull information from my teachers' and other performers' memories. The same performers frequently provided different dates for the same change in performance practice or their own biography on different occasions. Given that some were remembering decades into the past, this is not surprising. References to years varied, with performers giving specific years, saying something was around a certain year, or giving decades. Sometimes performers used historical markers such as "it was during the Japanese era" (the Japanese occupation, 1942–1945). Sometimes they referred to stages in their own lives or in the lives of others they knew—"I was still a bachelor" or "so-and-so was still alive." They also referred to other people they knew I knew: "so-and-so was still married to so-and-so" or "so-and-so was already born; she was still little." Some individuals may not have wanted to provide specific dates for reasons they did not share with me. In some cases, it was up to me to situate or approximate their memories in a particular decade or time period as I interpreted their narratives.

Some individuals did not pay much attention to years. More important for some were particular days on the Javanese calendar. Also, musicians and dancers themselves relied on oral tradition passed on to them from their elders. Because many of these elders were already deceased at the time of my fieldwork, I was not able to cross-check information by talking to them. Furthermore, in using personal memories to legitimize knowledge, sometimes the same individual re-remembered an aspect of a dance or musical composition differently in different conversations in order to support the point that he or she was making at the time. In other words, what an individual thought he or she heard and saw in the past was subject to change, or he or she heard and saw different things at different moments—tendencies that were facilitated by the flexibility of dances and music as performed in Malang. Seemingly contradictory statements were sometimes references to different points in the past, which performers strategically recalled.

The distinction that V. Narayana Rao makes between "recorded" and "received" texts in his work on South Asian literature (referenced in Sears and Flueckiger 1991: 4) is helpful in thinking about the seeming contradictions in performers' senses of the past. A recorded text is one that "has been written down or recited" while a received text is one that "an audience or consumer of the text hears or *thinks* has been recorded" (emphasis in original; Sears and Flueckiger 1991: 4). Rao's idea of received texts is particularly relevant because in Malang, performers received (that is, perceived) choreographies and musical compositions in particular ways (Sunardi 2010a: 113), using their memories and senses of the past as a basis of evaluation for performance in the present, as Lisa Gold found was the case in Bali (1998: 38–44).

Drawing attention to the importance of interpreting "memory as a self-fashioning act of the person" that reveals more about the present than about the past, Ann Stoler with Karen Strassler emphasizes the importance of considering "not only *what* is remembered but *how*" (original emphasis, 2002: 170). As Theresa Buckland points out, dance offers an embodied manifestation of personal memory (2006: 11). Likewise, music offers an aural manifestation. This is not to suggest that human bodies (dancing, singing, or playing instruments) are stable repositories of stable memories or histories. Since the body is constantly changing (ibid.: 15), a dancer may perform differently in the present than in the past as "age, injury, and health may transform earlier practices, and as a living, moving source, the body may not always replicate with exactitude the moves of the past" (ibid.: 13). The same can be said for musicians who speak of performing in particular ways in the past, but due to the ways their bodies change, may perform differently in the present. And yet, in remembering through dancing, playing music, and talking about performance, performers were doing important ideological work, using their bodies to produce, maintain, store, and transmit knowledge, including senses of tradition and the past, through performance (Taylor 2003: 21, 24).

I am less concerned with determining the veracity of specific dates or the details of the performance practice than with analyzing the meanings about performance that musicians and dancers constructed through their memories and senses of history at the moment I consulted them. Like Mary Zurbuchen, I recognize that in some cases personal memory affects individuals' senses of the past, "shaping and transforming past experience" (2005: 7). In other words, I am more interested in personal memories and performers' historical narratives for what they reveal about "the meanings that can be construed for its participants" (Neuman 1993: 276). At stake for musicians and dancers in the performance of certain dances—and in teaching me older ways to perform these dances and their music—was their social memory as Malangan people. For some, dance technique functioned as "an archive that links subjectivities and socialities to history" (Hamera 2002: 65). Building upon Paul Connerton to take bodily actions to be central to the construction and transmission of social memory through performance (1989: 71), I show that performers relied on their own senses of the past, including the social memories they shared as Malangan people as well as their personal memories, to legitimize their ideas of correctness about the performance and history of particular dances and their music—which included what they believed were correct and appropriate ways to embody maleness and femaleness.

I thus approach "tradition" as a complex, shifting construct that involves the intentional and unintentional inclusion and exclusion of practices and histories (Williams 1977; Hobsbawm 1983; Brinner 1995: 321; Coplan 1993). Drawing attention to tradition as a process, Felicia Hughes-Freeland advocates for a view of tradition "as an ideology that attributes precedents to practices that may have recently been revived, recast, or reinvented, even if the label or contents refer back to a previous practice" (2006: 55; see also 1993: 90). Approaching tradition as a process and as a way of thinking allows me to appreciate, take seriously, and value the authenticity and/or age that performers attributed to particular dances or ways of performing particular dances, while also recognizing that traditions are in flux, subject to choices people make about what to include or exclude.

To underline individuals' agency in making decisions about what is included, I adopt the notions of "selecting," "selection," and "selected" from Raymond Williams's discussion of tradition as "selective" (1977: 115–117) and Tomie Hahn's description of the coexistence of modernization and tradition in Japan "as an interesting dance of selection and prioritization" (2007: 28). Viewing selection as part of the cultural process by and through which traditions are produced, I examine how performers made selections through performance practice and their verbal discourse, showing that in the process of selecting tradition, performers articulated masculinity and femininity in particular ways. I thus approach gender and tradition as mutually constitutive.

Equally pertinent are the ways performers made selections through interactions. Benjamin Brinner writes,

> To the extent that a musical tradition resides in the minds of the bearers of that tradition, we can define it in terms of performer competence and interaction as

an aggregate of musical knowledge, skills, and ways of making music that are "bundled" together by a group of musicians, enabling them to interact within their community. (1995: 321)

Extending Brinner's focus on musicians to musicians and dancers, I approach tradition as neither singular nor fixed, but a product of specific interactions between individual performers, each with his or her own abilities and knowledge. I also consider the impact of interactions between performers and audiences, and between performers, and a foreign researcher (me) who, in asking questions and writing about performers, has also contributed to what is articulated and in some ways archived as "tradition."

No less important are the stakes of selecting tradition in particular ways. Felicia Hughes-Freeland is right to emphasize that "ideas of tradition, and the concomitant view of continuity and discontinuity are also subject to interpretive processes which are contingent on contemporary political concerns" (1991: 136). The "political concerns" I foreground are performers' concerns about the maintenance of local tradition and identity. It is my contention that as musicians and dancers continuously re-created east Javanese dance traditions, in part as expressions of regional culture and to maintain regional culture through expressions of gender, they negotiated cultural ambivalence surrounding female power—doing so in a Muslim-majority context.

Approaching Islam

No less of an impetus in writing this book has been to complicate assumptions about what it means to be a man, a woman, someone in between, or simply an artist in a Muslim-majority society, where the presence of Islam in the performing arts was strong (Sunardi 2012, 2013). Almost every performer I consulted was Muslim, albeit of different degrees of piety. Performances were held for Muslim celebrations such as circumcisions to celebrate a boy's transition into adulthood and supported by Muslim individuals, including those who were devout. Performances were also sometimes held in explicitly Muslim spaces: I once attended a performance of *ludruk* theater at an Islamic boarding school. Several performers said that the director (and financial backbone) of that *ludruk* group had made the *haj*, in effect linking a Muslim figure to the life of an artistic organization that featured males who played female roles. Many, if not all, of such males embodied femaleness to different degrees in their daily lives, too (as will be explored in chapter three). By providing a source of livelihood for such artists, the director had a hand in making cultural space for males to embody femaleness both on- and offstage.

Islam was present in additional ways. In many cases, lessons, rehearsals, and performances were scheduled so as not to conflict with the call to prayer after sunset, at nightfall, and before sunrise. If a lesson, practice session, rehearsal, or performance (including performances that lasted well into the night or all night) did not end before the call to prayer at these particular times, a break was usually taken during the call, during which the beautiful and eerie heterophony of the call emanating from the numerous mosques and prayer rooms within hearing distance rose into the sky through loudspeakers. Anne Rasmussen vividly describes and analyzes the presence of Islam in the soundscape, observing that "[h]earing Islam in Indonesia is not an option. It is a certainty" (2010: 39). Whether or not performers prayed, most used call to prayer times as points of reference. For example, to indicate that a rehearsal was more or less over, my gamelan teacher Kusnadi or another frequently said, "It's already *maghrib* [the call to prayer after sunset]." Often, when I asked what time an evening rehearsal or performance was going to start, many said, "After *isyak* [the call to prayer at nightfall]." Like Rasmussen, I found there was simply no doubt, no lack of reminder, and no forgetting that one was in a place where most people identified as Muslim in some way.

Despite the importance of Islam in daily life, or perhaps because it was taken for granted, most, but not all, artists infrequently discussed Islam with me as an issue of controversy. Given that one of my initial research goals was to examine how performers negotiated cross-gender performance in a Muslim context, I was surprised (and initially a bit disappointed) to find that unless I brought up the subject of Islam during interviews, most performers—with a few exceptions—did not often talk about it as an issue of concern. Due to my own mistaken assumptions, I was struck that in conversations with performers about *Ngremo, Beskalan,* and masked dance performed as cross-gender dances, no one brought up prohibitions against "mixing male and female elements in public" (Peacock 1987: 19) or "the Qur'anic concept *khuntsa,* an in-between gendered person whose behavior is condemned" (Oetomo 2000: 51; see also 1996: 263–264).

There may have been a number of reasons that Islam seemed to be a nonissue in most of my conversations with performers. My interest in performance practice may have encouraged performers to focus on playing, singing, and dancing techniques, or perhaps they assumed that I was more interested in the details of performance practice than in Islam. Perhaps Islam was not always a pressing concern at the time of my fieldwork for the performers I consulted because many of the communities in which I worked were relatively tolerant in terms of religion and supportive of the arts. This is not to suggest, however, that Islam was never an issue.

Some artists voiced their concerns about Islam (sometimes without prompting from me) because they perceived that increasing orthodoxy and piety had a tangible impact on their professional activities—that is, their ability to earn a living as professional musicians and dancers. Some performers, including those who were themselves Muslim, connected a decline in performance activity in their neighborhoods over the years to the increasing presence of Muslims who were orthodox in their beliefs and practices. Such perspectives corroborate Robert Hefner's findings that increasing orthodoxy in Islamic practice contributed to a decline in frequency of *tayuban* in rural east Java, a decline he observed between the late 1970s and the mid-1980s (1987a, 1987b). A puppeteer Tony Day consulted in the early 1990s identified the "leaders of the East Javanese Muslim community" as a significant "threat to traditional East Javanese culture" (2002: 191). Indeed, performers I consulted were speaking to the Islamic resurgence in Southeast Asia since the 1970s (Hefner 1997: 5), "an unprecedented deepening of Islamic piety since the 1980s" in Indonesia (Hefner 1997: 30), as well as an intensification of debate about the place of Islam in Indonesia since the fall of the New Order regime in 1998 (Harnish and Rasmussen 2011: 8; Hefner 2008; Houben 2003: 164).

While increasing Islamic piety was a strong cultural pressure at the time of my fieldwork, I suggest that the blame performers placed upon orthodox and/or devout Muslims for the decreased popularity of the performing arts belied the many factors affecting changing practices in the performing arts, including shifts in the popularity of particular genres. While older performers talked about the decline in the popularity of particular forms of theater such as masked dance drama and *ludruk*, they recognized that *jaranan* (hobby-horse dance), *dangdut*, and *campur sari* continued to be in demand, which I also noticed while in Malang.

Furthermore, since 1997 economic factors such as the devaluation of the Indonesian currency and dramatic increases in the price of oil products, had made it difficult for average families to afford sponsoring live performances that featured large numbers of musicians and dancers such as *ludruk*. Such economic factors have similarly contributed to preferences in central Java for the usually smaller *campur sari* ensembles over full gamelan ensembles (Brinner 2008: 19; Supanggah 2003: 3–4). Performers in Malang also identified local government regulations as a financial consideration. As they explained, and as I learned from sponsoring performances myself, patrons must obtain permission from the village, local police department, and local military headquarters, usually in the form of a permit, to host events that feature performing arts (see also Widodo 1995: 18). This permit is often more expensive for types of performance that are believed to encourage fights and drunken behavior, such as *tayuban* (see also Widodo 1995: 18).

Although Robert Hefner focuses on the impact of increasing Islamic orthodoxy and piety on ritual activity—including *tayuban*—in rural east Java, he also recognizes other complex cultural and economic factors that contributed to the decline in *tayuban* and other ritual activity he observed in the late 1970s to mid-1980s, including shifts in patterns of consumption. That is, people became more likely to display their wealth through "more privatized status goods, like radios, televisions, and motorcycles" rather than costly rituals (Hefner 1987a: 548; see also 1987b: 93–94). He also acknowledges the impact of poverty, government policies, and notions of modernity (1987a). In short, many factors and pressures have been affecting potential hosts' decisions about what kind of performance to sponsor, including personal preferences, the reactions of other people in a particular neighborhood, and the costs of the performance—not just the presence of Islam.

The ways that performers talked about Islam, however, invite exploration into how they made sense of Islam, performance, and dominant gender ideologies in their own ways, thereby mediating religious piety and shaping the practice, expression, and experience of Islam in Indonesia (Brenner 1996; Boellstorff 2005a, 2007; Blackburn 2008; Blackburn, Smith, and Syamsiyatun 2008; Smith 2008; Rasmussen 2010; van Doorn-Harder 2006; Weintraub 2011; Daniels 2013; Sunardi 2013). Such negotiations add a layer of complexity to the cultural and ideological work that dancers and musicians were doing in a place were cross-gender performance was a part of tradition, expected by some to maintain tradition, and a cultural mechanism by and through which performers contended with cultural ambivalence surrounding the magnetic power of femaleness.

2. Maintaining Female Power through Male Style Dance

This chapter explores some of the ways female dancers, as well as the mostly male musicians who accompanied them, were maintaining and making cultural space for the expression of women's magnetic female power through women's performance of male style dance, building from earlier analyses (Sunardi 2009, 2013). I first establish that for centuries, women in Java have expressed and embodied a magnetic power that is connected to their femaleness and that they have done so in myriad ways, including sexually, economically, and martially (i.e., abilities as fighters). I show that a certain ambivalence in the Javanese imagination has surrounded these expressions of female power. This ambivalence has contributed to the cultural contradictions surrounding womanhood in the twentieth and twenty-first centuries with which the performers I consulted have had to contend. I argue that, by performing male style dance, female dancers and (mostly) male musicians negotiated boundaries of gender and sex visually and sonically, maintaining and making cultural space for women's expression of female power despite pressures from state and society to control and subdue it.

Ambivalence toward Manifestations of Women's Power

Sexual Power

On the one hand, women's power to affect men through their sexuality has been recognized and celebrated in Java. For hundreds of years, the performance of female style dance in the context of harvest/fertility rituals throughout Java has represented the necessity of female sexual power to the prosperity, well-being, and continuity of the community (Hughes-Freeland 1997: 478–480; Hidajat 2006: 179, 181–183; Spiller 2008: 162). *Tayuban* dance events and female singer-dancers, with their connections to female sexuality, have also been linked with healing (Hughes-Freeland 1993: 108–110; 2008c: 145). In some cases, popular singer-dancers are "often honoured and admired by the villagers" (Koentjaraningrat 1985: 228 n175).

Stories and legends about sexual encounters between powerful men and women have signified that such unions were key to the sociopolitical stability within the realm, legitimizing kings' political power and authority. Dhedhes, a thirteenth-century queen of Singosari was known for her beauty and "as a 'woman with a flaming womb' whose magic would ensure its possessor's control over the throne" (Holt 1967: 78; see also Carey and Houben 1987: 15; Weiss 2006: 85–87). The potency of female sexual power can also be understood in the story that situates the origins of *bedhaya*, a type of central Javanese female style court dance, "in the encounter between the first king of the [central Javanese] Mataram dynasty, Sultan Agung (seventeenth century) and the goddess of the south sea, Kangjeng Ratu Kidul" (Becker 1991: 113). This story, which exists in multiple versions, written and oral, suggests that performance of some *bedhaya* dances symbolizes, among other things, the sexualized relationship between the male ruler and the goddess, as well as the unification of male and female energy believed essential to the success of his rule (Becker 1991: 113, 116–117; 1993: 123–131; Carey and Houben 1987: 17; Brakel-Papenhuyzen 1995: 26–27; Hughes-Freeland 1995: 200; Weiss 2006: 62–63; see also Brakel-Papenhuijzen 1992: 45). In certain performances in the court of Surakarta, if one of the *bedhaya* dancers is believed to be possessed by the queen's spirit, the king may use that dancer's body to consummate the relationship with his supernatural lover (Carey and Houben 1987: 17; Weiss 2006: 62–63; see also Hughes-Freeland 2008b: 148).

The presence and power of the goddess of the south sea is present in other ways. Javanese rulers of the central Javanese courts in current times make regular offerings to her (Brakel 1997: 266–267; Hughes-Freeland 2007: 189). Popular media, including magazines, films, and television, include regular references to her, reinforcing the awareness that many people in Java have of her and her power, connected largely to her sexuality (Wessing 2006: 51–52; Hughes-Freeland 2007: 189–190).

On the other hand, women's sexual power has also inspired apprehension, in part because (assuming a heterosexual framework) one way that men make sense of their own power is through their desires for women and, importantly, in resisting those desires (Browne 2000; Cooper 2000; Spiller 2008, 2010). As Nancy Cooper shows in central Java, in some cases, female gamelan vocalists draw on their magnetic power to flirt with other males in front of their husbands or boyfriends, testing their husbands' or boyfriends' ability to resist reacting and the other men's ability to resist temptation (2000: 617). These tests are processes by and through which men gain and protect spiritual power and are also mechanisms that maintain social harmony by encouraging individual self-control (ibid.: 617). Similarly, in West Java, men can show their power by resisting the seduction of female singer-dancers in Sundanese dance (Spiller 2008: 166). At *dangdut* performances in Yogyakarta, Jakarta, and other cities, many men refrain from applauding and "maintain a 'poker-face' expression," thus also demonstrating their restraint (Browne 2000: 3, 17). Exercising restraint and self-control, aspects of refinement, are ways through which a person may accumulate spiritual power in Java and also show that he or she possesses it (Anderson 1990a: 50–51). On some level, men expect and need women to be powerful and to exude this power through their sexuality, recognizing that women's power is necessary to their own power and their status (Cooper 2000: 628). At the same time, women's power is also threatening because of the potential for men to give in to temptation and thereby expose their lack of spiritual power (Cooper 2000: 617).

While female singer-dancers have been in some ways culturally valued for their roles in rituals, they have also been assumed to be of loose sexual morals as, historically, they have been associated with sexual freedom and prostitution (Raffles 1988: 342; Koentjaraningrat 1985: 204; Choy 1984: 60; Sutton 1984: 124). Foregrounding contradictions in Sundanese gender ideologies in his analysis of Sundanese dance in West Java, Henry Spiller has shown that the figure of the female singer-dancer simultaneously embodies and evokes the contradictory images of a sacred, benevolent, fertile rice goddess and also a profane, greedy prostitute (2010: 76–103). Writing about Sundanese music in West Java, Sean Williams enriches understandings of the complex position a female performer (as a singer or dancer) assumes when she takes center stage. "Because she must interact with both the audience and the (usually male) accompanists," Williams writes, "she must tread the thin line of respectability, answering to the mainstream interests of the audience members while responding to the instrumentalists behind her" (1998: 77). Building from Spiller and Williams, I suggest that female performers in Malang were negotiating conflicting expectations for women to be powerful and yet also submissive to men's authority.

Economic Power

Women's economic power has also been a source of cultural ambivalence. For centuries, women in Java have exerted economic power and influence. According to Barbara Andaya, "[e]xamination of ninth- and tenth-century inscriptions from Java show . . . that women entered into contracts, incurred debts, owned property in their own right, and played a part in village decision-making" (2007: 119). In the seventeenth century, women were active as traders (Brenner 1998: 74), and in the early nineteenth century, women controlled their husbands' money, bought and sold items at the markets, and were regarded as superior to men in financial matters (Raffles, 1817, I: 353, quoted in Carey and Houben 1987: 21, and in Brenner 1998: 74). Twentieth-century observers have noted the many occupations open to women, women's importance in making decisions for the family, and women's management of household finances (often including their husbands' earnings) (Geertz 1961: 46, 123–125; Keeler 1990: 129; Hatley 1990: 180; Brenner 1995; 1998: 155–156).

Women's economic power and clout, however, have been double-edged swords. While women have been lauded for their ability to manage money well, their handling of money and attention to financial matters has been used against them in terms of spiritual power, status, and prestige (Djajadiningrat-Nieuwenhuis 1987: 47; Errington 1990: 6–7; Keeler 1990: 140; Hatley 1990: 182; Brenner 1995: 25–26; 1998: 140–141; Browne 2000: 16). As explained in chapter one, following the dominant ideology of Javanese spiritual power, money should flow to spiritually powerful people as if without effort on their parts (Anderson 1990a: 53). Those who visibly exchange money—such as those who work at markets (including many women)—as well as those who appear to be concerned about money (including many women who work at markets and/or manage household finances) may be perceived as less spiritually powerful, less refined (even crude or coarse), and have less status than those who just seem to have money and appear unconcerned about it (Brenner 1998: 140–141).

At the same time, women play instrumental roles in producing status for their families through their handling of money, as shown by Suzanne Brenner (1998). For example, in Javanese merchant families, in many cases it is women's economic power and responsibility in running the family business as well as in the marketplace that produces not only wealth but also social status for their families, including the status of their husbands (Brenner 1998: 9, 142–143). "By insulating her husband from trade and, more broadly, from most matters having to do with money," Brenner explains, "a wife protects her husband's status, and by extension protects her entire family's position in the social hierarchy" (ibid.: 143). Furthermore, women in general are recognized to be better financial managers because they can better control their own desires and therefore better protect the financial welfare and security of their families (ibid.: 149–156). While many men thus need and expect women to be economically powerful, some also feel ambivalent about women's economic power and authoritative roles "ruling the roost" in the household (Brenner 1995; 1998: 136–138).

Martial Power

Women's physical and emotional strength as fighters has similarly occupied an ambiguous place in the Javanese imagination. As with sexual and economic power, there is a long history of women's martial power in Java. Through the course of the seventeenth to the nineteenth centuries, female soldiers in the central Javanese courts were highly trained in the use of weapons and cavalry maneuvers, and female bodyguards were entrusted with the duty to protect the ruler (Kumar 1980: 3–8, 31; Carey and Houben 1987: 18–19; Sumarsam 1995: 26–27; Weiss 2006: 61). During the Java War (1825–1830), a Javanese rebellion against Dutch rule, the "well-born lady" Radèn Ayu Sérang showed her bravery and prowess as a warrior by leading a cavalry squadron (Carey and Houben 1987: 21). In the twentieth century, women have been active as rebels, guerrilla fighters, soldiers, social and political organizers, and leaders of Islamic organizations, in some cases risking jail time, their well-being, and their lives (Anderson 1965: 26; Walton 1996: 135–136; Wieringa 2002; Blackburn 2008: 85).

One cultural model for such "strong" women exists in the figure of Srikandi, a female character in Javanese theater who is well known for her confidence, colorful speech, direct social interaction, and skill as a warrior (Carey and Houben 1987: 13–15; Pausacker 1991; Wieringa 2002: 233).[1] There are tales, too, in which she is transformed into a man and even fathers a child, suggesting cultural space for the crossing of conceptual and physical boundaries of sex and gender in Javanese theater stories (Pausacker 1991: 281–282, 286–287). Significantly, the figure of Srikandi was also referenced in official discourse. According to Benedict Anderson, "not only have the women's units in the Indonesian National Army taken Srikandi as their model, but also the first woman guerrilla who landed in West Irian during the 1962 liberation campaign was widely referred to as 'our Srikandi,' both by President Sukarno and by the general public" (1965: 26). At the same time, holding up the figure of Srikandi as a model has belied a cultural ambivalence surrounding women's power in the form of their strength as fighters, as well as other expressions of women's magnetic female power, contributing to dominant discourses stemming from the Indonesian state—a male-controlled structure of power—in which women have been portrayed as loyal, submissive wives and mothers.

Efforts from State and Society to Control the Magnetic Power of Femaleness

In official discourses after the Indonesian revolution (1945–1949), and during the reign of Soekarno (1945–1966), Indonesia's first president, women were encouraged to be like particular representations of the Javanese noblewoman Raden Adjeng Kartini (1879–1904) and the legendary princess Sumbadra: refined, polite, quiet, and dedicated to the home and their social roles as wives and mothers (Wieringa 2002: 99, 130–132; Shiraishi 1997: 90–91).[2] Such images of Kartini and Sumbadra as ideal wives and mothers were a marked contrast to women's historical roles in trade at markets; managing businesses and households; as headstrong, confident warriors who in some cases physically guarded and protected males; as well as wives and mothers.

Images of ideal women like Kartini were themselves constructions (Tiwon 1996). In private letters, Kartini expressed her longing to be free from the patriarchal structures of aristocratic life in Java and to never marry, and although she did marry and did become a mother, her time as a mother was very brief as she died a few days after the birth of her only child (Tiwon 1996: 49, 54–55). In Javanese theater stories, Sumbadra is portrayed as spiritually powerful and "quite able to gainsay her husband" (Carey and Houben 1987: 15). There are stories in which she, like Srikandi, assumes male forms, either in disguise as a man or transformed into a man, and is a good fighter when in male forms (Pausacker 1991: 272, 282, 287). Despite the existence of multiple femininities, the representation of gender crossings in theater stories, and the complex dimensions of a historical figure like Kartini and a literary figure like Sumbadra, the constructed images of Kartini, Sumbadra, and Kartini- and Sumbadra-like figures were the selected ideals promoted through male-dominated power structures.

Evincing the ambivalence surrounding female power during the Soekarno era, Andrew Weintraub analyzes what was termed a "crisis" in the late 1950s and early 1960s in West Java when the popularity of male puppeteers was overshadowed by that of the female vocalists in the accompanying gamelan ensemble (2004a: 58). In response, male puppeteers formed an organization sponsored by the government and supported by the army and the police, and at a 1964 conference, put forth a code of ethics to control the ways the vocalists performed (Weintraub 2004a: 58–59). As Weintraub explains, "[t]he conference led to the shaping of public policy to contain female performers' behavior, movements, songs, and dress onstage" (2004a: 59). Weintraub provides a sobering picture of what lies within the realm of possibility when male performers feel too threatened by women's power as well as the state's involvement in controlling it.

Violence has also played a role in state attempts to control women's power, particularly evident during the bloody transition from Soekarno's reign to that of Soeharto, Indonesia's second president. On the early morning of October 1, 1965, six generals and a lieutenant taken by mistake were kidnapped and murdered by a group of others in the military who identified itself as the September 30th Movement and professed to be protecting Soekarno from a coup (Heryanto 2006: 8; Roosa 2006: 3; Larasati 2013: 3). The movement was quickly suppressed by the military under the leadership of Major General Suharto, and the Indonesian Communist Party was blamed for the murders and for masterminding the movement, leading to the systematic kidnapping, imprisonment, intimidation, exile, and murder of hundreds of thousands of communists or suspected communists (Roosa 2006: 4; Larasati 2013: 2–3). It is believed that five hundred thousand to one million people, perhaps more, were killed—although the actual number remains unknown; the violence was particularly brutal in Central Java, East Java, and Bali (Wieringa 2002: 281; Roosa 2006: 4; Ricklefs 2008: 326–327; Larasati 2013: 3). Soekarno transferred power to Soeharto on March 11, 1966. As Soeharto established what came to be called the "New Order," which spanned from 1966 to 1998, the Soekarno years came to be referred to as the "Old Order" era (Steinberg 1987: 425; Ricklefs 2008: 322).

Along with the Indonesian Communist Party, the progressive women's organization Gerwani was blamed for the disorder that engulfed Indonesian politics and society in 1965–1966. Members of Gerwani had been active "fighters" in politics and had their own ideas about morality, womanhood, and the family, thereby disrupting official ideologies about women's roles as subordinate wives and mothers in both public and domestic spheres (Wieringa 2002: 232–279). Images of women dancing naked and sexually torturing the generals as they died were fabricated, circulated, and used to justify the imprisonment, torture, and murder of Gerwani members. Saskia Wieringa presents in chilling detail the sexualized nature of the violence against these women, showing that ambivalence about women's political power and women's power as fighters was closely connected to ambivalence about the power of female sexuality (2002). In the context of the turmoil of the 1960s, ambivalence about women's power contributed to the destruction of Gerwani and continuing state regulation of women's political activity thereafter (Wieringa 2002: 281).

By targeting Srikandis, the New Order regime tried to ensure that the women who remained were Sumbadras (Wieringa 2002: 327). In other words, the narrower roles for women established during the Soekarno years were more strongly enforced by the state and the threat or memory of violence during the New Order era. The government and the Indonesian women's organizations it sanctioned—such as Dharma Wanita, the national association of civil servants' wives—emphasized what the government considered to be women's correct roles and behaviors as submissive wives devoted to their husbands and as mothers (Tiwon 1996: 65; Suryakusuma 1996: 99; Sunindyo 1996: 124–125; Wieringa 2002: 309). With women thereby subordinated, men's roles as figures of authority at the top of the social and political hierarchies were articulated and enforced (Suryakusuma 1996: 95; Shiraishi 1997: 90–93).

The 1980s also saw several highly publicized cases of murder or attempted murder of women, including those portrayed as "women who have crossed the line drawn by tradition and the state's ideology of womanhood" (Sunindyo 1996: 137). This, as well as other images of women in the media, such as on television, in advertisements, and in films, contributed to social pressures for women to conform to roles as wives and mothers in the interests of preserving national order (Hughes-Freeland 2008c: 141, 145–147; Larasati 2013: 140). By promoting women's roles as wives and mothers and men's roles as fathers, the government solidified the nuclear family and heterosexuality as the foundation of social order necessary for the survival and prosperity of the nation, insisting on clear boundaries separating femaleness and maleness (Blackwood 2005; 2007: 185–186).

Performance was a key site in which official constructions of gender were reinforced and female bodies were controlled. As Felicia Hughes-Freeland explores, female singer-dancers served as "a source of fascination for the urban-based print media" by the late 1980s "as representing the antithesis to respectable New Order femininity" (2008c: 141). Also, the government instituted programs rooted in the government's ideas of orderliness to "upgrade" dance traditions, such as mandatory courses for performers in New Order ideology and "proper" ways of performing; permits required to host performances; and surveillance of performances and performers by police and government officials (Widodo 1995; Lysloff 2001/2002; Larasati 2013). Drawing on interviews with women in Malang and Bali, Rachmi Diyah Larasati brings to light the sobering reality that not only were some artists (those suspected of association with the Indonesian Communist Party or left-leaning organizations) prohibited from performing publicly, but that they also had to report weekly to the local military office for over thirty years; many women were subject to abuse and rape during these visits (2013: 57, 123–24). The control of which bodies were permitted to perform and in which ways took a variety of forms—including those that were violent.

From my observations of *tayub* and *campur sari* performances in Malang, it seems that such efforts made during New Order times have continued to affect performance in Reformation era times (1998–present). If guests or audience members danced too closely or attempted to kiss female singer-dancers, the singer-dancers and the men in the group took measures to stop this behavior from continuing. Sometimes the women simply moved away from the male perpetrator, either continuing to perform or stopping briefly, looking at the other singers or musicians with visible expressions of exasperation. In extreme cases, men who were ready as "bodyguards" of sorts would physically remove men behaving this way from the performing space. I noticed that at least one of the musicians in the group usually kept a protective eye on stage—either in a "brotherly" or "fatherly" capacity, as a particular female artist's boyfriend or husband, or because he had taken a romantic interest of his own in a particular female artist. Demonstrating another approach, Kusnadi taught me how to play extra walking patterns on the drum as a means to separate male guests who were dancing too closely to the female dancers at *tayub* events. The drummer may monitor *tayub* performances in central Java as well by cueing the musicians to stop if a male crosses the line of appropriateness with the female dancer(s) (Hughes-Freeland 2008c: 157).

Efforts to discourage physical contact between male guests or audience members and female artists further suggest beliefs that the potentially disruptive and dangerous magnetism of female sexuality had to be controlled (see also Hughes-Freeland 1997: 480; 2008c: 156–158). In such cases, performance onstage had offstage implications. From a New Order perspective, illicit relationships between men and women—including what could be perceived as forms of prostitution—had to be contained in order to maintain the integrity of the nuclear family and to prevent conflicts resulting from jealousy that might threaten social order.

Despite strong pressures from the state and society, women have negotiated contradictory expectations for women to be powerful but submissive to men's authority as wives and mothers of their children. Some women have not married, an act that is thus simultaneously personal and political. Many women who do marry have continued their historical roles of taking the lead in managing their household economies, often wielding strong economic influence over their husbands, and working outside the home (Brenner 1995, 1998). Thus, in New Order times, many women assumed (and embraced) roles as wives and mothers, but they were neither necessarily subservient to their husbands nor confined to domestic spheres.

In the Reformation era (1998–present)—which has been a period of radical change in political and social culture ushered in by student demonstrations and by Soeharto's resignation in May of 1998 (see Heryanto 2008a, 2008b; Ricklefs 2008: 379–413)—women have been more visibly taking leadership roles both on and offstage. Jan Mrázek has highlighted that women have redefined their roles as leaders in shadow theater: a female puppeteer performed a story about a woman leading and managing a country in support of Megawati Soekarnoputri's candidacy for president of Indonesia (2000: 156). Megawati (a woman) was president from 2001–2004. Women have also been taking advantage of opportunities to speak for and represent themselves in various theater traditions as performers and directors, including in modern theater and *ketoprak*, a type of central Javanese popular theater (Hatley 2007: 176; 2008: 278–279). At the same time, debates about female *dangdut* singers and pornography suggest that ambivalence about the expression of women's power, particularly in terms of female sexuality, remains an issue (Hatley 2007: 174–175; Daniels 2009: 81–94; Weintraub 2010: 173–200; 2011).

In the Reformation era, many Javanese have felt uncertain, anxious, and confused about the social and political changes taking place (Mrázek 2000: 163). Democratic elections, increased social and political activism, and ongoing economic crisis have also inspired anxiety and eruptions of violence targeting groups believed to threaten social order, such as women, ethnic Chinese (including ethnic Chinese women) (Cooper 2000: 610–611, 631 n8), alleged witches (Siegel 2006), homosexuals (Boellstorff 2004a), and foreign visitors. My teachers and friends expressed disappointment with the slow pace of economic recovery, and, due to an onset of natural disasters in 2004–2006 including earthquakes and a tsunami, a sense that political leadership was out of sync with nature. Some pointed out that when Soeharto was president, bombings or raids of hotels by mobs seeking to rid the area of foreigners did not occur, the economy was stable, and villagers benefited from state aid. Andrew Weintraub has found that performances of wooden-rod puppet theater on cassettes and VCDs from West Java revealed a distrust of political leadership and emphasized self-reliance following Soeharto's resignation (2004b: 218–219). Clearly, not everyone was certain that change had been for the better.

I believe that performers in Malang were contributing to the opening of cultural spaces that made it possible for Indonesia to have a female president in the early 2000s. As female dancers and the mostly male musicians who accompanied them contested official boundaries of gender through male style dance, they were contending with ambivalence toward women's power in the twentieth and early twenty-first centuries, pushing against pressures from state and society that sought to contain it. They were also contributing to the feeling of uncertainty that has come to characterize the Reformation era as they built on and departed from pre-established conventions of performance, reinforcing an anxiety about the loss of tradition discussed in chapter one.

Negotiating Boundaries of Gender

In performing male style dance, females have articulated senses of female masculinity—distinct senses of masculinity expressed by females (Halberstam 1998)—that entailed keeping their femaleness visible and audible. Building further from Judith Halberstam, I view such approaches as forms of "layering," a theatrical strategy in which a performed gendered role is noticeably superimposed—layered—onto an actor's own gendered self (Halberstam 1998: 260–261). One form of layering occurs "[w]hen a drag king performs as a recognizable male persona" and "choose[s] to allow her femaleness to peek through" (ibid.: 260). Similarly, female dancers in Malang "layered" masculinity onto their female bodies when performing the recognizable male personas portrayed through male style dances, allowing their femaleness to "peek through" a male veneer. They were thereby showing that women could be like men (be physically strong, take the lead), but without being men. In other words, women were insisting on their power as women, thereby maintaining the magnetic power of femaleness. In so doing, women were pushing tradition in particular directions visually and sonically.

Negotiating Boundaries of the Body's Appearance

Movement   *Ngremo Tayub* offers one of the most obvious examples of the ways women layered maleness onto their femaleness through movements. Movements associated with masculinity—higher arm positions, wider leg stances, and larger head movements—included those drawn from various male style dances[3] and from a form of martial arts called *pencak silat*.[4] However, females tended to articulate these movements in a more supple manner than males did for male style dances and martial arts, allowing a certain grace and fluidity that are associated with female style dances (and femaleness more broadly) to permeate the execution of their movements. Other movements were associated more directly with femaleness, such as movements drawn from aerobics—typically a woman's activity—and from "pat-a-cake" hand games—movements associated with children's activities. Movements associated with femaleness juxtaposed with those associated with maleness but executed in a more supple manner in the context of a male style dance performed by female bodies produced a complex sense of gender indeed.

When women performed other male style dances, such as *Ngremo Lanang*, *Beskalan Lanang*, and male style masked dances, they tended to execute the movements less sharply and less forcefully than male dancers, similarly allowing their femaleness to "peek through." Speaking to this femaleness, the dancer Luluk Ratna Herawati (b. 1967) explained that for male style dances she preferred "a man who really looks strong" because the dance looks manly and strong. If women dance, Luluk said, "even if she is strong [in a manly way], her womanliness is still there" ("*Kalau putri biarpun dia gagah, tapi kan masih ada keputriannnya, itu ada*") (p.c., January 4, 2006). This womanliness in the context of a male style dance supports Halberstam's point that layering—making visible both the performer's femaleness and the role's maleness—"reveals the permeable boundaries between acting and being" as well as "the artificiality of conventional gender roles" (1998: 261).

The feminization of the movements of male style dance also makes the performance of *Ngremo Lanang* more refined, in effect creating a refined male style of *Ngremo*. That this refinement was not necessarily valued, however, was evident in some performers' critiques of *Ngremo Tayub* for looking too feminine. One dancer and vocalist, a woman born in the 1950s, criticized *Ngremo Tayub* dancers "nowadays" for executing a head roll inappropriately for male style dance. She found that their head movements were not sharp or clearly articulated enough—too supple—for male style dance, declaring that the movement was from *Ngremo Putri* (*Ngremo* in the female style). Another dancer, a man born in the 1960s, commented that the movements did not fit the knightly character being portrayed and made the dance too coquettish. In critiquing the ways in which female dancers combined masculinity and femininity, these artists in effect expressed their discomfort with the ways dancers were disrupting boundaries of maleness and femaleness that they had come to accept as normal and fitting for male and female styles of *Ngremo*. These critiques also demonstrate that "alusness [refinement] is both polysemous and multivalent" in Javanese culture, and not necessarily always valued as ideal or appropriate (Benamou 2002: 280).

Paradoxically, some older dancers remembered female dancers of the past as having danced male styles "just like men," thereby situating maleness in women's bodies. Djupri described his grandmother Muskayah (c. 1890s–1990s[?]) as strong in a manly way (*gagah*) and handsome when she danced *Ngremo Lanang* (p.c., January 6, 2006). While statements about women of the past are subject to perception, interpretation, and the filtering of memory, performers consistently recalled their movements as sharper and more strongly articulated than the movements of dancers "nowadays." They perceived that many female performers in more current times—particularly since the 1990s, they recalled—were not performing male style dance—and *Ngremo Tayub* in particular—in a manly enough manner.

While Djupri and other performers situated maleness in female bodies of the past, many seemed to have also been affected by sensibilities of the

Old and New Order eras that separated maleness from femaleness, defined maleness as "strong," and kept physical strength associated with masculinity located in male bodies. One musician, born in the mid-1940s, articulated his discomfort with one of the movements that has become characteristic of *Ngremo Tayub*—lifting the fist above the head. He repeatedly explained that according to traditional conventions, lifting the hand above the head was impolite because this movement displayed the armpit. He implied that it was inappropriate for women to display their armpits—which were clearly visible when the arms were lifted up high because the costume was sleeveless. His comment indicated that he was seeing the dancers' femaleness first and foremost. He saw that the maleness was layered onto the dancer's female bodies, but he still held the dancers to normative standards of "polite" womanhood, thereby reinforcing a separation between maleness and femaleness while also speaking to the magnetic power of the dancers' femaleness.

The ways in which females pushed at assumptions about gender—in effect combining maleness and femaleness—made their performances of male style dance interesting for many viewers. Karen Elizabeth Sekararum interpreted the subversion of gender in *Ngremo Tayub* as part of the dance's appeal (p.c., November 29, 2005). Muliono expressed his own pleasure in watching females perform male style dances. Indicating his enjoyment of how females undermined the mapping of masculine physical strength to male bodies, he said that if a woman dances male style dance, he enjoys the dance more because, asking rhetorically, how is it that a woman can dance male style dance, and how is it that she can be strong in a manly sense (*gagah*)? He went on to say more animatedly that he really likes it when a woman performs male style dance and there is a coquettishness to the dance (p.c., January 3, 2006). Muliono thus identified and enjoyed the power of femaleness that females may bring to the performance of male style dance.

When women performed male style dance, in most cases, but not all, performers and audiences were aware that dancers were female. Paradoxically, this awareness reinforced the separation of maleness and femaleness even as performers undermined conceptual and physical boundaries of gender through their production of female masculinity. For the most part, performing male style dance did not detract from the performers' womanhood because usually the femaleness of the dancer's biological sex had a stronger impact on those watching than the maleness of the dance style. One musician, Stefanus Yacobus Suryantono, explained that when he sees women perform male style dance, the feminine aspects of the dancer and the dance affect him, and he finds the dancer beautiful, not handsome (p.c., July 31, 2006).[5]

Photograph 2.1. Tri Wahyuningtyas in costume for *Beskalan Lanang*, 2006.

Muliono, however, did say that sometimes he can forget that the dancer is a woman (p.c., January 3, 2006).

Makeup and Costuming   Many females enhanced their womanly beauty while producing senses of masculinity through makeup. Tri Wahyuningtyas (b. 1973) talked about her conscious decision to do her makeup for male style dance in a feminine way. During a video session I sponsored to document her performing *Beskalan Lanang*, she explained that she does her makeup "beautifully" for male style dance. When I asked her why she did this, she said that she did not know; it was normal for her to do so (p.c., Tri Wahyuningtyas, July 10, 2006). The "beautiful" approach she took for that recording session is evident in Photograph 2.1 in the lines of the eye shadow and liner as well as the "feminine" style of blush. This "beautiful" approach along with the carefully drawn mustache, facial hair below the lower lip, masculine eyebrows, and sideburns makes for a striking juxtaposition of masculinity and femininity.

Dancers highlighted their femininity more explicitly through the costume and makeup for *Ngremo Tayub*. Karen Elizabeth Sekararum explained that the womanhood of the dancer is emphasized through the costume, jewelry, and makeup, despite the mustache that is penciled on and the maleness of the dance style (p.c., November 29, 2005). The femininity that Karen Elizabeth identified, and that I also observed in performances of *Ngremo Tayub*, can be seen by comparing photographs of a female modeling a *Ngremo Tayub* costume (Photograph 2.2) and male *Ngremo Lanang* dancers performing in *ludruk*, a type of theater (Photograph 2.3). As seen in Photograph 2.2, the dancer Sri Handayani (b. 1982) does not look like a biological male, but instead looks like a woman trying to look sort of like a man. Sri's costume, with its strapless top and vest differs from the males' long-sleeved shirts, and her female figure is enhanced through the cut of the top and the way she has fastened it. Sri's bare arms reinforce her womanliness and are rather erotic in a Muslim context in which many women cover their shoulders and the top part of their arms, if not most of or all of their arms, in public. She has on a wig of short hair, and a male style head cloth.

Makeup was another means some *Ngremo Tayub* dancers undermined ideological separations between maleness and femaleness. Sri used cosmetics to make her femaleness apparent. The false eyelashes and the pink and purple colors of the eye makeup are recognizably feminine according to conventions of east Javanese dance makeup. The blush on her cheeks is softer than the blush on the men's faces, and her mustache and eyebrows feature finer lines. Although

Photograph 2.2: Sri Handayani (a female) models a costume and makeup for *Ngremo Tayub*, 2006.

Photograph 2.3: Males perform *Ngremo Lanang* for a performance of *ludruk*, 2006.

not clearly visible in this photograph, she has not used a pencil to thicken the fine hairs on the side of her face to create thick, more "manly" sideburns.

While some *Ngremo Tayub* dancers were expressing a sense of female masculinity by doing their makeup in a more "feminine" manner, one reason they did so was practical, related to the convention of changing gendered outfits in the course of a performance event. In many cases, after the dancer(s) performed *Ngremo Tayub*, she or they left the stage and changed into feminine attire of a long batik cloth wrapped tightly around the lower body and tightly fitting blouse, often made of lace. They redid their hair, replacing their male style wig with a large bun, and adjusted their makeup to appear like Sri in Photograph 2.4.

Returning to the stage, they performed as female vocalists seated with the gamelan (e.g., for shadow puppet performances) or female singer-dancers (e.g., for *tayub* or *campur sari*). By doing their makeup in a more feminine manner for *Ngremo Tayub*, the dancers could more quickly change from their *Ngremo* costume and makeup to female style dress. Speaking further to practical considerations and also to economic ones, Sri explained that changing quickly for *tayuban* is necessary; otherwise, the guests will go home and the dancers will not earn as much money (p.c., March 29, 2006). Sometimes

Photograph 2.4: Sri Handayani, performing as a singer-dancer for a *tayub* event, wears feminine attire, 2006.

other women who had not performed *Ngremo* were already dressed in female attire and performed while the *Ngremo* dancer(s) changed outfits. The *Ngremo* dancers, once changed, joined these women—although sometimes a dancer was hired just to perform *Ngremo*.

The convention of changing gendered outfits was another means by and through which *Ngremo Tayub* dancers subverted conceptual and physical boundaries separating maleness from femaleness and also expressed contingent senses of gender. Women embodied different gendered personas during different points in the performance, showing that masculinity and femininity were, in part, the product of makeup and dress, not fixed, inherent aspects of the anatomy, and also contingent upon context (Blackwood 2010). Furthermore, through the transformation in the dressing room, the dancers were able to reemerge in all of their feminine glory, assuming a hyperfeminine persona characteristic of the stage image cultivated by female singers and dancers in many parts of Java (Spiller 2007: 41). *Ngremo Tayub* dancers thereby reinforced their magnetic power as females.

Furthermore, *Ngremo Tayub* dancers, as other cross-dressed performers, played with dominant expectations about gender. Writing about drag kinging in the United States (with some reference to London), Judith Halberstam observes that "mainstream coverage of the scene tends to evince the sincere hope that even though girls will be boys, they will eventually return to being very attractive girls" (1998: 261). Likewise, I suggest that viewers in Java imagined the attractive femininity that lay under the "surface" of the *Ngremo Tayub* costume. The contrast of the dancers' appearance in the *Ngremo* costume and in female attire ultimately enhanced the dancers' beauty when they reappeared in female dress, reinforcing both the dancers' womanhood as well as the contingent female masculinity of *Ngremo Tayub*.

The *Ngremo Tayub* dancer's appearance both reinforced and undermined dominant norms as dancers interacted with guests (usually male) during what was called the *tembelan* section, named after the tipping practice called *nembel*. This section—in which viewers may tip the performers, request a song, and dance with the dancers—may be inserted into *Ngremo Tayub*. The *tembelan* section reinforced heterosexuality and also allowed space for homoerotic imaginations. Usually those who requested songs were men. The interaction of these men and the dancers' "male"-looking bodies in the performance space displayed a type of male homoeroticism, but one tempered by the knowledge that the dancers were female and, in many cases, would reappear later in the evening in feminine attire. This homoeroticism was permissible because the representation of a heterosexual relationship underlay the interaction. In cases where a woman danced with the *Ngremo Tayub* dancers (which I observed only once), a female homoeroticism was evoked as everyone knew the *Ngremo Tayub* dancers were women, too. Complicating matters, women dancing with female dancers in male style costumes reinforced images of heterosexuality. This cultural space for the simultaneous imagination of both homoeroticism and heterosexuality was another way participants in the performance event (including dancers, musicians, and guests) negotiated boundaries of gender, pushing at dominant social norms that insisted on the normalcy of heterosexuality, and made space for gender pluralism within the dominant framework of gender dualism (Peletz 2006).

Writing about Sundanese dance events in West Java that feature female entertainers, Henry Spiller has argued that the image of the hyperfeminine singer-dancer "brings the imagined oppositions of masculine and feminine, so vital to gender ideology, into sharp relief" (2007: 41). In many performances featuring *Ngremo Tayub*, the conceptual and physical boundaries of maleness and femaleness were brought into "sharp relief," too, albeit in some different ways—the "feminine-masculine" appearance of the *Ngremo Tayub* dancer, participants' knowledge that in many cases, the *Ngremo Tayub* dancer would reappear as a beautiful woman, and as I address next, hearing a female voice emanate from the dancer's quasi–male-looking body.

Negotiating Boundaries Sonically

Singing Female singer-dancers negotiated sonic boundaries of gender through musical conventions, including conventions of singing for *Ngremo*. One type of singing performed in *Ngremo* is called *kidungan*, which tends to feature a flat contour in a higher register followed by a more melodically elaborate cadence to the gong tone (see Sutton 1991: 164–165).

As I learned from Kusnadi, Stefanus Yacobus Suryantono, Supriono, and Sumi'anah, there were several aspects of *kidungan* singing that distinguished melodies appropriate for *Ngremo Lanang* from melodies appropriate for *Ngremo Putri*. For example, melodies going to the gong tone illustrated in Figure 2.1 for *Ngremo Lanang* tended to use the high, middle, and low registers, while singing in the high and middle registers (and in falsetto when performed by male dancers) was more appropriate for *Ngremo Putri*. Another characteristic of *kidungan* singing for *Ngremo Lanang* is that the last word or part of the last word was often repeated (text in boldface in Figure 2.1, "**sekeca**"). I suggest that such repetition renders the *kidungan* for *Ngremo Lanang* a bit "stronger" sounding because the last word is in effect sung with less *melisma* than in *Ngremo Putri*.

Despite the ways my teachers identified differences between *kidungan* singing for *Ngremo Lanang* and *Ngremo Putri*, different aspects of the melodies may have struck different performers as appropriate for *Ngremo Putri* and

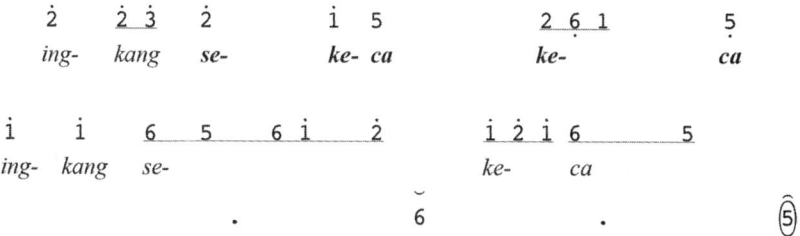

Figure 2.1: Sample basic *kidungan* phrases, roughly indicated, for *Ngremo Lanang* (top) and *Ngremo Putri* (bottom) going to one of the two gong tones of the composition "Jula Juli," as learned from Kusnadi and B. Supriono Hadi Prasetya. (The *sléndro* tuning system is used. For the entire skeletal melody of "Jula Juli," see Figure 4.1 in chapter four.)

Ngremo Lanang, and a particular melody was not exclusively performed in the gendered dance style with which some associated it.

Nonetheless, women could negotiate the physical capabilities of the female voice box in order to embody maleness by singing *kidungan* in ways that were associated with maleness, sonically expressing and producing female masculinity. Sumi'anah said that she started to sing *kidungan* lower in order to sound stronger in a manly sense (*gagah*; p.c., February 24, 2006). Reinforcing the goal of singing in a more manly manner for *Ngremo* in the male style, she said that when heading into the singing section, one should stand in basic position, wait a couple of gong cycles, and then make the voice low like a man's (p.c., March 3, 2006). However, the femaleness of women's voices subverted the maleness of the dance style and approach to singing, making it obvious to audiences and the other performers that the dancer was a woman. Djupri recalled his grandmother's vocal register was that of a woman but that "she imitated a man precisely" ("*meniru orang pria, ya précis*") and "the melody was like a man's" ("*lagunya ya, seperti orang laki-laki*") (p.c., January 6, 2006). Through the use of the voice, females embodied maleness, claiming the physical strength that maleness implied, but also maintained their femaleness and its power as women.

Through *kidungan* melodies associated with *Ngremo Tayub*, dancers layered maleness sonically by using lower pitches. *Kidungan* phrases for *Ngremo Tayub* typically started a bit lower, emphasizing pitch 6, rather than starting in a higher register on pitch 2, as do many melodies used for *Ngremo Putri* and *Ngremo Lanang* (Figure 2.2).

A number of performers attributed this innovation to the influential singer-dancer Sri Utami (b. 1957). Sri Utami, based in the East Javanese regency of Blitar, said that she sounded better singing lower, but was clever at finding her own melodies, highlighting her creativity. Sri Utami in effect defined her femaleness on her own terms, challenging cultural and artistic expectations that females should sing high, while also expressing a sense of female masculinity through performance. Strikingly, it was something that Sri Utami connected to her biological capacity as a female that contributed to her ability to articulate female masculinity through *Ngremo Tayub*—saying that after the birth of her third child her voice changed and sounded better when she sang lower (p.c., August 3, 2006).

Expressing an ambivalence about a departure from what he saw as Malangan, one musician explained that what Sri Utami sings has become what *Ngremo Tayub* dancers sing because she is creative, a "prima donna" (*primadona*), and other dancers imitate her.[6] Malangan *kidungan*, however, were like those sung in *ludruk*, implying that Malangan *kidungan* started on or around high 2. This musician, like other similarly minded performers, perceived that developments made in *Ngremo Tayub* were departures from

Maintaining Female Power through Male Style Dance

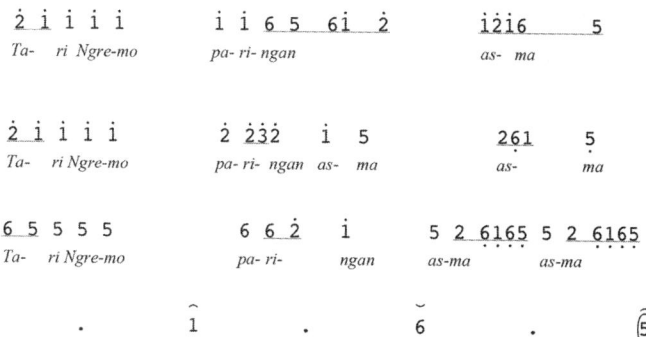

Figure 2.2: Basic *kidungan* melodies for *Ngremo Putri* (top), *Ngremo Lanang* (middle), and *Ngremo Tayub* (bottom), roughly indicated, with a sample text set over one gong cycle of the composition "Jula Juli," as learned from Kusnadi and B. Supriono Hadi Prasetya. (The *sléndro* tuning system is used.) The text, "*Amirsani kesenian kula, Tari Ngremo paringan asma*" may be translated as "Watch my art, *Ngremo* Dance is the name bestowed."

tradition, which he talked about in terms of established Malangan conventions. His critiques may have been rooted in a concern about the disappearance of local tradition, suggesting that concerns about the representation of gender and concerns about tradition were integrally connected. I cannot help but wonder to what extent, if at all, this musician's critiques were gendered, as in effect he was putting tradition in the mouths, so to speak, of the primarily male singer-dancers of *ludruk*.

Although *Ngremo Tayub* dancers evoked female masculinity through their exploitation of lower pitches for *kidungan* singing, they sang requested songs "like women" during the *tembelan* section. Sumi'anah reported that she sang requested songs the same way for *Ngremo* as she did when wearing female style dress (p.c., April 22, 2006). A former female singer-dancer (a woman) and two male musicians did not underscore differences in repertoire for the requested songs based on the maleness of *Ngremo*, explaining that guests requested whatever was popular (p.c., Cuci Indrawati, December 21, 2005; Supriadi, May 14, 2006; Panoto, May 16, 2006). The implication is that *Ngremo Tayub* dancers sang in a somewhat more manly manner for the *kidungan*, but not for requested songs, layering maleness onto their femaleness sonically as they moved between maleness and femaleness in the course of the dance. Again we find the expression of gender to be contingent. I suggest that the sound of the female voice emanating from a female body in the *Ngremo* costume (and makeup)—with its juxtapositions of maleness and femaleness—further contributed to the pleasure and disruption of this dance as the dancers pushed at the conceptual and physical boundaries of gender. Although the *Ngremo Tayub* dancers did not appear as hyperfeminine figures when in the *Ngremo* costume, their singing reminded viewers that hyperfeminine women—that is, women who manifested the power of their femaleness through their sexuality—were under the "surface" of masculinity.

Women negotiated boundaries of gender through singing for *Ngremo Tayub* in other ways. For one, they expressed their creativity and agency, thereby undermining dominant ideologies that women should be submissive to male authority and leadership. Going beyond the welcoming texts and *parikan* (a form of poetry) traditionally sung for the *kidungan* sections of *Ngremo*, Sri Utami incorporated texts from other cultural regions. Karen Elizabeth Sekararum highlighted Sri Utami's inclusion of a central Javanese poetic text (titled "Asmarandani") and Madurese style *kidungan* (p.c., January 6, 2006).

Indicating women's power to influence the popularity of particular songs, Karen Elizabeth explained that *tayub* dancers can introduce audiences to new repertoire through *Ngremo Tayub* as well as at other points during the *tayub* event. If the audience liked these songs, they might come to request them in subsequent performances (p.c., January 6, 2006). Women thereby assumed leading roles. In cases where dancers were tipped for a song they introduced, they ultimately shaped flows of money as well as flows of repertoire, also exerting economic power. That most guests who requested songs were men indicates that introducing repertoire was a means by and through which women exerted their power over men in the form of influencing the direction of change, and in some ways, leading the direction of innovation.

The ways performers talked about *Ngremo Tayub*'s history also has implications related to women's power and their singing. Performers recalled that by the late 1970s to mid-1980s, a section in which viewers could tip the performers, request a song, and dance with the dancers was incorporated into *Ngremo Lanang*, which female singer-dancers performed as an opening dance for *tayub* events.[7] By the 1990s, a distinct substyle that came to be called *Ngremo Tayub* had emerged. Although this style was named for *tayub*, it has been performed for a variety of types of performances, not just for *tayub*, and may be performed with or without a tipping section.

The incorporation of a section in which guests could request a song inspired a bit of controversy among performers. Some said almost with disgust that this was just a way for the dancers to make more money. They seemed to be implying that this innovation to *Ngremo* was economically driven and had little artistic merit, suggesting that they were interpreting this change through the lens of the dominant, male-oriented Javanese ideology of power that links concerns with money to crudeness. Performers may have also internalized official views that the presence of "desire and cash" is what makes female singer-dancers and their performances "deemed unsuitable as approved national culture" (Hughes-Freeland 2008c: 144). In the eyes of some, inserting a tipping section was inappropriate for the brave, proud, knightly male character of *Ngremo Lanang*, a dance that was usually performed to welcome and honor guests; a tipping section effectively degraded the dance into a display of money.

The ambivalence about the tipping innovation may also lie in women's control of the money. Significantly more tip money went to the female dancers, rather than to the male musicians, and it was largely a dancer's decision as to whether she would share her tips and how much she would share with the musicians (usually with the drummer). In other words, females made an innovation that augmented women's economic power, even though it may not have augmented their status. Similarly, Susan Browne found that the tip money earned by female *dangdut* singers in nightclubs, although providing a means of giving them economic status, "does not enhance their social status" (2000: 16). However, guests' requests for songs and paying tips did give women a certain economic authority to "rule the roost" as they performed *Ngremo*, like many women have done in the home (Brenner 1995).

Musical Accompaniment Male musicians, as well as female dancers, were agents in the production of female masculinity, and contributed to the process of sonic layering. For example, musicians contributed to the production of female masculinity through their drumming. Dennis Suwarno (b. 1957) said that the character and feeling of *Ngremo Tayub* was still coquettish even though women were wearing a male costume. For this reason, he explained, he plays the drum "coquettishly" by making the strokes sound higher and lighter, and by playing relatively sparsely (p.c., August 8, 2006). He, like the central Javanese musicians Marc Benamou consulted, connected coquettishness, lightness, and femininity (2010: 74, 77). By drumming in a way that he believed was appropriate for the male style dance at hand but also expressed the coquettishness—and thus the femininity—of the dancers, he contributed to the expression of female masculinity. That he described the feeling of *Ngremo Tayub* and the drumming in terms of coquettishness also suggests the sexual power of the female dancers that affected him even though they were performing a male style dance.

Similarly, Kusnadi was affected by the femaleness of female dancers who performed male style dance, but articulated a different approach to playing the drum. Although for him, the feeling was different when a female performed male style dance, he still believed that the drummer and the drumming should convey the maleness of the character. At the same time, he emphasized that one had to pay attention to the abilities of the dancer. Giving the example of the strong male style masked dance *Klana*, he said that the tempo should not be too fast because a female would not be able to do it (p.c., February 4, 2006). I do not believe that Kusnadi was trying to insult or belittle female artists but was demonstrating his sensitivity to female dancers who perform male style dances in their own ways. In maintaining the maleness of the character while drumming at a slower tempo he believed better accommodated female dancers, Kusnadi was also contributing to processes of layering maleness over femaleness in performance. The male strength came from the character of the dance while femaleness came from the slower tempo. By saying that the feeling was different, he indicated that a certain femininity was still visible through the male veneer of the costume, movement, and musical accompaniment, thereby also identifying and in effect contributing to the expression of female masculinity.

Achmad Suwarno (b. 1952) talked about the contributions he made to *Ngremo* drumming, thereby identifying ways that he as a musician contributed to the production of female masculinity. He was talking about drum patterns played on the east Javanese drum (*kendhang*) that imitated rhythmic patterns of the popular music called *dangdut*, and thus called *dangdutan* (Figure 2.3).

Figure 2.3: Basic *dangdutan* drum pattern, set over one phrase of "Jula Juli," as taught by Kusnadi.

Kusnadi recalled the use of the basic *dangdutan* drum patterns on the east Javanese drum for *Ngremo* in the late 1970s or 1980s, explaining that performers have added variations to this basic pattern since then (p.c., May 3, 10, 2007). Achmad Suwarno, it seems, was one of these performers. Achmad Suwarno said that working with his friends, he "perfected" *dangdutan* drumming for *Ngremo* in about 1986 in the context of *tayub*. While recognizing the creative interaction between men and women, he described the process of working on *dangdutan* drumming with the dancers in the dressing room, talking with them as they did their makeup. He highlighted his own agency and creativity, however, by explaining that he sought to make the drumming better by trying out different ideas (p.c., April 3, 2006).

Tellingly, I did not hear this sort of *dangdutan* drumming—innovations made in consultation with, or under the authority of male musicians—critiqued for taking *Ngremo* too far from tradition. However, the use of instruments influenced by popular music such as the set of two small drums from *dangdut*, electric bass, electric keyboard, and the performance of *campur sari* songs were seen as departing too far from tradition. These were innovations that performers remember making their way into *Ngremo Tayub* more recently as a result of audience demand and female performers taking requests. For example, Kusnadi recalled the use of the *dangdut* drums and electric instruments starting in the 1990s with *campur sari*. He said that the keyboard began to be used in southern Malang in the 2000s, and was for young people who did not know how to dance to gamelan compositions (*gendhing*) but could dance to *dangdut* and *campur sari* (p.c., May 3, 2007). Such changes contributed to some performers' concerns about the maintenance of "tradition."

It seems that when it came to the issues of innovation and change, some performers invoked double standards. Although they criticized dancers "nowadays" for changing (and "ruining") *Ngremo Lanang*, they underscored the flexibility of this dance, repeatedly explaining how they made changes so that they and audiences would not become bored. As performers recalled that, during busy months, they sometimes performed *Ngremo Lanang* almost every day—and sometimes twice a day—it became clear that the potential for boredom was very real. As performers recalled inserting other compositions, using different types of song texts, and incorporating different movements, it was apparent that *Ngremo* has been a remarkably flexible dance, subject to current trends since at least the 1950s. Departure from the "original" was not unique to *Ngremo Tayub*, but some performers perceived some changes to tradition as acceptable and others as not, revealing their ambivalence about women's power, women's authority, and some expressions of female masculinity.

Negotiating Gender On- and Offstage

Female performers' negotiations of gender through dance have intersected with other aspects of their lives since "times past." Djupri expressed his wonder and admiration as he recounted his grandmother's life (c. 1890s–1990s) and career, saying that she looked strong in a manly way (*gagah*) when she did *pencak silat* martial arts. He also remembered her drumming:

> Her drum strokes were distinct, pleasant to listen to—like a man's. "Oh, I have to be like a man," [she said]. She had to be like man, using whatever way worked. Indeed when she played "*tak*" it was like a man, just the same. That was the strange thing, but there was indeed, as it may be called, a sacred aspect, *ilmu*.[8]

Tak is the name of a drum stroke that is usually quite loud and sharp. Speaking from my own experiences drumming, it does require a particular strength in the form of a focused energy to execute. By attributing her abilities and physical strength as a drummer and as a dancer to her *ilmu*, Djupri underlined the possession of spiritual knowledge as a strategy of gender transgression in different realms of activity.

Muskayah also assumed a "male" role as spiritual teacher. Women have been recognized for their spiritual potency and potential, and sometimes have achieved high positions in mystic sects (Geertz 1960: 328–329; Beatty 1999: 202). The role of teacher or master, however, is gendered male as a father figure, and men have usually taken leading roles (Geertz 1960: 329; Mulder 2005: 55; Beatty 1999: 202). In talking about Muskayah as a master of spiritual knowledge herself as well as her abilities in martial arts and drumming, Djupri remembered and portrayed her as one who pushed at dominant ideas about what women's activities and behaviors should entail. By praising Muskayah, Djupri himself subverted Old and New Order ideology about womanhood with which he had grown up. The discrepancies between official ideas and social realities, and between official ideas and valued memories of an idolized family member, are striking.

Some women related their preferences for male style dance to aspects of their behavior and personalities in their everyday lives. Although the females I consulted who performed male style dances neither described themselves as a third gender nor lived as men in their daily lives, some did attribute their affinity for male style dance to their strong personalities. Warananingtyas Palupi (b. 1980) complicated senses of gender by recognizing that her personality did not map to the representation of femininity expressed through refined female styles of dance. In talking about her own preferences for male style dance (such as *Beskalan Lanang*), she tied aspects of dance to her character and behavior in her everyday life. Palupi said that she has a hard time with refined female style dances because they are too slow; she is not slow or relaxed (p.c., November 15–16, 2005). Tri Wahyuningtyas (pictured in Photograph 2.1) preferred male style dance (such as *Beskalan Lanang* and *Ngremo Lanang*) because of its strength and freer movements:

> Perhaps it is the character, too, the character from the movement that is stronger, also wider and more open. I just feel more comfortable performing it.... When I think of female [movement], it is smaller, more, I don't know, one has to—ah, too much! I think it's more intricate than male movement, which is freer and has strength.[9]

Women like Palupi and Tri could use the stage as a space to rehearse and formulate ways of moving and acting that they could also take to varying extents into their daily lives. As Sylvia Tiwon has argued, women make sense of their identities as women despite dominant ideologies that have portrayed them as either ideal models like Kartini or uncontrollable maniacs like Gerwani members (1996).

Women's expression of masculinity in Malang also speaks to a larger issue of how women in various parts of the world use performance as a means to embody different gendered identities. For example, Deborah Wong shows that performing taiko is a strategy that Asian American women use to embody an Asian American femaleness that is loud and assertive, challenging cultural expectations and stereotypes that Asian American women are quiet and demure (2004: 216–218). Tomie Hahn shows that Japanese women are able to take on multiple identities through *nihon buyo* dances in which a single dancer portrays different characters, including male and female (2004: 313). She argues, "the metaphoric shifting present in *nihon buyo* choreography offers women an embodied understanding of multiple identities as well as flexible notions of self within a society that has historically restricted their expression" (Hahn 2004: 323). Women's embodiment of different senses of gender through performance can be an important means of resisting dominant norms.

In Malang, women internalized the maleness of the characters they portrayed to different degrees, contributing to the expression of female masculinity in different ways. Tri, for example, embodied maleness by concentrating from the heart. She talked about the importance of becoming the character from the dancer's heart or soul, explaining that if there were no disturbances, she felt like the male character she was portraying and no longer herself. As a dancer, she expounded, one has to be able to feel the character and have enthusiasm from the inside; otherwise, the dance will not have form (p.c., Tri Wahyuningtyas, July 1, 2006).

For some, the degree to which masculinity was internalized was contingent upon the dance. Karen Elizabeth explained that she did not feel like a man when dancing *Ngremo Tayub*, emphasizing that it was not her goal to feel like a man because being a woman is part of this dance. For the male style masked dance *Bapang*, however, she does feel that she becomes the male character named Bapang. For masked dance, she said, the important thing is the mask and the goal is to be entered by the spirit of the mask (p.c., November 29, 2005). Karen Elizabeth was in effect identifying different approaches she took to the embodiment of masculinity for different dances. Making such choices was another means by and through which dancers expressed contingent senses of female masculinity.

Negotiating Islam

Performing male style dance was also a means by and through which women could negotiate Islamic orthodoxy and piety. "Because Islam has comprehensive teachings about women's role and place in society," Susan Blackburn instructively writes, "almost anything women do can be seen to be political in the sense of either accepting, supporting or challenging religious practices and beliefs" (2008: 84). Sri, who identified as Muslim, responded to my question as to whether she ever felt any incompatibility with her religious beliefs by explaining,

> No, that is our work, you know. Why should we feel ashamed, why? It is our work, right, our work in order to eat, right? As far as religious matters, that is between us and the one above. Yes, so [work and religion] cannot be all mixed up. The important thing is that we are right, yes?—Work a job that is *halal*. (p.c., March 29, 2006)[10]

In using the word "*halal*"—what is permitted or allowed by Islam—Sri was evoking the religion in order to legitimize her profession as an artist, in some ways a striking assertion given the immoral, licentious stereotype of female singer-dancers in Java, as well as her activity performing male style dance. Invoking Islamic discourse, she was insisting on the "rightness" of her profession.

Other Muslim female performers have drawn on religious discourse to legitimize their professions, offering further examples of "women shaping Islam" (van Doorn-Harder 2006). Such performers have included other East Javanese female singer-dancers (*tledhek*) that Robert Hefner encountered who performed at *tayuban* (including *tledhek* from Malang) (1987b: 77). He found that "[v]irtually all *tledhek* claim to be Muslim, some insisting quite strenuously that they are good Muslims" (1987b: 77). Female *dangdut* singers—including the infamous Inul Daratista who was at the center of national controversy in the early 2000s for a style of dancing that some Indonesians found to be too sexually provocative—have also positioned themselves as Muslims, maintaining that their art and their religion were separate matters (Daniels 2009: 88–89; Bader 2011: 346). Other *dangdut* singers negotiated Islam and their profession through their belief that the money earned as an entertainer at a place where alcohol was consumed was *halal* as long as they did not drink the alcohol themselves (Browne 2000: 29). As they negotiated Islam, Sri and other female performers were subverting dominant Indonesian gender ideologies that insisted that women be "proper wives and mothers," making cultural space for women—including Muslim women—to publically assert other roles (e.g., as artists) as well as their sexuality (Browne 2000: 2, 30). Doing so through the performance of male style dances, as Sri did when she performed *Ngremo Tayub*, made such negotiations of gender and religion all the more complex.

Being like Men without Being Men?

By performing male style dance, female dancers and the musicians (mostly male) who accompanied them negotiated boundaries of gender and sex visually and sonically, maintaining and making cultural space for women's expression of female power despite pressures from state and society to control and subdue it. In particular, performers were negotiating contradictory expectations that women should be powerful but also refined, submissive wives and mothers. Some women clearly did not identify exclusively with official representations of ideal femininity projected through figures like Sumbadra and Kartini, but instead they used male style dance as a means to embody alternative senses of womanhood. Given the precedent of violence against women who pushed too hard against official constructions—not only the destruction of Gerwani in the 1960s but also several highly publicized cases of murder in the 1980s (Sunindyo 1996)—dance was a "safer" strategy performers could employ to articulate alternatives to official gender ideologies in ways that did not overtly challenge the state's authority. Onstage, performing male style dance, women embodied and expressed their power as females in different ways—sexually, physically, and economically—as well as showed that they could be like men—be physically strong, move quickly and freely, and innovate artistically. In expressing their femaleness visually and sonically through a male veneer, women demonstrated that females could be like men without being male or living as men.

In some cases, however, the ways performers (especially *Ngremo Tayub* dancers) destabilized conceptual and physical boundaries of gender through male style dance reinforced anxieties and ambivalence among some performers about the loss of tradition—older ways of performing, and with older ways of performing, older ways of embodying gender sanctioned during Old Order and New Order times that had become normal for many performers. *Ngremo Tayub* was especially disruptive for many performers because of the ways female dancers pushed at boundaries of gender as they "layered" maleness onto their femaleness (Halberstam 1998). Indeed, performers negotiated a variety of pressures in terms of gender as they performed male style dances, as did males who performed female style dance, which I explore in the next chapter.

3. Negotiating Pressures in Terms of Gender

Male Dancers and Female Style Dance

This chapter develops some of my earlier analyses (Sunardi 2009, 2013) to further explore some of the ways in which male dancers who performed female style dance (or had performed female style dance prior to my fieldwork) have been pushing at dominant conceptual and physical boundaries of gender and sex by expressing, embodying, and representing male femininity in diverse ways on- and offstage. I argue that male dancers, in so doing, have been contributing to the ongoing cultural production of tradition and maintaining cultural space for males to access and make visible the magnetic power of femaleness. The ways male dancers negotiated boundaries of gender were made most clear to me through the ways they talked about various cultural pressures, indicating ways they contended with official discourses of gender.

Official Discourses of Gender by Era and Impact on Male Performers

As with the senses of femaleness explored in chapter two, ideologies of maleness in Java have shifted through the course of the twentieth and early twenty-first centuries, contributing to multiple senses of masculinity as well as cultural contradictions surrounding maleness with which performers in Java have had to contend (see also Spiller 2010: 23–27). Prior to the 1940s, more spaces existed for men to embody a wider spectrum of masculinity. Highly refined male characters from Javanese theater such as Arjuna served as models of ideal forms of masculinity (Anderson 1965: 28; Spiller 2010: 24–26). These characters, who embody potent spiritual power and are powerful fighters, have slender bodies and tend to move with slow, careful movements that bear many similarities to the movement styles of refined female characters (Brakel-Papenhuyzen 1995: 53–56; Hughes-Freeland 1995: 190–191; Benamou 2002: 275). Cultural spaces also existed for homosexuality and transvestism. James Peacock writes that "'Pure' Javanese tradition does not condemn homosexuality and regards a very wide range of behavior, from he-man to rather (in our terms) 'effeminate,' as properly masculine" (1987: 204 n3).

However, into the 1940s, 1950s, and 1960s—the times of the Indonesian revolution and the Old Order era of Soekarno's reign (1945–1966), a "strong" manly type came to be held up as the ideal model of masculinity in national and popular discourses as men were encouraged to assume positions of leadership within the family as household heads and within the new nation as political leaders and lawmakers (Wieringa 2002: 99; Shiraishi 1997: 90–91; Spiller 2010: 26). President Soekarno, a national hero, promoted a standard rooted in his own good looks, sexual prowess, bravery, loyalty to the nation, charisma, and as Shiraishi notes, "his deep baritone voice" (1997: 91). Dipping into Javanese theater, he held up as "the model for the new Indonesian Man" the character Gatotkaca, a legendary knight known for his physical strength, strong body type, determination, courage, loyalty, and patriotism (Anderson 1965: 28; see also Weintraub 2004b: 110). Acknowledging the influence of popular culture, Benedict Anderson, writing in the 1960s, observes that "the 'he-man' heroes" popularized in the movies contributed to changing perceptions of refined heroes in traditional theater, such as Arjuna, as effeminate (1965: 28). Some Islamic ideologies likely reinforced these other social pressures exerted on males to live as "manly" (Peacock 1987: 204 n3). In light of the changing standards that privileged visible "manly" strength and confidence, as well as larger, stronger body types, many believed that males with attributes perceived as feminine or effeminate fell short as men and as males.

James Peacock points to the impact that dominant discourses had on performers' behavior and lifestyles in 1960s Surabaya, the site of his fieldwork on *ludruk*. Noting that after the Indonesian revolution, it was considered more progressive and modern for *tandhak ludruk* to live as men, he cites two *tandhak* who had cut their long hair because of "progress" (1987: 206–207). Peacock emphasizes that cutting long hair was not without distress because long hair, as a part of the body, "may have signified a more sustained commitment to the womanly role than does interest in extra-somatic feminine trappings" (Peacock 1987: 207). Peacock also identifies contradictory expectations that *tandhak ludruk* faced in terms of their gender identities. On the one hand, they were encouraged to be ideal women when doing so contributed to national unity through performance by singing songs in support of the nation. On the other hand, they were discouraged from taking gender transgression into their daily lives; instead they were encouraged to be modern, Indonesian men—to have short hair, wear pants, and be heads of households (Peacock 1987: 206–207; see also Boellstorff 2007: 86–87).

Official ideologies that males should be "manly," "fatherly," and heterosexual were reinforced and more strictly enforced during the New Order era (1966–1998) (Shiraishi 1997; Boellstorff 2005b: 96, 196), paralleling the regulation of women's roles and behavior discussed in chapter two. For example, the sanctity of the nuclear family and heteronormativity was imposed through the government's efforts to control men's behavior in *Reog Ponorogo*, a tradition of East Javanese dance involving large, impressive masks. Ian Wilson (1999) writes that historically, the performers called *warok* have been spiritually powerful figures. To preserve their potency, *warok* avoided sexual intercourse; instead of living with women as wives, they took in young boys called *gemblak* to help with household chores. *Gemblak* also performed with *warok*, sometimes wearing female dress (Pigeaud 1938: 300–301; Kartomi 1976: 87). Further reflecting the changed political dynamics after 1965, the government and conservative Muslim groups viewed this *warok-gemblak* relationship in homosexual terms and thus as intolerable (Wilson 1999: par. 8–9). The New Order government was also suspicious of any powerful figures not under their direct influence. For these reasons, among others, *Reog Ponorogo* and *warok* lifestyles were adapted. More specifically, "[a]side from discouraging practices involving communication with ancestor spirits, the government outlawed the taking of gemblak in 1983, encouraging reog troupes to replace gemblak dancers with young girls" (Wilson 1999: par. 9). One result, Wilson argues, is that *Reog Ponorogo* was reconstructed to become an apolitical regional tradition rather than a practice that could potentially undermine official constructions of masculinity, fatherhood, and the family (1999).

The increasing separation of "male" and "female" and a tendency toward favoring "strong," heterosexual senses of masculinity since the 1940s has not been without resistance. Observing masked dance in Malang in 1963—during Old Order times—Onghokham mentions the role of a transvestite as an artistic aide to a troupe leader (1972: 117, 119). That this person was "a well situated villager" (ibid.: 119) suggests that s/he, in some ways at least, did not occupy a completely marginalized position within the community. James Peacock also describes that nearly all of the *tandhak ludruk* he consulted in the early 1960s embodied femininity in their daily lives by wearing women's attire and working jobs associated with women "such as tailoring women's clothes" (1987: 207), but many of these males "endur[ed] parents' discomfort and strangers' taunts to keep the role 'woman'" (1987: 207).

Since New Order times and into the Reformation era (1998–present), males who dress and live as female have insisted on their visibility and acceptance both socially and politically (Boellstorff 2004b; 2005b: 56–57; 2007). Such males are called *waria*—a composite of the Indonesian words *wanita* (woman) and *pria* (man)—or by less culturally sensitive terms such as *banci* or *béncong* (Boellstorff 2004b; 2005b: 9, 11; 2007: 80; Oetomo 1996, 2000). Strikingly, despite New Order gender ideologies, *waria* have been, to a certain extent, tolerated and supported by the government. *Waria* have received recognition and support from local governments since the second half of the 1960s (Oetomo 2000: 51). In fact, the term *waria* "originate[d] not in tradition but in government dictate and dates from 1978" (Boellstorff 2007: 83).

Tom Boellstorff productively discusses the challenges of using terms in English for *waria*, such as "transvestite," "transgender," and "transsexual" (2007: 82). While he explains his preference for "male transvestites," he does so with the recognition that, "[a]s is always the case with any act of interpretation, terms are always to be taken as contingent analytical devices. The goal is not to find a perfect or permanent term but to craft a working vocabulary—the modification and clarification of which is part of cultural critique itself" (Boellstorff 2007: 82). The "working vocabulary" I use as a gloss for *waria*—males who dress and lives as female—is meant to communicate the male femininity that is a key part of *waria* identity (Boellstorff 2004b, 2005b, 2007) and to allow for the recognition of *waria* as an identity that is distinct from that of "woman" (Boellstorff 2005b, 2007), points to which I return later in this chapter. At the same time, I do not mean to imply that there is any one way of living as female.

Since the mid-1960s, *waria* have been working to increase their visibility and social acceptance, seeing themselves as part of national culture, by more openly wearing women's clothes and establishing themselves in salon work (Boellstorff 2004b; 2007: 86–87). According to the *waria* Mama Samsu and her partner Totok Suprapto, *waria* have started to have the confidence to live openly since the 1970s as more *waria* started to appear nationally and internationally in events such as competitions in makeup, beauty, and fashion (p.c., May 9 and 16, 2006). Tom Boellstorff observes a "shift around 1980, when some people began identifying as waria on an ongoing basis in public (as opposed to more circumscribed contexts like theatrical performances)" (2005b: 56).

Indicative of increased visibility, a *waria* was a contender for mayor in the city of Malang in 2003 (Boellstorff 2004b: 187 n19; 2007: 226 n15). I also noticed *waria*'s visibility during my fieldwork, seeing *waria* working in salons, performing in *ludruk* shows, attending *ludruk* performances, and out and about in public. I also noticed representations of *waria* on television, corroborating the visibility in mass media that other analysts have also noted (Murtagh 2011: 392–393 n3; Boellstorff 2007: 88). Some *tandhak ludruk* identified openly as *waria* and went by feminine terms of address such as mama (*mama*), miss/sister (*mbak*), or missus (*nyonya*) (see also Pawestri 2006: 101–109), and as highlighted by Tjundomanik Tjatur Pawestri, some went by feminine names (ibid.: 101). This visibility suggests a reopening and expansion of social space that existed during pre-Indonesian revolution times for males to live as female.

Tolerance and visibility, however, were not synonymous with acceptance, and local pressures reinforced dominant, official ideologies pressuring males to live as "manly" men (Boellstorff 2005b: 11–12, 57; 2007: 78–113; Oetomo 2000: 49; Murtagh 2011: 392–393 n3). Such pressures and their impact on male performers become all the more clear through a closer look at the experiences of three individuals, each of whom negotiated their on- and offstage senses of gender in different ways.

Experiences of Individual Male Dancers

Muliono

I initially came to know Muliono (b. ca. 1976?), or Mul for short, as a dancer who specialized in strong male style masked dances. Several performers in Tumpang recognized his special ability to perform the strong male style masked dance *Klana* in particular. When I saw him perform *Klana*, I, too, was transfixed by his presence and energy as a dancer. M. Soleh Adi Pramono suggested that I study with him because he had a special inner strength as a dancer, which I did. I was pleasantly shocked, then, when Mul told me that he used to perform female characters for masked dance when he was younger and smaller in build. As he spoke with me, however, he seemed to be asserting his masculinity even as he talked about embodying femininity, which I have come to understand as one effect of the social pressures he felt to be manly.

Mul linked the femaleness he embodied in masked dance specifically to the stage in a number of ways. He talked about performing female characters out of necessity to the performance, explaining that female dancers at that time were shy about performing masked dance, and because no one else (i.e., other male masked dancers) could perform female style dance (p.c., January 3, 2006). He also talked about embodying femaleness in terms of his competence, explaining that he became "female" through the dance movement, saying that the movement had to be supple, like a woman. He also pointed to becoming the female character through the costume. Through these explanations, I suggest, he was asserting that he was a male who could perform female style dance because he had to and because of his skill dancing and transforming his appearance, not because he was somehow feminine or effeminate. Reinforcing his offstage masculinity, he explained that he felt the coquettishness of the female character he was dancing when he came out on to the stage, but the feeling of becoming a woman disappeared when he was finished performing (p.c., Muliono, January 3, 2006). In other words, he was making clear that his expression of femininity was contingent upon performance.

Mul accessed and legitimized the femininity he embodied onstage through spiritual practices as well. He said that he would ask for a mantra or magic words from his teacher, which he likened to meditating, so that the character could enter. He said that he truly felt like the female character he was portraying to the point where he did not remember dancing—indicating that he was in a trancelike state as a spirit possessed his body. Many Javanese artists value a performance given by a dancer believed to be entered by a character or spirit. Karen Elizabeth Schrieber found that, according to masked dancers in Tumpang, "[t]he times a dancer performs well or with great animation are contingent on his oneness with the spirit of the mask. With time the dancer comes to be associated with this spirit and is empowered by it" (1991: 26). Sarah Weiss has heard Javanese teachers talk about the necessity for a dancer to "empty himself of everything but the character which can then fill him up, enliven him" (2003: 37). In Mul's case, being entered, filled up, empowered, and/or enlivened by the character helped him to convincingly embody femaleness. He reported that after he performed, his friends said, "how was it that you were like a real woman?" (p.c., January 3, 2006). It also allowed Mul to distance himself from that femaleness—it was not his, but the character's.[1]

Muliono spoke to further gender-crossings in the course of one performance, relating one time when he performed a female role and then played the male character Gunung Sari. He did this because no one else could play Gunung Sari (p.c., January 3, 2006). Such a transformation likely entailed a costume change, a change in masks, as well as a change in demeanor. Like female *Ngremo Tayub* dancers when they change gendered outfits (see chapter two), Muliono's changing gendered characters demonstrates the expression and embodiment of gender to be contingent upon context, including different points within a single performance.

Although he separated his on- and offstage gender identity, Muliono indicated that others did not. He became associated with the femaleness of the female character(s) he was portraying, corroborating Schrieber's findings cited above. He recalled that his friends in the hamlet of Glagahdowo often jokingly called him "sister" or "miss" (*mbak*) (p.c., January 3, 2006). Such "jokes"—which may have bordered on taunts—likely functioned as a form of social pressure for Mul to conform to dominant expectations of maleness.

Over time and as he matured into his adult identity as a man, Muliono, it seemed, did not want to be associated with the femininity of female characters, but instead with the masculinity of male characters. Speaking further to the impact of social and familial pressures, he explained that he did not want to perform female roles after he married—that is, after he assumed the roles of husband and household head and was expected to soon become a father.[2] He said that he did not want to perform female roles in part because his wife Ning[3] joined the masked dance group in his hamlet of Dampul and performed those roles.

Continuing on, he spoke further about concerns related to his gender identity. Prior to his marriage, he explained, he often performed female roles, although up in the Tengger mountains, which was away from his home community. He did not want to perform female roles in his home area because Ning's parents were there, and he was *malu*—an Indonesian word that can be roughly translated as shy or embarrassed—in front of them, especially Ning's father. He said that her parents liked it when he performed *Klana* (p.c., January 3, 2006). He thus felt encouraged to embody a "manly" sense of masculinity, perhaps a gendered quality parents-in-law or potential parents-in-law were likely to find more appealing than feminine qualities in a man who would be or was their daughter's husband. Mul, too, may have wished to demonstrate that he was manly and thus capable of being a good husband, household head, and father. In other contexts, too, Mul reinforced and articulated his heterosexual, "manly" sense of masculinity. He explained that he did not want to perform female roles at PSMD (Padepokan Seni Mangun Dharma [Mangun Dharma Art Center]). He was *malu* because he had lots of female friends there (p.c., Muliono, January 3, 2006). In short, when he wished to be perceived as a heterosexual, "manly" male, he avoided performing female style dance.

Muliono's repeated use of the word *malu* is significant in other ways, and points to the complexity of its meaning. Acknowledging the limitations of translation, Henry Spiller writes, "the usual glosses [of malu], including shame, embarrassment, shyness, bashfulness, humility, and modesty, do not quite capture the subtleties of this important cultural concept" (2010: 27). Ward Keeler argues in an analysis of *isin*, a Javanese word that means *malu*, that underlying an individual's feelings of *isin* is a "sense of vulnerability to others' behavior" (1983: 153) and fear that one's status could be compromised (ibid.: 163; see also Spiller 2010: 27). This "status fright," as Keeler terms it (1983: 163), may include feelings of vulnerability about one's gendered status, which is in part related to the connections between feelings of *malu*, sexuality, gender identity, and socially acceptable behavior in Malay societies (Collins and Bahar 2000: 42; Spiller 2010: 35).

As Collins and Bahar explain, "[g]ender-inappropriate behavior causes both men and women to feel *malu*" (2000: 42). This is illustrated in Keeler's example of a Javanese man, "an accomplished clown" who performed the maidservant role in *ketoprak*, a type of central Javanese theater. After this man became a grandfather, he no longer wished to perform near his home because "he would feel *isin* to be seen performing by his own neighbors and kin" (Keeler 1983: 163). In addition to concerns about being seen performing a comic role, he may have been concerned that his embodiment of femaleness would compromise his status as a senior, male figure in his community whose seniority lay in part in the perception of his grandfatherhood, and by extension, his fatherhood and heterosexuality. Similarly, when Mul felt a sense of "status fright" and wished to protect his status as a heterosexual male, he avoided performing female style dance.

Supatman

The experiences of Supatman (b. 1945), a former *tandhak ludruk*, further point to pressures on male artists to live as men. In Supatman's case, the pressures came from his family and, in a roundabout way, other performers. Supatman, however, also recognized the femininity he once embodied in his offstage life.

Remembering decades into the past, he recalled performing *Ngremo Putri* in *lérok* (an older term for *ludruk*) in the late 1950s.[4] While he recalled his popularity—sometimes performing eighteen times a month—he also recalled that other performers, likely jealous, attacked him with black magic so that he would stop performing. Suffering the effects of this sorcery, he went crazy, and was in a state of distress for twenty-one days. His parents helped him to get cured, but made him promise to not perform in *lérok* anymore. After he stopped performing in *lérok*, he turned to a type of central Javanese theater called *wayang orang*, in which he performed *Ngremo Lanang* and other male roles for two years, from 1958 to 1960. He then turned to a form of sung poetry called *macapat* and by 1962 was performing it professionally (p.c., December 6, 2005; March 26, 2006).

Tellingly, Supatman was in his adolescence when he was moving from *Ngremo Putri* in *lérok* to *Ngremo Lanang* in *wayang orang* and then to *ma-*

capat. At this stage of his life he was likely beginning his physical, emotional, and sexual transformation from boyhood into manhood. Supatman recognized that he did not fit into a normative category of maleness, acknowledging that he straddled conceptual and physical boundaries separating the two official genders. When I asked Supatman whether he enjoyed performing *Ngremo Putri*, he said yes, disclosing that "In the past, I was almost, you know—almost not male.... I was almost like a woman—nowadays a *banci*" (*"Saya dulu hampir, koq—hampir ndak laki.... Saya ini sudah hampir seperti perempuan gitu—kalau sekarang banci gitu lho"*) (p.c., December 6, 2005). Expressing his understanding that others perceived him as effeminate, too, he reported that other people in his community said that he was "sweet" and "coquettish," adjectives often used to describe traits associated with femininity (p.c., December 6, 2005).

Although Supatman "experimented" with femaleness during this period of his life, he ultimately chose to stick with maleness. He explained that he was still performing *Ngremo Putri* as he learned *Ngremo Lanang*, but that as he learned the male style, his *Ngremo Putri* "disappeared" (p.c., December 6, 2005). That is, he gradually forgot *Ngremo Putri*. One implication is that the femaleness and its power that Supatman could embody also "disappeared" as he became more manly onstage as well as offstage.

Furthermore, in part from the pressure he felt from his parents, Supatman left the world of *lérok*, a type of performance strongly associated with not only onstage female impersonation, but offstage homosexual activity as well. What concerned Supatman's parents may have been more than jealousy of Supatman's ability as an artist—as this sort of envy is neither exclusive nor particular to *lérok*. They may have also been concerned about the femaleness they saw their son embodying so well, the attention he may have been receiving from other males in the group or in audiences, and/or the attention he was giving to other males. From my conversations with other Javanese about sorcery, the severity of the effects in Supatman's case—which may have also been related to his own distress—suggest that very strong, passionate emotions were involved, such as those stemming from one whose lover has turned his or her attention elsewhere, feelings coming from one whose romantic or sexual advances have been rejected or at least not reciprocated, or feelings coming from one whose object of desire is clearly in a relationship with another. Whether these hunches are correct or not, it is clear, by Supatman's own account, that familial pressures as well as pressures from other performers contributed to his decision to turn away from the male femininity he embodied in *Ngremo Putri* and *lérok*.

Mama Samsu

As indicated earlier, some male dancers lived as *waria* (males who dress and live as female). To better understand the perspectives and experiences of *waria* artists, I interviewed Samsuarto (b. 1955), a *waria* who began to study the arts as a child and actively performed in *ludruk* theater from 1978–1991.[5] An important figure in the *ludruk* and *waria* communities in Malang and popularly known as "Mama Samsu," she[6] talked about *waria*'s struggles to be accepted by their families and communities, as did the individuals Boellstorff consulted (2004b, 2007). Mama Samsu explained that many *tandhak ludruk* have women's hearts, but do not live openly as *waria*. The stage was an important socially acceptable space for males with women's hearts to embody womanhood, she and her partner Totok explained, if only temporarily (p.c., May 9, 2006).

Mama Samsu pointed to social pressures, particularly in village communities, to conform to dominant assumptions about gender. In villages, she said, people are still close-minded and the families of males with women's hearts often make them live as men and marry women, sometimes with tragic consequences. Mama Samsu did grant that people in the city were more tolerant of *waria* and that their work in makeup, fashion, and performance was appreciated. However, even in the city, Mama Samsu noted, not all males with women's hearts who were active in *ludruk* (or in general) had the confidence to live openly as *waria*.[7] She experienced discrimination by an institution of higher learning when her BA thesis was failed because she dressed like a woman, although she did graduate in 1982.

Work in the beauty industry has been part of *waria*'s larger efforts to more visibly negotiate cultural and economic space. Mama Samsu explained that these kinds of occupations appeal to *waria* because they can dress up and wear makeup daily. In other words, these occupations allowed *waria* to remain visible as *waria* in their working worlds, contributing to the visibility of *waria* in society more broadly (Boellstorff 2005b: 143). These careers also provided an important source of income. Mama Samsu had trained many *tandhak* who were *waria* as seamstresses and makeup artists so that they could supplement their earnings from performing and enter professions with steadier incomes—particularly as they aged and became less able to rely on their own beauty. Samsu indicated that *waria* can make positive contributions to their communities and improve their image through good work in the beauty industry (p.c., May 9 and 16, 2006). She voiced the responsibility that many Indonesian gay male, lesbian, and *waria* individuals take toward their acceptance in society by doing good deeds (Boellstorff 2005b: 212).

Mama Samsu also identified religious pressures, explaining that some orthodox Muslims deemed having one's makeup done by a *waria* to be filthy (p.c., May 9 and 16, 2006). She, however, drew on her personal approach to religion to counter negative ideas and to justify her male femininity in her offstage day-to-day life. Posing the question of who was judging, humans or God, she answered that God is the one to judge, and that everyone is God's creation. Referring to many *waria*'s and *tandhak ludruk*'s experiences of being forced to live as men and marry women, but unable to satisfy their wives (implying sexually), Samsu said that they cannot help it because they were made like that by God (p.c., May 9, 2006). In other words, God made some males feminine and sexually desire male partners, not females. Samsu was also speaking to an important aspect of *waria* identity—having a male body with a woman's heart, making the *waria* identity distinct from that of "woman" (Boellstorff 2005b: 57, 169, 171; 2007: 88, 90, 92, 99).

When I asked Samsu what her religion was, she replied, chuckling, "*nétral*"—implying her independent and open-minded approach. She went on to explain that at one time, she and her long-term partner Totok argued about religion. She questioned why one had to approach God through Islam, articulating her belief in a supreme God while also expressing reservation about choosing Islam as the way to practice monotheism. Mama Samsu decided, however, to "enter Islam" (*masuk Islam*) with Totok and they went to an Islamic boarding school, consulting an Islamic teacher (*kyai*). Totok, however, distanced himself from Samsu, which led to a fight that resulted in their temporary separation. Relating their reunification, she explained that Totok became ill and Samsu was asked to pick him up, concluding the narrative about their argument with the point that "the one to judge is God, not those people" (*"yang nilai Tuhan, bukan orang itu"*) (p.c., Samsuarto, May 9, 2006).

The example of Samsu and her relationship with Totok provides a productive comparison to the ways other Indonesians identifying with non-normative gender identities and sexual orientations have made sense of their sexuality, lifestyles, and Islam, as explored by Tom Boellstorff (2005a, 2007) and Evelyn Blackwood (2010). While some males who identified as *gay* (males who live as men and desire other males who live as men) did find being *gay* a sin, the predominant views Boellstorff found were that being *gay* was either not sinful or "a minor sin easily forgiven by God" (2005a: 580; 2005b: 183; 2007: 151).[8] Similar to Samsu, many of Boellstorff's *gay* Muslim interlocutors referenced ultimate judgment by God. Also in the same vein as Samsu, "many *gay* Muslims concluded they were created *gay* by God and, thus, that they were not sinning" (Boellstorff 2005a: 580; see also 2005b: 183).

Evelyn Blackwood's female Muslim homosexual interlocutors recognized "that according to Islam homosexuality is a sin, but they find their own accommodations between their religious beliefs and their desires" (2010: 15; see also p. 94). By making sense of Islam—and religion in general—in their own ways in order to legitimize gender identities and sexual desires that were nonnormative by the standards of dominant Indonesian (and Islamic) gender ideology, individuals such as Samsu, Totok, those consulted by Boellstorff, and those consulted by Blackwood, were contributing to the spectrum of beliefs, practices, and attitudes that comprise Islam in Java (Daniels 2009).

Although at the time of the interview, Mama Samsu articulated an independent approach to God and religion, she also described the importance of respect for the context, as when serving as a beautician for a wedding. She noted that when she goes to a mosque, she makes the effort to wear a headscarf. She also said that she wears appropriate attire when she goes to a church (p.c., May 9, 2006). Samsu's decision to wear women's attire to mosques is also significant because the issue of what *waria* should "wear when praying as Muslims" (Oetomo 2000: 54)—male attire because they are male, or female attire because they live as female—remains unresolved within *waria* communities (Oetomo 2000: 54–55). By specifying women's attire (a headscarf) to go to mosques (although not necessarily specifying to pray), Samsu was insisting that Muslim society recognize the femininity with which she identified. Moreover, she was providing an example to other *waria* who felt similarly about their femininity while also demonstrating her own respectability. In light of Suzanne Brenner's article showing that through veiling, some women in Java "refashion themselves to fit their image of modern Islamic womanhood" (1996: 691), Mama Samsu's decision to wear a veil also suggests that she was asserting a sense of modernity as she asserted her femininity.

In talking about her propriety, piety, and her long-term relationship with Totok (her partner of over twenty years at the time of my interviews with her), Mama Samsu was also implicitly countering negative assumptions about *waria*'s promiscuity and availability as prostitutes. Not only did *waria* have to contend with rumors and stereotypes about their licentiousness, they frequently faced forms of attention and teasing that sometimes bordered on sexual harassment and belittlement. I write here from personal experience. Taken to be a *waria*, I garnered some wide-eyed stares and comments from men, women, and children that ranged from "transvestite!" (*banci!*) to "my, so pretty" (*koq ayu*). I was also subject to hoots, hollers, pinches in the rear, a caress on the cheek, a pat to the crotch, and a few "offers" from men. The consistency of this attention, while physically and emotionally exhausting at times (I can only imagine what it might be like for many Javanese *waria* who do not have the luxury of simply being able to leave such environments), also indicated the appeal that male femininity had for many in the general public—and, paradoxically, the magnetic power of femaleness that some males were expected and encouraged to exude as they expressed femininity in their own ways.

Expectations for On- and Offstage Expressions of Gender

Expectations from audiences, other performers, and on the part of males who performed female style dance themselves also exerted pressures on male dancers, pressures that they navigated and negotiated. Despite male dancers' embodiment of femininity, other performers and audiences usually—but not always—recognized that their male femininity was distinguishable from female femininity. A female dancer (a woman) generalized that as good as *tandhak ludruk* were, they still looked different than females. She identified "a little stiffness... perhaps in the neck or somewhere else" (*"ada kaku-kakunya sedikit... mungkin di leher atau mungkin di apa itu ya"*). She also explained, "Sometimes we think, 'hey, she's beautiful, her body is good'—it seems. But if compared to a real woman sometimes the difference is still apparent" (*"Kadang-kadang, kita kan 'eh, cantik, bodinya bagus,'—kelihatannya. Tapi kalau dibandingkan sama putri asli itu kan kadang-kadang masih kelihatan berbedaannya"*) (p.c., 2006). By saying that "sometimes the difference is still apparent," she indicated that the difference between a male *tandhak* and a "real woman" was not always apparent.

My mother-in-law, a Javanese woman visiting from Yogyakarta, was convinced that a *tandhak* at a *ludruk* show we attended was female. Surprised to learn that the artist was male, she was impressed with his ability to look so womanly. She may have been convinced, too, because she was less familiar with *ludruk* casting conventions in Malang than local audiences, although, as I explore later, many audience members in Malang delighted in the confusion and, on some level, often allowed themselves to be fooled.

The photographs of a female dancer in a *Beskalan Putri* costume (Photograph 3.1) and male dancers in *Ngremo Putri* costumes (Photograph 3.2) help to illustrate some of the ways male femininity was perceived to be similar to and different from female femininity, despite the stunning beauty of some male *tandhak*. As highlighted through comments from other performers and people in the general public, male bodies tended to be bigger than female bodies, particularly noticeable in males' larger arms and hands, thicker wrists, broader shoulders, and thicker necks. Most males tended to be taller than most females as well.

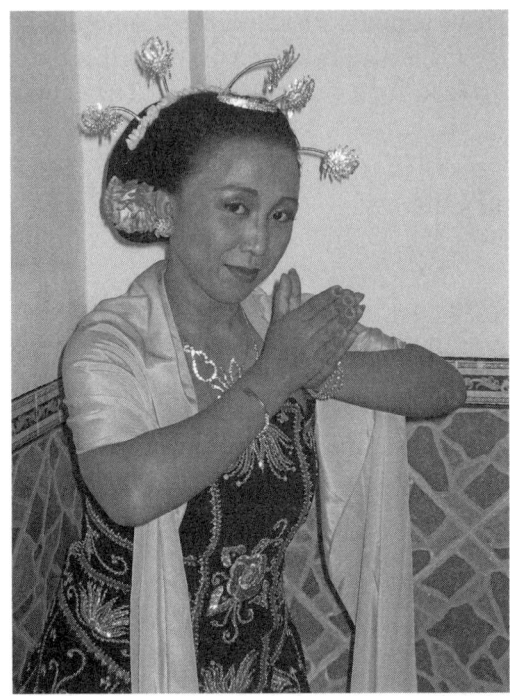

Photograph 3.1: Wahyu Winarti (a female) in a *Beskalan Putri* costume, 2006.

Photograph 3.2: *Tandhak ludruk* (males) perform *Ngremo Putri*, 2006.

While the dancer cited above acknowledged that some male *tandhak* can be more beautiful than "real women," she also identified several features that made them different from females: their voices, their movements, and their awkwardness (p.c., 2006). As she alluded, the sonic impact of a male *tandhak*'s singing in falsetto was usually different than a female's singing, as was a *tandhak*'s speaking voice. In fact, it was often when I spoke and people heard my voice that those who took me for a *waria* realized that I was a woman. For many in Malang, male femininity sounded different as well as looked different from female femininity. And yet, these differences were part of the appeal of male femininity, and, to a certain extent, expected.

Expectations of Male Tandhak *on the Part of Audiences*

Audiences have encouraged gender transgression through their patronage of and desires for cross-gender dancers since "times past," demonstrating their expectations for male *tandhak* to embody femaleness both on- and offstage despite dominant ideologies and social pressures for men to be manly. For some men in audiences, the refined, quiet wives and mothers-of-their-children modeled after Kartini and Sumbadra (see chapter two) fell short as "idealized women." Some preferred a sexualized hyperfemininity embodied by, ironically, male *tandhak*. From his observations of *ludruk* in 1950s east central Java, Clifford Geertz has written that people saw transvestism as "peculiar," and *ludruk* was popular in part because audiences could "wonder at the transvestites"—enchantment that sometimes led to homosexual activity (1960: 295).

Peacock analyzes audiences' comments concerning the beauty of *tandhak ludruk* in 1960s Surabaya, explicit references to their bodies, and desires for them, arguing that *tandhak* represented idealized women and "evoke[d] fantasies of *sexual* escape from adult responsibilities," partly because they could not bear children (original emphasis, 1987: 204). In other words, men could submit to the sexual desires that the female power of male *tandhak* aroused without the worry or responsibility of fathering a child. Providing further insight into the appeal of male *tandhak*, Peacock suggests that "the transvestite's stylized womanly mien forms a kind of blank screen onto which males can project fantasy images of qualities more womanly than those of any real woman" (1987: 206). Many people (males and females) in Malang, including other performers with whom I watched *ludruk* performances, said that *tandhak* could be more beautiful than "real women."

Speaking further to the infatuation and escapism that audiences desired, Djupri recounted an instance in the early 1960s when a man became so obsessed after seeing him dance that he followed Djupri around, forgetting about his own wife and children (p.c., June 15, 2006). Peacock also found that "[o]n occasion, a spectator becomes so aroused that he endeavors to marry the transvestite, and the transvestites are reputed to possess magical power to induce such arousal" (1978: 218). Peacock notes, however, that audiences were disgusted when any aspect of a *tandhak*'s maleness or age became apparent, pointing to audiences' high demands that *tandhak* live up to their expectations for "super-womanly" femininity in which they could revel (1987: 205–206).

Tandhak ludruk may have appealed to male audience members for the same reasons that *waria* appeal to males. Indeed, some *tandhak ludruk* were *waria*. As Oetomo explains, for some Muslims, a man's sexual relationship with a *waria* outside of marriage (to a woman) is not necessarily considered adulterous (2000: 49). Furthermore, similar to Peacock, Oetomo recognizes that "[o]ften, sex with waria is even perceived as 'safer' and 'cleaner,' since it does not result in pregnancy . . . and is perceived not to transmit commonly known STDs such as syphilis and gonorrhea" (Oetomo 2000: 49–50). Paradoxically, when audiences knew that *tandhak* were male, they could respond to the *tandhak*'s femaleness more freely than they would be able to do with a female. Djupri said that when he was performing as an itinerant female singer-dancer (mid-1950s to early 1960s), people in Malang knew that he was a young man because they knew him personally. He said that viewers preferred him to a female because they could dance more freely with a male and even kiss him, behaviors in which they could not indulge if the dancer were female (p.c., June 15, 2006). Taking such liberty with a male dancer performing female style dance was another manifestation of infatuation and escapism. It also suggests the magnetic pull of femaleness.

Audiences have continued to expect "super-womanly" expressions of femininity into Reformation era times. Comments from audiences at *ludruk* performances I attended indicated that they enjoyed male *tandhak*'s abilities to look like beautiful women even though most watching knew from convention or the *tandhak*'s appearance that they were male. When *tandhak* entered the stage one by one to sing as a group for an opening act of a *ludruk* show, I heard men in the audience and running the sound system whistle for the ones they found sexually attractive, calling out remarks such as "beautiful!" and "let's go, beautiful!"

Many in the audience—men, women, and children—seemed to relish their own confusion. Expecting and allowing themselves to be fooled or convinced, many were taken in by the *tandhak*'s feminine beauty. I frequently overheard men and women of all ages make comments about *tandhak* of a variety of ages—younger and more mature—such as "Is that really a woman?" or "That one looks like a real woman." At one performance, a man and I formed a brief friendship as we tried to determine whether a *tandhak* was a woman or not. (We concluded that the dancer was male.) Some of this fascination for *tandhak ludruk* was evident, too, when large crowds at *ludruk* shows parted on their own accord, allowing me to pass backstage unimpeded as they watched and whispered, "a *tandhak* is coming."

Expectations for male dancers to pass or virtually pass as female contrasted with audiences' expectations for female dancers performing male style dance. At the performances I attended, I did not hear audiences or guests make comments indicating that they were fooled or allowed themselves to be fooled into believing that Indonesian women performing male style dance were men, or that they were judging the dancers' handsomeness (although some people did mistake me for being male when I performed). Nor did I hear stories about women falling in love with women who performed male style dance. More research is necessary to ascertain why I did not encounter such stories and to determine whether it was a matter of females' sexual attraction to other females being less visible than males' sexual attraction to other males.

Playing into Audience Expectations Ludruk performers played into audience expectations for the sexual fantasy of male femininity, while also embodying femaleness for their own reasons. Most male dancers since "times past" have labored to look convincingly feminine. Supeno (1923–2009) and Djupri (b. 1939) talked about particular components of the dance costume that they or other male *tandhak* used to look more convincing as women in the past. Supeno described the use of padding by *tandhak* during his heyday (likely in the 1940s–1960s) to enhance their chests and buttocks. He also described a thin plastic mask that some *tandhak* used to make their faces look smooth. He said that he did not use this mask, however, because it was hot (p.c., June 27, 2006). Recalling his activities in the 1960s, Djupri talked about other items he used to transform his appearance, including wigs with real hair that could be glued on to the head and used to make a large bun. He specified that these wigs were from Japan, thereby implying their high quality and expense as well as the care that he took to look like he had long hair.

The use of *ilmu* (spiritual knowledge, often of a secretive nature; see chapter one) was also a strategy male dancers used to embody femaleness. Supeno recounted that he used *ilmu* in order to look beautiful and do his makeup well so that audiences would like him and invite him to perform often (p.c., June 27, 2006). Speaking about his own abilities, Djupri explained that he could dance and feel like a woman on stage because of his *ilmu*, which he took from a heavenly nymph (*dewi widadari*). His transformation to womanhood was so complete that when dancing, he felt like he hated women but liked handsome men (p.c., Djupri, January 6, 2006).[9] In talking about his attraction to handsome men (while in the mindset of a female), Djupri reinforced heterosexual norms even as he articulated what on some level was a homosexual desire.

Djupri also talked about a type of body suit, also from Japan—which I never saw, but which he described as a sort of outer skin complete with pores; body hair; and padding for breasts, hips, and buttocks.[10] Indicating a fairly widespread use of these suits in *ludruk*, Djupri said that lots of his *tandhak ludruk* friends had them, describing different models. His suit covered his upper arms and thighs, and went up the neck with padding to smooth over an Adam's apple. Some, which were more expensive, covered the entire arm and leg. Some also went up the face—perhaps similar to the thin mask that Supeno referenced. The suits came in a variety of colors and the pores made the "skin" look more realistic, while enabling one's natural skin to breathe (p.c., Djupri, June 15, 2006). His fascinating description reinforced the high value he placed on his and his peers' efforts to convincingly embody femaleness and its attracting power.

Some male artists visibly embodied femaleness offstage in public spheres, resisting dominant pressures to be "manly." Supeno and Djupri pointed to their own feminine appearance when they were active as *tandhak* by recalling that they wore their hair long in the course of their daily lives. Supeno reminisced that during his heyday (likely the 1940s–1960s) he had hair down to his waist or buttocks, which was good for making a large bun (p.c., June 27, 2006). Djupri said that when he was actively performing female style dance in the 1960s, sometimes he wore his wig of long hair for months at a time because it was more convenient than removing it and reattaching it every day (p.c., June 15, 2006).

Overcoming his initial shyness with laughs and smiles as he talked to me—his female student in a daughterly relation to him—and my husband, whose presence likely made him feel more at liberty to discuss sexual matters, Djupri explained that the above-mentioned body suit made the genital area look convincingly female as well. Not only was the front of the crotch area smoothed over, there was a pocket to contain a man's genitals. The suit also contained a hole and pubic hair designed to resemble female genitalia. Perhaps obviously, an anatomically correct genital area is more than what was necessary for public performances of female style dance, and Djupri referred to the use of this suit in private activity as well. He said that a man could have sex without the suit being taken off—reporting that it was said that sex was more pleasurable with the suit than with a female. (I took it that he meant for the person not wearing the suit.) He quickly reiterated that that was what people said—he did not know because he had never done this (p.c., June 15, 2006).

In talking about purchasing these suits, Djupri further attested to the effort and financial investment that he and his peers made to look as convincingly female as possible. He said that he bought his at a store in Malang (I assume that he meant the city of Malang) that sold makeup, wigs, and such. Again implying the expense and high quality, he highlighted that the store carried products from abroad and that the seller was Japanese. Noting that the suit was kept in the back, he speculated that perhaps the seller did not sell these suits to just anyone—perhaps just to *tandhak ludruk* (p.c., June 15, 2006). While thus indicating that the use of the suits was not unusual among *tandhak ludruk*, he implied that their use was not a part of general public knowledge, and thus a "secret" of performance that contributed to *tandhak*'s ability to affect their audience with the magnetic female power they could embody.

Although I neither heard about body suits like these from anyone else, nor noticed any being used for *ludruk* performances that I observed in the early twenty-first century, I did see that male *tandhak* worked quite hard to look feminine. Most wore figure-enhancing undergarments such as corsets. Some wore spandex or spandexlike shorts that gave their buttocks a shapelier, more feminine silhouette. Some males had full breasts, perhaps from hormone therapy or silicone injections (see Boellstorff 2007: 94), indicating that they had more permanently altered the appearance of their bodies. Most spent a considerable amount of time doing their makeup, expertly softening and smoothing their complexions through foundation and powder; enhancing their eyes with layers of eye shadow, with eye liner, and with false eyelashes; highlighting the bone structure of their faces with blush; and defining their lips with lipstick. Some *tandhak ludruk* were known to exercise in order to maintain their figures (p.c., Luluk Ratna Herawati, January 4, 2006).

To sound feminine, male *tandhak* cultivated their falsetto range in order to sing in the same high register as females. They also sang *kidungan* melodies that were associated with *Ngremo Putri*, such as melodies that exploited higher pitches, as discussed in chapter two. Lestari (b. 1954), who had been performing female roles since the early 1970s (and could dance *Ngremo Putri* by 1971), talked about little tricks that can be used to make a melody sound more like the way women sing (p.c., April 30, 2006).

Supriono, who did not perform as a *tandhak* himself but worked with me on my singing and helped me to transcribe and analyze vocal melodies from various recordings (including my field videos), identified a particular ornament as a characteristic of *kidungan* for *Ngremo Putri*. This ornament usually occurs about halfway through the first phrase of singing. Using the text in Figure 3.1 as an example, each syllable of the words "*sugeng rawuh*" is sung on high 2, but on the final syllable "*wuh*," there is a distinctive ornament up and then back to 2 (p.c., B. Supriono Hadi Prasetya, May 29, 2007).

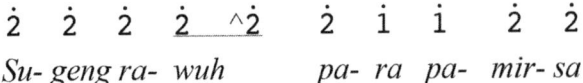

Figure 3.1: Typical basic first phrase of a *kidungan* sung by the dancer in the course of performing *Ngremo Putri*, roughly indicated with an ornament on the syllable *"wuh."* Borrowing from Marc Benamou's work, I use a ^ symbol to indicate this ornament (2010: xxxix). The text, *"Sugeng rawuh para pamirsa"* ("Welcome viewers"), is a typical welcoming text.

Supriono recognized that an ornament is also used for *kidungan* for *Ngremo Lanang*, but, he said, it was different (although he did not further specify the differences). He explained that for him the *putri*-ness is very apparent with the ornament as used for *Ngremo Putri* and encouraged me to use it in order to sound more coquettish (ibid.).

In rehearsals I attended and organized, male musicians often jokingly imitated *tandhak ludruk* by singing this phrase with this ornament—in falsetto—to the delight of the others present. This musical gesture in falsetto clearly evoked senses of femininity associated with male *tandhak*. The femaleness of some *tandhak*'s offstage lives was also evoked as performers knew (or assumed) that some *tandhak ludruk* were *waria*.

In the *ludruk* performances I observed, the comedians tended to take more liberties in their joking with male *tandhak* than with females—even kissing the *tandhak ludruk* to the delight of the audience. The *tandhak* played along, feigning the anger that a woman would be expected to display if such liberties were taken with her. Audiences reveled in comic scenes like this in part because taking such liberties with female artists was rarely funny or tolerated, as discussed in the previous chapter. The efforts to discourage physical contact between male guests or audience members and female artists—as well as the moments of tension that occurred when a male overstepped accepted bounds, rather than the humor evinced when male comedians or actors and male *tandhak* interacted in *ludruk*—further suggests that audiences expected male femininity to be different from female femininity and that male femininity was appealing because of this very difference. *Ludruk* performers understood this and played into these expectations.

Male *tandhak*'s efforts to make their bodies look and sound female differed from females' efforts to make their bodies look male. I did not observe or hear women talk about making their chests look more like men's (i.e., flatter and/or broader). Neither did I notice evidence of women taking male hormones to make their bodies look more masculine nor hear about women doing so. I did not hear talk of women exercising or lifting weights in order to make their figures look more "manly" by making their arm muscles more defined or their shoulders broader. Indeed, from looking at female dancers' arms, it did not seem as though they lifted weights. Women did not seem to regard their own bodies as "male" as they prepared to perform male style dance either. For example, I did not notice women wearing men's undergarments or allowing their chests to be exposed as men sometimes did as they applied their makeup. In many ways, male and female dancers employed different strategies to negotiate conceptual and physical boundaries of gender through performance of *Ngremo*, *Beskalan*, and masked dance, suggesting that the production of male femininity was not necessarily analogous to the production of female masculinity.

Expectations to Keep Up with Changing Audience Tastes Male *tandhak*, like their female counterparts, were also expected to keep up with changing audience tastes and demands, which they did in part through the use of *dangdutan* in *Ngremo Putri*. *Dangdutan* refers to drum patterns, instrumentation (e.g., incorporation of instruments used in *dangdut* and *campur sari* such as electric keyboard, bass, and *dangdut* drums), song genre (i.e., use of popular music), and a section of the *Ngremo* choreography in which these elements were incorporated. Performers consistently identified *dangdutan* as an influence from *Ngremo Tayub* (see chapter two). *Ngremo Tayub* conventions were used because they were popular in *tayub* and on cassettes and that is what audiences wanted (p.c., Kusnadi, 2006; Lestari, April 30, 2006). Here we find that innovations made in a "female" type of performance were incorporated into a "male" type of performance, again suggesting the impact of female artists in taking tradition in new directions.

Strikingly, *Ngremo Putri*, a female style dance that males have used as a means to articulate male femininity, has been strongly influenced by *Ngremo Tayub*, a male style dance that females have used to produce female masculinity, further complicating the articulation, representation, and perception of gender in *Ngremo Putri*. The movements used in most performances of *Ngremo Putri* that I observed exhibited influences from *Ngremo Tayub*, influences that for some detracted from the ideal femininity represented through older styles of *Ngremo Putri*. One musician (born in the 1940s) identified the raising of the arms and hands up past the eyebrows as inappropriate for female style dance: it was too strong and exposing the armpits was impolite. He also determined the dancers' leg position to be too wide; in the past the leg position was like that of *Beskalan Putri*. For this musician, the stance used for *Beskalan Putri* was an ideal stance for female style dance in which the legs are closer together. Although he found that *Ngremo Putri* was no longer appropriately "female," he was in effect identifying aspects of a contemporary male femininity.

Musically, this musician also found contemporary performances of *Ngremo Putri* too manly for his tastes. Accents played on a large drum (*jidhor*) and/or bass drum and crash cymbal from a drum kit or drum set had been incorporated into *Ngremo Putri*—another influence from *Ngremo Tayub*—in the early 1990s, he recalled. Furthermore, he found that the sweetness of the female style was not manifested because the tempo was too fast.

And yet, male dancers also projected more sexually overt forms of femininity through contemporary forms of *Ngremo Putri*, particularly in the *dangdutan* section. In the *dangdutan* sections I observed (and performed on one occasion as a *Ngremo Putri* dancer), the movements departed from the stylized, "traditional" movements of *Ngremo Putri* to feature movements associated more with dancing to popular music. For example, the hips and buttocks are swung in what is seen as a more overtly suggestive manner—too overtly sexy or silly in the eyes of some performers. Sometimes *tandhak* smiled, exposing their teeth; this also departed from tradition. One musician frequently voiced his opinion—which was shared by many performers—that smiling with the teeth exposed was inappropriate for the representation of a refined, elegant woman through traditional dance. Some male dancers tied their dance scarves (*sampur*) around their bodies, or draped them on in a way to more blatantly expose their shoulders and backs.

Thus in terms of movement and music, the performance of *Ngremo Putri* since the 1990s undermined some performers' assumptions about femininity. Pressures from audiences to perform *Ngremo Putri* in this *Ngremo Tayub*-influenced manner suggest that ideal senses of maleness and femaleness promulgated in the past did not capture the range of gender identities that were relevant and appealing to many from the 1990s onward. A stronger and more sexually assertive female persona—infused with a bit of masculinity and accompanied by the sounds of popular music, including the sounds of electric keyboard, electric bass, and *dangdut* drums, among other instruments—was more meaningful to audiences toward the end of the New Order era and into Reformation era times.

Expectations of Tandhak on the Part of Other Performers

Musicians and dancers valued male *tandhak*'s abilities to look like women, and not like males trying to look like women, pointing to their expectations that *tandhak* pass or virtually pass. As one artist and I watched footage from a *ludruk* performance that I had videotaped, I remarked that the *tandhak* were very coquettish. He replied that the *tandhak* used to be too coquettish and so looked like cross-dressers; their director told them to tone it down a bit, and now they were good (p.c., 2005). Similarly, another artist asserted that *tandhak* can be "*over*," implying that *tandhak* can overdo femaleness to the point of looking unconvincing as women (p.c., 2006). His tone clearly indicated that such exaggeration was not what he preferred.

Musicians reported that although they know most *tandhak ludruk* are male, the way they play and feel can be affected by *tandhak* who are particularly believable as women. Kusnadi explained that because *tandhak ludruk* can embody the soul of a woman, and are coquettish, he does not feel like he is drumming for a man (p.c., August 12, 2006). Similarly, Dennis Suwarno said that when he drums for *Ngremo Putri* in *ludruk*, he does not forget that *tandhak* are male, but he looks at the way they dance. If they dance coquettishly, he considers them coquettish (p.c., August 8, 2006). He also explained, however, that the drumming for *Ngremo Putri* has to be made to precisely fit the dance in order to avoid the exaggeration noted above, reinforcing the goal of the performance to make the males look as convincingly female as possible (p.c., Dennis Suwarno, August 8, 2006).

Performers also recognized the particular effect that male *tandhak* gave to *ludruk*. The dancer Warananingtyas Palupi said that *tandhak* made *ludruk* unique (p.c., January 1, 2006). B. Supriono Hadi Prasetya said that if men do not play the female roles, the aura was different, speculating that the Surabaya Radio Republik Indonesia group was not so popular nowadays because women performed female roles (p.c., November 10, 2005).

Males' embodiment of femaleness was arousing for some. One musician (b. 1950s) articulated his sexual desire for male *tandhak*, providing insight into how he negotiated the boundaries of his own sexual desires. He explained that when he sees a man perform female style dance, he is affected by the femininity of the dance and the dancer, not the dancer's maleness. When he sees *tandhak ludruk*, he finds them beautiful, not handsome. Admitting that his passion (*nafsu*) cannot always be controlled, he confessed that he has fallen in love with *tandhak*, even though he knows they are male. He clarified that he fell in love "just in his heart," inferring that although *tandhak* aroused and/or attracted him, he did not try to pursue a relationship. Asserting his assumptions about the normalcy of heterosexuality and yet recognizing the sexual appeal of *tandhak*, he said that falling in love with a *tandhak* is actually not permitted, but that his feelings were pushed from passion. He indicated that his desires were not unique by reporting that he has many friends who become infatuated with *tandhak* because they have large breasts and are incredibly sexy, even though they are male (p.c., 2006).

By talking about the appeal of male *tandhak* in terms of desire for women, men like this musician and audiences in Peacock's (1987) study simultaneously reinforced and subverted official discourses promoting heterosexuality in different eras. Gender categories and with them ideas about gendered behavior and conventions of performing that behavior, were not challenged even as homosexual desires were articulated, and in some cases (although not in the case of the musician cited above), acted upon. The core of the issue was maintaining appearances: men appeared to conform to heterosexuality by what they said even as they undercut it by what they did (including the bodies they desired) to negotiate boundaries of gender, sexuality, and sexual desire.

Ambivalence toward Waria on the Part of Other Performers While other performers were affected by *tandhak*'s femaleness, some expressed their ambivalence about *waria*. One performer said that he enjoyed watching *tandhak* perform, including those who were *waria*, but that he was afraid of *waria* and did not want to talk to them. Some musicians and dancers indicated that the behavior of *tandhak* who were *waria* went beyond propriety and that *waria* could not control their emotions or sexual desires. Some performers said that having a *waria* as a girlfriend was dangerous because a *waria*'s character is "hard" and emotions are "strong." They generalized that when *waria* fall in love, it is difficult for them to let go of the people they love and they become jealous easily. One man said that he did not want to dance *Ngremo Putri* when he was in *ludruk* because of *waria*: he did not want to be around them so he just performed *Ngremo Lanang*. A drummer agreed, saying that *waria* were also what made him reluctant to play for *ludruk*. Since most performers knew that many *tandhak* at the time of my fieldwork were *waria*, their gender transgression in their daily lives was imagined when they were seen performing. This caused some discomfort, evident in performers' criticisms of *tandhak* for their assumed offstage behaviors. One drummer said that nowadays it is as though *tandhak* are possessed by mischievous spirits; it is not *ludruk*, but *waria* looking for men.

Dédé Oetomo provides further insight into the discomfort some performers voiced regarding *waria*, observing that "some waria can be aggressive in pursuing their men—a practice normally considered unfeminine in women—grabbing men by their arms, shoulders, hips, or even crotch. It is cases like these that make one think not all waria are consistently so-called 'imitators of women'" (2000: 50). Of particular importance is the distinction Oetomo highlights between *waria* and women. Similarly, the performers referenced above were identifying ways in which they understood the femininity embodied by *waria* as different from femininity embodied by females, perceiving male femininity as distinct from female femininity. *Waria* were thus perceived not only to cross boundaries separating maleness and femaleness in their daily lives, but also to push at the boundaries of accepted norms of femininity.

Many performers insisted that before the 1990s, *tandhak* were not *waria* (even though other evidence discussed earlier suggests otherwise), linking their presence to the disintegration of *ludruk*. Several performers pointed to the irony that most *tandhak* "nowadays" cannot perform female style dance well even though they dress and live as women. One musician considered *Ngremo Putri* better in the past when men who were not *waria* performed it, saying that *Ngremo* in the past was standard or basic (*baku*)—in other words, not the *Ngremo Tayub*-inspired transformation that was usually performed at the time of my fieldwork. Pointing to his perception of *waria*'s limited musical competence, he asserted that *tandhak* used to be able to play gamelan, whereas now they cannot, and that *kidungan* singing was better in the past. He held that now if *tandhak* can dance a little, they are arrogant, implying that despite this arrogance, they are mediocre performers. A *tandhak ludruk* who had been performing in *ludruk* since the 1970s said that nowadays, dancers come to the performance already dressed as women, but to no avail because they cannot perform female style dance well. Ironically, in the eyes of some performers, *tandhak* at the time of my fieldwork were too womanly offstage and not womanly enough onstage.

Talking in terms of an aesthetic of "unrecognizability," some performers expressed their expectations for transformations from manhood to womanhood to be temporary and limited to the context of performance as well as to emphasize that performers of the past who were not *waria* performed female roles better than performers "nowadays" who were *waria*. They used the word "*pangling*" to describe the success of artists in the past to embody femaleness so completely that others in the *ludruk* group and people in the audience did not recognize them. "*Pangling*" is a Javanese word used to comment on a person's appearance, meaning that they look so different than usual that the person commenting does not recognize him or her. One critique two musicians voiced (on separate occasions) was that, in comparison to "regular men," *waria* could not look unrecognizable because they looked the same on and offstage. The performers making these critiques valued onstage expressions of male femininity—a contingent male femininity—but were uncomfortable when it was taken offstage.

Expectations on the Part of Male Dancers of Themselves and Their Relationships with Others

Many male dancers held themselves to high standards of convincingly embodying femaleness, taking the male femininity they embodied quite seriously. Some performers emitted a sense of pride in being able to fool others into believing that they were biological females. Djupri recounted that when he was young and frequently performing female style dance many people believed that he was a girl when he was in female attire (p.c., June 15, 2006). He related that one time he wore women's clothes in public, posing as a man's second wife, and even fooled Supeno, his own uncle, at the market. According to Djupri, the man had seen Djupri perform female style dance. He asked Djupri to stay in female dress and pose as his second wife in order to see how his first wife would handle such a situation (p.c., June 15, 2006). Djupri was thus also further speaking to ways he blurred his on- and offstage gender identity.

Djupri declined to perform the female style dances *Beskalan Putri* and *Ngremo Putri* for my video recording sessions in 2005–2006, however, because he believed that he was no longer convincing as a woman. He said repeatedly that in the past when he had on his makeup and costume, he was beautiful, but now he was too old, no longer slim, and no longer pretty. He also said since he had not performed female style dance for so long (over ten years) he felt stiff (p.c., Djupri, December 1, 2005; January 6, 2006; March 27, 2006). Djupri's references to his stiffness underline the importance of a graceful flow that is a preferred aesthetic of female style dance.

Djupri also expressed the expectation that he had of himself to live as a man. He referenced his grandmother's religiously inspired instruction to become a woman only when he performed, but not in daily life because God had made him a man (p.c., January 6, 2006). Like other artists I have referenced in this chapter, he identified familial and religious pressures to conform to dominant notions of manhood.

Interestingly, in a context of shifting senses of masculinity, it seems as though Djupri's grandmother sanctioned his nonconformity to some aspects of dominant religious ideology—such as not to cross-dress at all—but at the same time, she insisted that he conform to others—such as not to cross-dress in his offstage life. This suggests her own conflicted relationship with the religious convictions circulating in their community, the limits of gender transgression she approved, as well as her concern for Djupri to be socially accepted. (She may have heard of Djupri's activities posing as a female offstage.)

Some male dancers attributed their abilities to perform convincingly as women to their abilities to locate and draw on their feminine qualities—that is, the male femininity they identified and thus expected in their own selves. For example, Kadam (1939–2014) said that he naturally had a high voice, so he was suitable for female roles. Generalizing that male *tandhak*'s ability to perform female roles stemmed from their own feminine attributes, he explained that most males who perform female roles are able to do so because they have "women's blood" or "women's hearts"; this kind of man can be satisfied by dressing as a woman (p.c., May 23, 2006).

Lestari (b. 1954), who lived as a man, explained that dancers have to find the character of *Ngremo Putri* and its coquettishness from their own selves—that one has to search for the ways to move in order to be more beautiful, such as the way to move the neck coquettishly and how to smile sweetly. He still felt like himself when he did his makeup, but when he stepped on stage, he felt like a woman. Sometimes when he exited from the stage, that feeling did not disappear, especially if he knew that he would appear again for another part of the performance, such as to sing or act in the play. When he was completely done performing he felt like himself again (p.c., April 30, 2006). He thereby expressed contingent male femininity.

I suggest that moving between maleness and femaleness in the course of preparing for performance, during performance, and after performance, was one way that Lestari negotiated the femininity he expected of himself as an artist who specialized in female roles and his religious orientation as a Muslim. He said that he has never had a problem with religion and being a *ludruk* artist who specializes in female roles, indicating his piety by noting that he also participates in the Islamic ritual prayers (*ikut solat*) (p.c., April 30, 2006). Furthermore, he said that everyone in his neighborhood knows that he is a *ludruk* performer who specializes in female roles, and he has never had a problem in his community. He related that when he departs to go somewhere, people sometimes ask him in a friendly and familiar manner whether he is performing. Lestari took this as a gesture of support and acceptance of his profession (p.c., April 30, 2006).[11]

Such acceptance may have been related to the fact that he lived as a man in his daily life and thus conformed to dominant cultural expectations for males to live as men even though he embodied femininity as a profession. Artists who were *waria* did not necessarily experience the same degree of acceptance in their communities, as we have seen, suggesting that generally artists involved with cross-gender dance performance were accepted as along as they did not push at ideological boundaries of gender beyond certain limits in their daily lives. Nonetheless, as a Muslim man who recognized the femaleness of his own self, Lestari complicated dominant ideologies that separated maleness and femaleness into distinct gendered and sexed categories as well as what it meant to live as a Muslim male.

For some males, the makeup process was a crucial step in embodying the femaleness of their hearts. Suradi (1945–2009) and Kadam divulged that they started to feel like women when they began to do their hair and makeup. Kadam said that by smiling sweetly in front of the mirror as he drew his eyebrows, he started to act like a woman even before he stepped onto stage. Suradi and Kadam reported that they felt like men again when their hair and makeup had been removed (p.c., Suradi, May 3, 2006; Kadam, May 23, 2006). Lestari and Kadam reinforced their female roles onstage and their feminine tendencies in general by referring to themselves and other male *tandhak* as *seniwati*, the feminine form of the word *seniman*, or artist (p.c., Lestari, April 30, 2006; Kadam, May 23, 2006). This is analogous to a man referring to himself as an actress rather than an actor. In this manner, they linked their temporary transformations to womanhood to their identities as professional, gendered performers, articulating yet another sense of male femininity despite cultural pressures to be manly.

The backstage behavior of some male *tandhak ludruk* indicated that many considered their bodies visually feminine, reinforcing their expectation that they and others respect them as feminine, too. As I was photographing *tandhak* doing their makeup at a *ludruk* performance, one covered his bare chest with his hands, shaking his head when I pointed my camera his way. I was struck by his reaction because I had been given permission to take photographs, many *tandhak* seemed to be enjoying posing for the pictures I was taking, and he did not appear to have womanly breasts. He behaved as though his bare chest—although physically seemingly "male"—was a private part of his body, like a woman's. My photographing him at that particular moment was thus inappropriate, impolite, and almost pornographic. Many *tandhak* kept their chests covered as they did their hair and makeup by wearing feminine attire such as a blouse or loose dress, or by wrapping a sarong around their body. As mentioned earlier, I also noticed *tandhak* wearing feminine shape-enhancing undergarments such as corsets. Many *tandhak* were quite visibly embodying femaleness in front of other performers and audience members who peered at them.

Tandhak also established physical spaces backstage in which they expressed their femininity. Usually the *tandhak* sat together doing their makeup and dressing a bit apart from the "men" performers who were preparing to go onstage, making distinct dressing spaces for those embodying femaleness. This does not mean that *tandhak* and "men" did not interact or cross into each other's spaces. I observed *tandhak* and men flirting with each other, and in one case, a *tandhak* lavishing attention on a *Ngremo Lanang* dancer by helping him with his makeup and costume. *Tandhak* were in effect reiterating their femininity through their interactions with men, further indicating that they thought of themselves as feminine and expected others to interact with them as such.

Tandhak of different generations also had different ideas about how *tandhak* and *waria* should appropriately embody femaleness, pointing to generational differences in expectations for the expression of gender. Mama Samsu (b. 1955) articulated her concern about the images that *tandhak* and *waria* projected and the ways these images affected society's perceptions of *waria* on- and offstage. She did not care for the fashion show that was part of the opening acts of some contemporary *ludruk* performances, finding that the short skirts and tight clothing (often internationally inspired) that *tandhak* often modeled were not appropriate. As *tandhak* and *waria*, she believed that they should be smooth and graceful and so should wear a long batik cloth, traditional Javanese blouse, and large hair bun (p.c., May 9 and 16, 2006). This is a "classic" and "traditional" Javanese woman's outfit and hairstyle, although subject to changing trends, too. Mama Samsu was speaking to an expectation of feminine refinement consistent with Old Order and New Order gender ideologies—ideologies with which she had grown up—even as she called for the embodiment and expression of such feminine refinement by males.

Furthermore, identifying offstage behavior that she did not like among younger *waria* currently active in *ludruk*, Mama Samsu noted that many do not "know themselves" and that they are not faithful to their partners, which can cause problems of jealousy within the *ludruk* community, and even within one group. She did not like the carefree lifestyle she said that many *waria* lead, saying that most do not think about the future and how they will earn a living after their beauty fades. Samsu's concerns about the behavior and future of other *waria* were not unlike the concerns that Tom Boellstorff encountered among gay male and lesbian Indonesians who, feeling a sense of responsibility for bettering the image that larger society had of them, "would castigate each other for only caring about throwing parties, or stealing each other's girlfriends or boyfriends, or gossiping, rather than doing something 'positive' (*positip*)" (2005b: 212). Mama Samsu, too, also felt that *waria* needed to take responsibility for themselves and perceptions that others had of them.

Not every male was comfortable with the femaleness he recognized in himself. Speaking frankly about his offstage femaleness, Kadam divulged that he had a woman's feeling and the "seed" for his woman's heart since he was a little boy. He explained that because all of his mother's twelve children were male, and she did not have a daughter to help with housework, she dressed him in girls' clothes and had him help her (p.c., Kadam, May 23, 2006). Such work is understood in Java to be women's household duties and includes cooking, washing dishes, doing the laundry, and ironing—work with which girls typically help (Geertz 1961: 119, 126). Wearing women's clothes became normal for him, and his friends were all girls (p.c., May 23, 2006). Kadam's experience taking such female roles offstage was not unique in Old Order times: most of the *tandhak ludruk* that James Peacock consulted in the course of his research in Surabaya in the early 1960s "[had] taken feminine roles since childhood," such as playing girls' games and helping their mothers in the kitchen (1987: 207).

Kadam recognized that gender and sex do not necessarily map to each other in a simple one-to-one correlation as they do in official discourses, but that some men and women embody gendered attributes of the opposite sex. Accounting for why males with women's hearts—including himself— and females with men's hearts existed, Kadam explained that during sexual intercourse sometimes one parent wishes for a baby of one sex while the other parent wishes for the opposite (p.c., May 23, 2006). Kadam recognized different types of males with women's hearts, as well as a range of lifestyles, recognizing a continuum of male femininity. Some males, such as himself, lived as men; others lived as women; and still others had sex-change operations and husbands (p.c., May 23, 2006). In identifying a range of ways males embody femininity, Kadam was recognizing gender pluralism within a framework of gender dualism.[12]

Despite his frankness, Kadam expressed ambivalence about his own male femininity in his offstage life. He clarified that although in his soul he felt like a woman, he did not want to become one. He explained that when he saw women as a young man, he wanted to marry (often a euphemism for sexual intercourse), which meant that his blood was more than fifty percent male.[13] At the same time, he identified limitations in his own sexual desires for women and that living as a "true man"—one who has a productive sexual relationship with a wife that results in children—was a struggle. He also explained that the only woman he could love was his wife, and that he could not seduce other women "in a manly way" (p.c., May 23, 2006). Throughout our conversation, Kadam compared his gender and sexuality to that of "other men," or "normal men," pointing to his recognition of his own difference and also implying what he believed existing as a "normal man" entailed: sexual prowess and conquest of women.

Kadam's references to his blood and inner self also signify his struggle to negotiate his sense of destiny to be a man and the pressures to live visibly as a man in the terms of official discourses about masculinity. In Kadam's case, tensions between inner and outer selves and between onstage and offstage personas mirrored each other, further blurring the edges of on- and offstage realms of cultural production and personal experience.[14] Implying that a male could and should be prevented from having a woman's heart, he instructed that if I have a son in the future, I must not allow him to wear women's clothes (p.c., Kadam, May 23, 2006).

Negotiating Pressures, Redefining Gender

Male dancers since "times past" negotiated a variety of pressures—social, familial, religious, institutional, discursive—as they embodied femininity in different ways. They accomplished this through particular strategies of gender transgression, which included rearticulating state-, community-, and family-sanctioned ideals in their own ways. Some conformed to dominant expectations of womanhood through their performances of female style dance and to dominant expectations of manhood by living as men. Others upheld state-sanctioned notions of femininity by performing and living as "proper" women, but embodied that femaleness through their male bodies. Still others pushed at dominant ideals of femininity by wearing more overtly suggestive clothing and by expressing a femaleness that departed from dominant Old Order and New Order ideals. Some males transgressed gender in different ways at different times in their lives, as we saw with Muliono and Supatman.

While some were motivated to do so in order to express the femaleness of their hearts and souls, others did so for the sake of performance (and employment), connecting their embodiment of womanhood to the physical space of the stage and moment of performance. All, however, in effect challenged dominant ideologies about which kinds of bodies could and should occupy femaleness and its magnetic power, as well as made socially acceptable space for male femininity, albeit sometimes contingent upon the context of performance. In embodying femininity through their male bodies, performers were not only disrupting dominant ideas about gender and articulating gendered constructs in their own ways, they were also negotiating east Javanese tradition, sometimes in ways that many performers I consulted did not like, evident in their critiques of *tandhak ludruk* and *Ngremo Putri* "nowadays." At the heart of what concerned those who critiqued *Ngremo Putri* "nowadays," as well as *Ngremo Tayub* (seen in the previous chapter), was a concern about the preservation of Malangan tradition. And their senses of Malangan tradition were bound up in their senses of history, the subject of the next chapter.

4. Constructing Gender and Tradition through Senses of History

This chapter explores how performers constructed senses of gender—including boundaries of femaleness and maleness—as they established what comprised tradition through their senses of history. I argue that the ways performers connected femaleness, the female style dance *Beskalan Putri*, the past, spiritual power, and Malang as they talked to me indicates ways of thinking that in effect maintain cultural space for the magnetic power of femaleness and connect female power to Malangan identity. The senses of femaleness and its power that performers associated with *Beskalan Putri* were so strong, I further posit, that they shaped the ways performers understood and talked about the histories of other dances discussed in this chapter, including *Ngremo Lanang*, *Ngremo Putri*, and *Beskalan Lanang*, as well as the expression of gender in these dances. These perceptions also provide deeper insight into what has concerned performers about the performance of *Ngremo Tayub* and *Ngremo Putri* since the 1990s discussed in preceding chapters.

Senses of Gender, Senses of History

Beskalan and femaleness seemed almost inseparable for many performers. Their references to "*Beskalan*" generically were frequently references to the female style, *Beskalan Putri*. Reinforcing preferred aesthetics for female style dances, they explained that the character and feel should be refined, smooth, coquettish, sweet, and polite. Several explained that the tempo of the music should be slow, so as to bring out *Beskalan*'s sweetness. Women were also imagined. *Beskalan Putri*, one dancer explained, was about the beauty of everything that a woman has. Another said that the dance was specifically for women. Strikingly, these connections to femaleness belie histories of *Beskalan* in a male style and performance of both female and male styles by both female and male dancers. In fact, the former dancer Supeno emphasized that a woman should or must (*harus*) dance *Beskalan Putri* even though he performed it himself for many years. These associations of *Beskalan* to femaleness have led me to explore performers' senses of history in terms of gender, and to think more about how people's senses of the past influence their senses of the present and vice versa (Connerton 1989: 2).

My thinking has been influenced by Sarah Weiss's analyses of gender and performers' senses of the past in her studies of female musicians who play the *gendèr* (a type of metallophone played with two mallets) for central Javanese shadow-puppet performances (2002, 2006). She explores the cultural contradictions surrounding a *gendèr* playing style that has been gendered female because it has been historically associated with women *gendèr* players, recognizing that females and males can and do play "female style." Weiss shows that, paradoxically, while central Javanese performers associate female style *gendèr* playing with "village style," and village style in general is usually denigrated by musicians trained in the urban traditions of the courts and arts academies, female-style *gendèr* playing is also connected to an older style of performance and thus valued (2002: 299–300; 2006).[1] This older style is characterized by an "aesthetic . . . of following the *rasa*, or feeling, of the performance as it changes and develops," rather than the "schooled precision" typically associated with more recent, urban styles that are associated with mostly male musicians (Weiss 2002: 300; 2006). Weiss's work suggests that the connections between femaleness, the past, and *rasa*-ful performance—that is, performance full of feeling, affective power, and deep knowledge (see chapter one)—is one way in which performers have recognized magnetic female power through their senses of the past and thus maintained space for the recognition of female power in the present. Applying these perspectives to dance performance in Malang and developing a previously published analysis of performers' senses of history (Sunardi 2010a, 2010b), I show that performers recognized female power in the present as they connected *Beskalan Putri* to the past, spiritual power, and female figures, doing so in different ways through their individual senses of history.

Connecting Femaleness, *Beskalan Putri*, and Malang

Local Tradition, Female Power, and Islam in Djupri's Narratives

Djupri (b. 1939), one of my principal dance teachers, put women at the center of his verbal narratives about *Beskalan Putri*'s history by connecting the dance to his grandmother Muskayah and to the spirit of a female warrior from past times. As I learned from him in bits over the course of many months, Muskayah was born in the 1890s. When she was nine years old, she fell ill, slipping into a dreamlike trance state. At that time, her name was Sukanthi. While in this alternate state of consciousness, the spirit of the legendary princess or noblewoman Prabaretna from the thirteenth-century east Javanese kingdom Singosari came to her. Prabaretna called upon Sukanthi to heal people by becoming a dancer. Sukanthi was instructed to perform *andhong*, a type of itinerant performance. An *andhong* group usually included one or two professional female dancers (also called *andhong*) who sang as well as danced. *Andhong* groups wandered from village to village looking for places to perform, and viewers, usually male, who would pay to request a song and dance with the female singer-dancers. By performers' accounts, *andhong* was a tradition that for the most part fell out of practice in the late 1950s to mid-1960s.[2] According to Djupri, the spirit of Prabaretna gave Sukanthi *Beskalan Putri*. This dance, Prabaretna's spirit explained to Sukanthi, existed in the past but was lost when Majapahit, the last of the great courts of east Java, fell (1478 or c. 1520).[3]

Upon awakening a few days after she had fallen ill, Djupri explained, Sukanthi could immediately perform *Beskalan Putri*, its songs, and its music. She trained an ensemble and began to perform, changing her name to Muskayah as a reflection of her new identity as a dancer and healer.[4] Initially performing as an *andhong*, Muskayah became famous for her beauty, grace, difficult movements, and efficacious spiritual power to heal through performance. She was also asked to perform at particular events, indicating that her status as a dancer increased. She spread *Beskalan Putri* throughout Malang and other parts of Java through her many students and her many performances, including performances in sacred or ritual contexts such as exorcisms, vow fulfillment ceremonies, and village purification ceremonies. She performed at increasingly prestigious venues as she was hired by the subdistrict, the regency, and went all the way to Banyuwangi and Yogyakarta. The sultans of Yogyakarta hired her for her spiritual knowledge, including her abilities to exorcise and make offerings. The Dutch hired her, too, and she performed abroad in the Netherlands, China, and Japan. From Djupri's narratives, it seems that Muskayah healed and entertained many during her long career as an artist, the height of which was likely to have spanned from some time between 1899 and 1908 to the 1940s, before she passed away in the late 1980s or mid-1990s.[5]

Analyzing Djupri's narratives in further detail offers a means to explore the cultural and ideological work he was doing in terms of elevating Malangan tradition, identifying female power, and negotiating Islam. For one, Djupri exemplified a cultural value placed on antiquity, giving cultural legitimacy to *Beskalan Putri* by situating it as a centuries-old tradition (Hobsbawm 1983). While Sylvia Tiwon also notes beliefs about *Beskalan Putri*'s antiquity, writing that the dance is "believed to date back to the 13th/14th century kingdom of Majapahit" (2005: 111), I have not located other historical evidence to either support or refute the antiquity of this dance. What is more important for me, however, is that Djupri talked about it as a centuries-old dance, thereby elevating its status.

Djupri was also elevating *Beskalan Putri* by linking it to the culture of courts that once flourished in east Java, and in the case of Singosari, a court that was located in the Malang area. In Java, images of female singer-dancers performing in villages typically stand in stark contrast to images of female dancers trained in the courts of urban central Java who perform court dances such as *bedhaya* (Hughes-Freeland 1997: 478; 2008b: 144). Furthermore, itinerant performers are, in general, considered particularly low class, often viewed as beggars, and in the case of the female singer-dancers, as prostitutes (Geertz 1960: 296; Sutton 1984: 123–124). By underscoring Prabaretna's courtly rank, Djupri elevated *andhong* and *Beskalan* dancers as performers, *Beskalan* as a dance, and the knowledge he believed Prabaretna's spirit gave to his grandmother about it (p.c., February 7, 2006; March 22, 2006; August 7, 2006).

Indicative of the need that many performers in East Java feel to legitimize their traditions by associating them with court culture, Victoria M. Clara van Groenendael found that *jaranan* (hobbyhorse) performers in the East Javanese regency of Kediri linked stories about the origins of *jaranan* to the Panji legend (2008: 169–184). She highlights that the Panji legend is connected to court culture both in terms of content (the stories center around the legendary East Javanese prince Panji) and in terms of enactment (the stories are performed through theater traditions associated with court cultures) (2008: 184). By telling legends that link *jaranan* to the Panji story, performers elevated *jaranan*. In Clara van Groenendael's words, *jaranan* was "lifted to a level above that of 'uncultured' folk entertainment and associated, be it only symbolically, with the official (court) culture" (2008: 184). In Kediri, as in Malang, performers drew on their senses of the past to assert the cultural value of their traditions. Strikingly, they did not seem to question the value placed on court culture.

As Djupri talked about *Beskalan*'s history, he connected the dance to female power in multiple ways, including the power females may embody through spiritual knowledge, or *ilmu* (see chapter one). He related that while Muskayah (at that time, Sukanthi) was in a dreamlike trance state, the spirit of Prabaretna instructed her to revive *Beskalan Putri*—several hundred years after it had been lost—and gave her *ilmu* about the dance, instructing her to find a man named Baswara. One implication is that in being given such *ilmu*, Muskayah was also given the ability to access spiritual power (or more spiritual power in addition to what she might have already had). The *ilmu* included the dance's movements, songs, and musical accompaniment as well as the philosophical meanings of the dance, including the dance's portrayal of Prabaretna's own search for Baswara, alias Jaka Umbaran, her true love. One implication is that Muskayah was either a reincarnation of Prabaretna or a medium for Prabaretna's spirit, who was still searching. In linking Prabaretna to Muskayah, Djupri in effect located two women of different pasts in the body of one girl, reinforcing *Beskalan*'s connections to *ilmu* and spiritual power associated with female figures.[6]

The story of Prabaretna's search also represents female power and agency. Although the details of the story varied on different occasions that I consulted Djupri, the basic outline is that Prabaretna and Jaka Umbaran were in love with each other.[7] Their parents, however, did not accept their relationship and separated them. Determined to be together, Prabaretna and Baswara each set out to find the other, spending years searching high and low through the forests. *Beskalan Putri* portrays Prabaretna's search (p.c., Djupri, February 7, 2006; August 7, 2006). Prabaretna neither heeds her father's wishes, nor does she wait as a subservient wife-to-be for her lover to rescue her or figure out what to do. Instead, Prabaretna is portrayed as taking the initiative to locate the man she desires—a striking contrast to constructions of ideal women in Old Order and New Order ideologies who were portrayed as subservient to males as fathers or husbands.

Prabaretna's power in the form of her strength as a warrior is further represented through the costume pictured in Photographs 1.2 and 3.1 (in chapters one and three, respectively). This costume is similar to that used for male knights, princes, and kings in masked dance, further aligning the female character portrayed in *Beskalan Putri* with a physical strength and readiness to do battle that is frequently associated with male warriors (Photograph 4.1). Like these knightly men, Prabaretna is portrayed as wearing pants. Some of my teachers also said that a dagger (*keris*) could be worn behind the back, as masked dancers do for male style dance. Djupri explained that the layers of material worn as aprons of sorts around the lower body represent fabric

Constructing Gender and Tradition through Senses of History 99

Photograph 4.1: Muliono in costume for *Gunung Sari*, a refined male style masked dance. Note that the lower tip of his dagger's sheath can be seen just behind his left hip, 2006.

torn from Prabaretna's search through forests. The many beaded strands on the costume symbolize the threads of her ripped clothing, indicating the years she has spent searching (p.c., Djupri, February 7, 2006).[8] As I imagine, following Djupri's narratives, she presumably has nicks and scratches on her skin from the same branches and thorns that have ripped her clothing. She has likely not been eating well. Despite these tests of physical and emotional endurance, she perseveres.

The dance movements, too, symbolize Prabaretna's strength. A warrior, she manipulates her bow and shoots an arrow. Perhaps she is hunting for food or warding off an attack from a dangerous animal or demon. She looks out in the distance, searching for Jaka Umbaran, attentive to her environment. She is also attentive to her appearance, adjusting her hair or ornaments around her ears, showing that she retains her dignity, pride, and hope. One interpretation is that every time Muskayah, or anyone else, danced *Beskalan*, she or he was performing Prabaretna, on some level embodying the spirit of this woman and the power she expressed through her strength as a warrior. I cannot help but recall the female soldiers of the seventeenth to nineteenth century central Javanese courts discussed in chapter two.

Djupri's narratives also contained possible references to Islam. He described the spirit who visited Muskayah as wearing a white robe (*jubah putih*), white turban (*serban putih*), white shoes and, later in the conversation, a white shirt and white pants,[9] thereby suggesting that the figure had some connection to Islam, and perhaps was Muslim (p.c., November 12, 2005). The pants suggest that the spirit was clad in a type of dress appropriate for fighting—perhaps as a female Muslim warrior—which may be related to the portrayal of a female warrior in the dance.

Djupri further evoked Islam by relating that while in trance, Sukanthi held a small book that was the size of a lighter. Suggesting the mysterious involvement of the supernatural world, he explained:

> She was in trance then suddenly holding it. The ones who knew were regular people, who were healthy [i.e., those not in trance]: "Lho! Where did this child get that thing she's holding so? She's holding that book." Like that.[10]

This small book can be interpreted as a *Qur'an* (p.c., Sunardi and B. Supriono Hadi Prasetya, 2007). The surprise of the onlookers in Djupri's narrative suggests that this book appeared out of nowhere, reinforcing the sense that the supernatural world—perhaps a Muslim supernatural world—was involved in the transmission of this dance as well as Muskayah's *ilmu* and power as a healer.

The hints of Islamic imagery are striking for what they suggest about the place of the religion in the east Javanese courts of the past. On the one hand, the courts that Djupri referenced, Singosari and Majapahit, were Hindu-Buddhist. Muslim polities in Java—including Demak and Mataram—rose to dominance in the sixteenth century, after the fall of Majapahit (Koentjaraningrat 1985: 44–56; Sumarsam 1995: 18; Spiller 2008: 45, 47; Ricklefs 2008: 38–39). On the other hand, the Islamic influence in the Hindu-Buddhist courts that Djupri's narratives imply may have very well indeed been true. According to M. C. Ricklefs, gravestones in two graveyards "near the site of the Hindu-Buddhist court of Majapahit. . . . suggest that some members of the Javanese elite adopted Islam at a time when the Hindu-Buddhist state of Majapahit was at the very height of its glory" (2008: 5; see also Houben 2003: 153). Moreover, Vincent Houben writes that "[r]ecent studies have shown" the presence of Islamic consultants at the Majapahit court (2003: 154).

Whether or not Djupri knew about these Muslim graves or Islamic consultants, was drawing on other historical evidence, or otherwise took a Muslim presence in the Majapahit court to imply a Muslim presence in Singosari (from where Prabaretna was said to have come) by implying Prabaretna's connections to Islam, Djupri drew on his sense of the past in order to negotiate Islam and the performing arts in contemporary times. He consistently mentioned that devout Muslims in his community disapproved of women's activity in the performing arts and criticized Muskayah for her involvement. Such criticisms were likely connected to negative assumptions about female singer-dancers, especially those who were itinerant. He said that Muskayah did not want her own daughters to become dancers because she did not want them to feel the pain of such denunciation, indicating that she was deeply affected. Djupri seemed to be responding as much to her hurt as to the censure from members of the community.

Through his narratives about Muskayah's call to become a singer-dancer, Djupri implied that she was neither low class nor a prostitute but was a potent healer given an important and morally virtuous duty by a spirit with some connection to Islam. In situating the command to perform as an *andhong* to such a spirit, Djupri further elevated the status of *andhong* as a tradition. Furthermore, since Muskayah's power and knowledge came from a spirit with a connection to Islam, the power and knowledge that she embodied also had a connection to Islam, suggesting the importance of the religion to Malangan tradition. Speaking to her ultimate triumph within her community, Djupri recounted that even the most devout Muslims—the same people who criticized her—came to her when they needed her help as a healer.

Performers' senses of history in other regions of Java further show connections musicians and dancers have made between performing arts, spiritual power, and Islam, thereby legitimizing the art forms. For example, the master gamelan musician Warsadiningrat (1882–1975) of the Surakarta court situated the origins of gamelan *sekaten*, a type of ensemble that is played in the courtyard of the court mosque as part of the celebrations commemorating the birth of the Muslim Prophet Muhammad, to the Islamic saint Sunan Kalijaga in the sixteenth century (Sumarsam 1995: 29, plate 13; 2011: 48). While there is no historical evidence to support this, linking gamelan *sekaten* to Islam enhances the spiritual power and status of the instruments (Sumarsam 2011: 48–49). As Sumarsam explains, "linking the origin and use of gamelan *sekaten* to the rise of Islam is common among the Javanese and scholars of Javanese culture" (2011: 48). In Cirebon, West Java, the curative power of masked dancers of pedigree, who may be female or male, is believed to stem in part from their Muslim lineage, which they trace to Sunan Kalijaga (Ross 2011: 146–147).

The manner in which Djupri talked about Muskayah—her curative powers stemming from a figure who appeared in seemingly Muslim dress, suggesting a Muslim lineage of sorts—also demonstrates the way he connected spiritual power, Islam, the past, and performance. In short, through his narratives about Muskayah's dreamlike experience as a child, Djupri elevated *andhong* and *Beskalan Putri*, represented Islam and gender in ways that justified his grandmother's activity as an artist and asserted her importance in the history of Malangan traditions.

A strikingly similar narrative exists about Semi (1885–1973), one of the first female dancers to perform a type of social dance called *gandrung* in Banyuwangi (a regency at the eastern end of Java) (Sutton 1993: 136–137; see also Yampolsky 1991a).[11] Although the details differ, the basic trajectory is that a young girl falls ill, goes into trance, begins to dance, and afterward becomes a dancer (Sutton 1993: 136–137). The remarkable similarities in the narratives about Semi and Muskayah—not only the elements of illness, trance, recovery, and becoming a dancer, but also the year in which Semi was born and the point in her life when she fell ill—suggest a number of things. For one, a young girl falling ill and being "called" to become a dancer, in addition to occurring in some way, may be a sort of trope in local dance histories in different parts of East Java. Also, the late nineteenth and early twentieth centuries may have been times of changes in social norms that contributed to shifts in the sex of dancers who performed certain female style dances. In addition, such stories may have been a means by which their tellers made sense of and/or justified girls' roles as dancers as well as the spiritual power attributed to them.

Other Performers' Narratives, Other Representations of Female Power

M. Soleh Adi Pramono (b. 1951) reinforced Djupri's history about *Beskalan Putri*, but told it differently by linking *Beskalan Putri*, the past, Malang, and femaleness in his own way. When I was still fairly new to Malang, in November 2005, Soleh invited me to accompany him and his daughter to interview Djupri, explaining that it was important to meet Djupri because Djupri's grandmother created *Beskalan Putri*. In an interview with Soleh about eight months later in July 2006, he again referenced Djupri and Muskayah to tell me a history similar to Djupri's, also emphasizing that *Beskalan* is hundreds of years old and tied to Malang. However, while he recognized Muskayah's spiritual power and interactions with the supernatural world, Soleh explained that Muskayah created *Beskalan Putri* by developing it over time as she performed as an itinerant dancer. Soleh thereby emphasized a more "rational" creative process and implied her activities in secular contexts (p.c., July 27, 2006).

Also different was that while Soleh pointed to Prabaretna's connection to Malang, he referred to her connection to Malang in the seventeenth century, which was after the fall of Majapahit. In talking about the seventeenth century, he was situating Malang as a contemporary of the central Javanese kingdom Mataram. On previous occasions, he had referred to historical connections between the performing arts of Malang and those of the central

Javanese court city of Yogyakarta, which many Javanese position as an heir to Mataram. Through his sense of history, Soleh may have been implicitly reinforcing his case for a relationship between Malangan traditions and those from central Javanese courts.

Other performers' narratives about Muskayah were different and also similar in other ways. Timan (b. 1930), who was one of Muskayah's accompanying musicians as a boy, and Supeno (1923–2009), Muskayah's son, insisted that she was not an itinerant performer but was requested. In other words, they implied that she was hired for specific occasions, thereby raising her status as a dancer (p.c., Supeno, June 27, 2006; Timan, July 4, 2006). Furthermore, Muskayah did not play a central role in every performer's understanding of *Beskalan*'s history. Chattam Amat Redjo (1943–2013), a respected dancer and dance expert based in the city of Malang, acknowledged that Muskayah was likely a *Beskalan Putri* dancer, but he did not believe the accounts that credited her with creating the dance (or reviving a dance that had been extinct). Nonetheless, like Djupri and Soleh, Chattam connected the history of *Beskalan* to female dancers, and positioned it as a Malangan tradition by situating its antiquity in the Malang area. He, too, asserted that *Beskalan Putri* has existed for centuries, and similar to Djupri, referenced the thirteenth century kingdom of Singosari.

Using some different kinds of sources from Djupri's and Soleh's oral narratives, Chattam pointed to the costume as evidence of *Beskalan Putri*'s antiquity, arguing that its materials were proof of the trade abroad that has characterized Javanese history since at least the times of Singosari. Referencing more recent history, he showed me a photograph of a female *Beskalan Putri* dancer that he said was taken in the 1930s,[12] speculating that if the costume were as elaborate as it was in the photograph, most likely the dance had emerged some years prior to the photo, before what he believed was Muskayah's time. Further establishing its existence before he believed Muskayah was active as a dancer, he cited a conversation he had with a woman named Markunah who was dancing *Beskalan* by the 1920s. Chattam's implication that Muskayah was not active as a dancer before the 1920s, however, contrasts with Djupri's history. Following Djupri's narrative, if Muskayah were born in the 1890s, she would have had her dream experience and become a dancer sometime between 1899 and 1908 (at nine years old), and thus would have had many years of experience as a dancer by the 1920s and 1930s.[13]

Like Djupri, however, Chattam connected *Beskalan* to the power of femaleness by connecting it to women's spiritual power and sacred contexts. Chattam highlighted *Beskalan*'s connection to ritual by explaining that *Beskalan* had existed for centuries as a ceremonial dance and by referencing one of Markunah's performances for a ceremony in the 1920s that involved the use of a water buffalo's head (p.c., April 14, 2006). In a previous conversation with both Chattam and Soleh, the use of the water buffalo head had also come up for discussion. Chattam was explaining to me that *Beskalan Putri* was used in ceremonies during Dutch times (that is, prior to 1942). The head of a water buffalo was wrapped in white cloth and put in a hole to keep away evil spirits. Soleh offered his interpretation of why the buffalo head was used, reinforcing *Beskalan*'s connections to east Javanese court culture of past times as well as to the supernatural world. Soleh explained that the water buffalo was connected to the Hindu goddess Durga, who rode a water buffalo during the time she spent in the underworld, specifying that the Durga to which he was referring came from Majapahit (p.c., Chattam Amat Redjo and M. Soleh Adi Pramono, April 9, 2006). In the course of the conversation, both men underlined *Beskalan*'s use for ceremonial, ritual purposes, emphasizing the spiritual dimensions of the dance in relation to a feminine power represented by a female deity.[14] Chattam and Soleh were thus speaking to the power of femaleness on multiple levels as they recognized the power of the dancer, of the dance, and of the deity.

The Malang-based Indonesian dance scholar Robby Hidajat also links *Beskalan Putri*, Malangan identity, and ritual (2006). His work helps us to understand that historically, fertility rituals (including those featuring *Beskalan Putri*) have been important to people in Malang because the economy in Malang has been based on agriculture (2006). As introduced in chapter two of this book, female dancers have long played important roles in fertility rituals in many parts of Java, on one level personifying the goddess of rice. The ritual function of *Beskalan Putri* in fertility rituals further connects the dance to femaleness both in terms of female dancers as well as in terms of female sexuality. Henry Spiller has highlighted that in Sundanese dance events in West Java, the fertility of the land is represented by and mapped to the sexuality of the female dancer's body (2010: 10, 82). This seems to be the case in east Java, too.

The drummer Sumantri (b. 1954) also linked *Beskalan Putri* to the fertility of the land, doing so through an etymology of the word "*Beskalan*." He linked "*Beskalan*" to the word "*cikal*," a coconut tree sapling. He explained that the actual name of the composition that accompanies *Beskalan* is "*Klapa ndhèk*," from "*Klapa pendhèk*," which literally means "short coconut" (p.c., April 20, 2006; see also Hidajat 2006: 180). The reference to a coconut tree sapling also links the dance to agriculture and fertility (the sapling, if in fertile soil, will grow). Such Javanese folk etymology is called *jarwa dhosok* (Becker 2000) or *kérta basa* (Beatty 1996: 281). In casual everyday joking, many Javanese delight in similar kinds of riddles, puns, and other plays on words.

Despite the differences in details between the individual narratives of the performers cited above, there did seem to be a consensus that by the 1920s,

Beskalan Putri was being performed by women. Like Djupri and Soleh, Chattam connected this dance to women of the past—the woman in the photograph and a woman he consulted—referencing *Beskalan*'s connections to the spiritual world through its uses for ceremonial and sacred performance. Reinforcing the importance of female dancers, performers seemed to suggest that *Beskalan Putri* was initially performed by females and then came to be performed by males. Chattam explained that *Beskalan Putri* entered *ludruk* theater in the 1930s (p.c., April 14, 2006). At that time, the performers playing male and female roles were male (see chapter one). The work of the *ludruk* scholar Supriyanto supports Chattam's narrative, indicating the influence of female dancers on *ludruk* performers. Supriyanto writes that after what he terms the "Besut period" of *ludruk* history (c. 1915–1920s), "*ludruk* presented a female style opening dance that imitated the movements of *andhong* dancers (itinerant female singer-dancers). This style of female dance was named Beskalan Malangan Dance" ("*ludruk menyajikan tari pembukaan putri yang menirukan gerak penari* andhong *[tandak ngamen]. Gaya tari putri itu dinamakan* Tari Beskalan Malangan") (2001: 24).

As different performers talked about the past in different ways, it became clear to me that their senses of *Beskalan Putri*'s history were often quite personal—rooted in their personal memories, their own experiences, and oral histories that they had learned from those older than they. In Djupri's case, his sense of *Beskalan Putri*'s history was inseparable from the history of his own family. Although performers' senses of history varied, on some level, many needed *Beskalan*'s femaleness and its power because *Beskalan Putri*'s femaleness and its power were so closely connected to their senses of the past, what constituted Malangan tradition, and thus what constituted their heritage and identity as Malangan people. The connections performers drew between femaleness, *Beskalan Putri*, and Malang were all the more evident in the ways they talked about other dances, including *Ngremo Lanang*.

Ngremo Lanang *as a foil to* Beskalan Putri

In sharp contrast to many performers' beliefs about *Beskalan Putri*'s origins in Malang, connections to femaleness, and connections to the spiritual world, many situated *Ngremo*'s origins outside Malang, connected the dance to maleness, and connected it to the secular world, thereby establishing it as a sort of foil to *Beskalan Putri*. Many performers situated *Ngremo*'s origins in Surabaya or Jombang, explaining that the original *Ngremo* was the male dance style, *Ngremo Lanang*. By their accounts, it initially developed in forms of performance that fed into the development of *ludruk*, and in *ludruk*, corroborating Hidajat (2006: 183–185). While such performance forms were likely performed in Malang by the 1920s (Supriyanto 2001: 22–23), artists recalled that *Ngremo Lanang* began to replace *Beskalan Putri* in popularity in Malang in the 1950s (p.c., Kusnadi, January 23, 2006; Djupri, July 6, 2006) and 1960s (p.c., Achmad Suwarno, April 3, 2006; Panoto, May 16, 2006). Although performers did not necessarily claim to know when exactly *Ngremo* was created in Surabaya or Jombang, their sense of its importation and memories of its increasing popularity in Malang contributed to their senses that it was a newer dance than *Beskalan Putri*, at least in Malang. *Ngremo*'s strong connections to *ludruk* reinforced a sense of maleness that *Ngremo* evoked because it was initially associated with male performers.

By associating *Ngremo*'s history with *ludruk*, performers also connected this dance to performance contexts that have tended to be thought of as secular. While *ludruk* can be sponsored for sacred purposes—such as the performances for village purification ceremonies I attended (including a couple in which I performed)—performers did not talk about *ludruk* as sacred. This contrasted with the ways they connected other types of performance (including shadow puppet theater, masked dance, *Beskalan Putri*, and *jaranan* [hobbyhorse dance]) to sacred contexts as well as entertainment contexts. Djupri often said that *Beskalan* was used for sacred performances while *Ngremo* was used for entertainment. Talking about Muskayah's activities, he explained that *Ngremo* was not fitting for the sacred context of exorcism; for this reason, Muskayah performed *Beskalan Putri*, *Beskalan Lanang* (discussed later in this chapter), or a dance called *Srimpi Lima* (p.c., December 30, 2005).

As performers linked femaleness and maleness to *Beskalan* and *Ngremo* through their senses of history and the origins of these dances, they constructed boundaries of femaleness and maleness: femaleness was connected to *Beskalan*, female dancers, Malang, antiquity, and sacred or secular contexts while maleness was connected to *Ngremo*, male dancers, Surabaya or Jombang, modernity, and secular contexts. Performers further constructed these senses of femaleness and maleness as they talked about the history of *Ngremo* in the female style, *Ngremo Putri*.

Understanding *Ngremo Putri* in Relation to *Beskalan Putri*

Although performers expressed differences of opinion about *Ngremo Putri*'s history, they emphasized influences from *Beskalan Putri*, among other Malangan dances.[15] For performers, the incorporation of influences from *Beskalan* "Malangized" and further feminized *Ngremo Putri*, imbuing *Ngremo Putri* with the power of femaleness that they associated with *Beskalan Putri*.

Their understandings of influences from *Beskalan Putri* also made *Ngremo Putri* more meaningful to them because it allowed them to view the dance in terms of Malangan tradition. Sutrisno (d. 2009), Sumi'anah's husband, described *Ngremo Putri* as she was teaching me as the "original *Ngremo Putri* specific to Malang that came from *Beskalan*" ("*asli Tari Ngremo Putri khas Malang, yang berangkatnya dari Beskalan*") (p.c., March 3, 2006). One of the most visible influences from *Beskalan Putri* that performers consistently identified was the costume.

The Costume

Some performers emphasized that the costume used for *Ngremo Putri* was taken from *Beskalan Putri*. Chattam explained that *Ngremo Putri* originated in Surabaya, where it derived from *Ngremo Lanang*. Drawing on his own memories, he recalled that *Ngremo Putri* came to Malang through *ludruk* performers from Surabaya in the late 1950s to early 1960s. At that time the dance was called *Tari Jombangan*—after Jombang. Dancers initially wore a long cloth wrapped around the lower body (*kain panjang*)—I assume he meant batik—cloth wrapped around the torso (*angkin*), and a scarf or sash (*slendang*). In Malang, dancers from Surabaya saw *Beskalan Putri* and started to order the same or very similar costumes. By about 1963, most dancers were using this costume and the dance came to be called *Ngremo Putri* (p.c., Chattam Amat Redjo, April 14, 2006; July 24, 2007).

Sumantri tentatively offered a slightly different version of *Ngremo Putri*'s history, one with stronger overtones of local pride but no less attention to the costume. He ventured that performers from Surabaya sought to imitate *Beskalan Putri*, but they could not do so entirely because the drumming was too difficult. As a result, they created *Ngremo Putri* by adapting the movements of *Ngremo Lanang* to a female style. Recognizing the lack of documentation and consensus among living senior performers, he admitted that he did not know whether this history was true and encouraged me to consult other sources, including other people. What was clear for him, as he stressed the influence from *Beskalan Putri* and from Malang, was that *Beskalan Putri* was from Malang and that Surabayans took the costume for *Ngremo Putri* from it (p.c., April 20 and 23, 2006).

The *ludruk* scholar Henri Supriyanto also draws attention to beliefs that *Ngremo Putri* was influenced by *Beskalan Putri*, writing that "Malangan Ngremo Putri is believed to be a development from *Beskalan Malangan* [*Beskalan Putri*], distinctive for using *sémbong* [a type of batik garment] and a strapless bodice" ("*Tari Ngremo Putri Malangan diyakini merupakan perkembangan dari tari Beskalan Malangan, ciri khas memakai sembong dan mekak)*" (2001: 63). Clearly the costume was associated with Malang for performers in Malang and was of great significance to them.

The importance performers attached to the costume may have been connected to their senses of antiquity. Asbari (b. 1948) and B. Supriono Hadi Prasetya (b. 1976) speculated that *Ngremo Putri* had its origins in *Beskalan Putri*. Asbari said that he did not know from where *Ngremo Putri* originated, but his feeling was that it came from *Beskalan Putri* since the costume was the same. (He believed that the musical accompaniment for *Ngremo Putri* was Surabayan.) He and Supriono supported this hunch by noting that Malang is an older place than Surabaya (p.c., Asbari and B. Supriono Hadi Prasetya, June 29, 2006). They implied that since Malang was the older place, Malangan arts were older and thus similarities between *Ngremo* and *Beskalan* most likely stemmed from roots in Malang.

That performers recalled this costume—that of a female warrior—gaining currency for *Ngremo Putri* by the early 1960s is also significant because it suggests a resistance to dominant gender ideology toward the end of the Soekarno period. This was just prior to the murder of the generals and lieutenant in 1965 that would be used to justify the destruction of Gerwani, an organization of women who were seen by some as pushing too hard against gender norms. Strikingly, as power associated with femaleness located in the bodies of women became increasingly monitored by the state while Indonesia moved into New Order times, female martial power associated with the *Beskalan Putri* costume continued to be embodied by male performers as they danced *Ngremo Putri*. *Ngremo Putri* was thus a site of resistance to dominant gender norms in multiple ways—in terms of the types of sexed bodies that were representing femaleness, in terms of the representation of female power, and in terms of the representation of a "strong" female persona, on some level evoking a history of female fighters (see chapter two). Equally important was that the female martial power represented in *Ngremo Putri* continued to be perceived by performers in Malang as they saw *Ngremo Putri* in relation to *Beskalan Putri*. In other words, they perceived female power through their local tradition, suggesting that their local senses of identity were connected to their senses of female power.

Other Aspects

Performers identified other ways the representation of femaleness in *Ngremo Putri* was influenced or may have been influenced by *Beskalan Putri*, including the past practice of the dancers holding the dance scarf in front of their mouths during sections in which the dancer stood in place to sing. This was most likely to politely cover open mouths and teeth (p.c., Supatman, March 26, 2006; Kusnadi, 2006; Djupri 2006; Asbari, July 5, 2007). That this practice was not used for male style *Ngremo* indicates that covering the mouth was associated specifically with the performance of femaleness. Chattam believed that this practice in *Ngremo Putri* was taken from *Beskalan Putri*. Why dancers stopped doing this remains a mystery, but Chattam believed that it fell out of use after the mid-1960s because *Beskalan* was no longer performed in *ludruk* or *tayub* (p.c., July 24, 2007). Chattam implied that after the mid-1960s, *Ngremo Putri* dancers either followed the performance practices established by *Beskalan* dancers, or, since they were not "reminded" by *Beskalan Putri* dancers to cover their mouths, most *Ngremo Putri* dancers stopped doing so. This change in performance practice may have also been related to the political events of 1965–1966 that contributed to a new generation of performers taking the stage after the mid-1960s and bringing with them different approaches to performance, which is discussed further in the next chapter.

Sumantri pointed to the drumming in *Ngremo Putri* as evidence of influence from *Beskalan Putri*, and in particular, an aspect of *Beskalan*'s femaleness that was used to more effectively feminize *Ngremo*. Sumantri explained that the drumming is the same for *Ngremo Lanang* and *Ngremo Putri* with the exception of a pattern used for a particular way of walking. Sumantri speculated that since this drum pattern—which occurs in *Ngremo Putri* but not *Ngremo Lanang*—is the same as a drum pattern in *Beskalan Putri*, it may have been taken from *Beskalan Putri* and inserted into *Ngremo Putri* in order to distinguish it from *Ngremo Lanang*. He qualified this hypothesis, however, saying that he did not know whether this was true (p.c., April 23, 2006).

Although this was conjecture on Sumantri's part, he was in a sense speculating that femaleness associated with *Beskalan Putri* was intentionally incorporated into *Ngremo Putri* in order to enhance its femininity and to distinguish its femininity from the masculinity of *Ngremo Lanang*. In other words, adapting *Ngremo Lanang*'s movement was not enough to satisfactorily feminize the dance; *Ngremo Putri* needed a "boost" of femininity from *Beskalan*, and along with this boost of femininity, a boost of female power. This particular walking movement in both dances involves the dancer swaying the hips, a motion that my teachers (and other dancers, including females) consistently encouraged me to emphasize in both dances in order to better express the femaleness of the dance style. For them, this movement signified a sensual, but not overtly erotic, female beauty.

In terms of the musical compositions, Kusnadi explained that the original, complete, authentic *Ngremo Putri* was accompanied just by the composition "Jula Juli," whereas the original, complete, authentic *Beskalan Putri* used a roster of compositions, beginning with "Gendhing Beskalan" (Figure 4.1).[16]

Ngremo Putri (sléndro)	Beskalan Putri (pélog or sléndro; if sléndro 7 = 1; 4 = 3)
	Part One
"Jula Juli"	"Gendhing Beskalan"
. 2 . 1 . 2 . 6 . 2 . 1 . 6 . (5)	. 2 . 1 . 2 . 6 . 2 . 1 . 6 . (5)
. 6 . 5 . 6 . 2 . 6 . 5 . 2 . (1)	. 6 . 5 . 4 . 2 . 6 . 5 . 2 . (1)
	"Ijo-Ijo"
	6 5 6 1 3 2 1 6 4 5 6 1 2 1 6 (5)
	2 1 6 5 3 1 3 2 5 6 5 4 2 6 2 (1)
"Ganggong"	"Ganggong"
2 1 6 5 2 1 6 5 2 1 5 6 1 2 3 (2)	2 1 6 5 2 1 6 5 2 1 5 6 1 2 3 (2)
3 1 2 3 5 6 5 3 5 6 1 6 5 3 2 (1)	3 1 2 3 5 6 5 3 5 6 7 6 5 4 2 (1)
5 3 2 1 5 3 2 1 5 3 1 2 3 5 6 (5)	5 4 2 1 5 4 2 1 5 4 1 2 4 5 6 (5)
6 3 5 6 1 6 5 6 5 3 2 3 2 1 6 (5)	6 3 5 6 7 6 5 6 5 4 2 4 2 1 6 (5)
	"Janur Kuning"
	2 1 6 5 2 1 6 5 2 1 6 5 1 2 1 (6)
	1 2 1 6 1 2 1 6 1 2 1 6 2 1 6 (5)

Figure 4.1: Compositions that accompany *Ngremo Putri* and *Beskalan Putri*, as taught by Kusnadi. (For "Kembang Jeruk" I have notated a more basic skeletal melody with colotomic structure and, over this in italics and smaller font, a more filled-in melody, both as taught to me by Kusnadi.)

The addition of other pieces to "Jula Juli" made the musical accompaniment for *Ngremo Putri* more similar to the roster of pieces that accompanies the first part of *Beskalan Putri*. From what Kusnadi remembered, *trompongan*—which he defined as music that accompanies the last section of *Ngremo Putri*—started to be used in *ludruk* in the 1970s (p.c., June 14, 2007). As Kusnadi explained, the specific composition used could vary: usually a musician playing one of the metallophones called *saron* or *demung* just started to play a piece and the other musicians followed. "Ganggong," however, was a typical choice (p.c., Kusnadi, May 31, 2006). This was the piece that I heard

Part Two (also called Ricik-Ricik)

"Ricik-Ricik"

. 1 . 5   . 1 . 5   . 1 . 5   . 2 . ⑥

. 2 . 6   . 2 . 6   . 2 . 6   . 1 . ⑤

"Kembang Jeruk"

. . 5 4   2 1 3 2   . . 5 6   5 2 1 6

. . . 4   . . . 2   . . . 1   . . . ⑥

. . 2 2   1 3 2 1   6 6 6 6   5 2 4 5

. . . 2   . . . 1   . . . 6   . . . ⑤

---OR---

. . 5 4   2 1 3 2   . . 5 6   5 2 1 6

. . . 4   . . . 2   . . . 1   . . . 6

. . 2 2   1 3 2 1   6 6 6 6   5 2 4 5

. . . 2   . . . 1   . . . 6   . . . ⑤

(Back to "Ricik-Ricik")

Figure 4.1 (*continued*)

consistently as I worked with musicians to learn older forms of *Ngremo Putri*. Strikingly, "Ganggong" is the same piece that is played toward the end of the first part of *Beskalan Putri* (see Figure 4.1).[17] With its denser melody, "Ganggong" contributes to the increasing momentum of both dances to the end. Kusnadi's narrative suggests that the use of "Ganggong" in this manner may have been an influence from *Beskalan*.

Furthermore, performers' senses of *Ngremo Putri* in the past were infused with their ideas about *Beskalan Putri*. Kusnadi repeatedly explained that

Ngremo Putri used to be slow, like *Beskalan Putri*, implying that the femaleness associated with *Beskalan Putri* was key to the expression of femaleness in *Ngremo Putri*. The musician Komari (b. 1957) characterized the slower tempo of Kusnadi's drumming for *Ngremo Putri* as sweet, saying that in the past *Ngremo Putri* was the sweetest. He also generalized that most women are calm, suggesting this was why *Ngremo Putri* should be drummed at a slow, calm tempo (p.c., May 24, 2006).

Recognizing Differences, Identifying Malangness

Performers were also aware of the differences in the musical accompaniment and dance movements for *Ngremo Putri* and *Beskalan Putri*, which they used to distinguish *Beskalan Putri* as a Malangan dance (also discussed in Sunardi 2010a and 2010b). For example, although "Jula Juli" and "Gendhing Beskalan" are nearly identical structurally and melodically (see Figure 4.1), performers heard "Gendhing Beskalan" and "Jula Juli" as different in part because "Gendhing Beskalan" has also been used to accompany the masked dance *Bapang*, and has thus been used for another dance that performers believed was characteristically Malangan (p.c., Budi Utomo, December 26, 2006; Gimun, December 26, 2006; Kusnadi, May 2006). "Gendhing Beskalan" is thus part of a musical repertoire that performers perceived as Malangan. In contrast, performers heard "Jula Juli" as part of a general east Javanese repertoire. Perhaps because "Gendhing Beskalan" and "Jula Juli" are so similar melodically, performers drew on their sense of history to underscore differences in characteristic tuning systems.

Tuning System   Performers explained the basic differences between *Beskalan* and *Ngremo* by polarizing the dances in terms of tuning. They said repeatedly that *Beskalan Putri* is performed in *pélog*, a seven-toned system with larger and smaller intervals, while *Ngremo* is performed in *sléndro*, a five-toned system with more or less equally spaced intervals. Associating tuning system with place, they linked *pélog*, *Beskalan*, and Malang and opposed these to *sléndro*, *Ngremo*, and Surabaya/Jombang.

Performers and researchers have emphasized the use of *pélog* in Malang. Jaap Kunst's tabulations of complete bronze *sléndro* and *pélog* sets in several areas of east Java (along with other information, including the number of inhabitants based on the 1930 census) confirm the prevalence of *pélog* gamelan ensembles in Malang historically. The predominance of *pélog* distinguished Malangan music from that of neighboring areas, where there were significantly more *sléndro* sets (Kunst 1949: 564–567; Sutton 1991: 132). Decades later in the 1980s, R. Anderson Sutton also observed that *sléndro* was the predominant tuning system in east Java with the exception of Malang, finding that "[t]he preference for *pélog* in Malang is one of the strongest points in favor of positing a distinct Malang tradition" (1991: 132).

Most musicians and dancers I consulted preferred and felt more comfortable with *Beskalan Putri* in *pélog*, believing that the "original" *Beskalan* was performed in *pélog*. Many, including M. Soleh Adi Pramono and Timan, claimed that in Malang gamelan sets in general were originally *pélog* (p.c., M. Soleh Adi Pramono, September 2005; Timan, July 4, 2006). After two recording sessions I sponsored in which *sléndro* gamelans were used because those were the instruments available on those specific occasions, the participating musicians and dancers indicated that *Beskalan* was more pleasing in *pélog*, and should be in *pélog*. They said that in *sléndro* it sounded odd, the feeling was not right, it was too similar to *Ngremo*, and they did not perform well, gently encouraging me to rerecord them using *pélog*. After we found the instruments and space that met our particular needs, I did.

Evidence from Kunst, Sutton, and the performers with whom I worked indicates that *Beskalan Putri* has shifted since the early twentieth century from being performed primarily in *pélog* to primarily in *sléndro* and back to *pélog*. When I asked performers more specifically about which tuning system they remembered being used in the past, they recalled performing and observing *Beskalan Putri* in *sléndro* as well as in *pélog*—striking details given that most had so clearly associated *pélog* with Malang and had insisted on its use for *Beskalan Putri*. Some musicians and dancers remembered performing more often in *sléndro* because most gamelan sets used to be *sléndro* sets.[18] In fact, Supeno, who was born in 1923 and was the oldest dancer I consulted, felt comfortable practicing only in *sléndro*. He said that he had never danced or drummed *Beskalan* in *pélog* when he was actively performing as a dancer (likely the 1940s to 1960s) (p.c., June 2006).

While bits of suggestive evidence appear to contrast with performers' senses of history, it is important that many associated the use of *pélog* with Malangan performing arts traditions despite changes in the tuning system used in response to external influences. Djupri offered a convincing explanation of why the tuning system used has shifted. Because purchasing a gamelan ensemble in both tunings was expensive, most individuals, villages, organizations, and/or institutions owned a set in *pélog* or *sléndro*. Up to the 1940s, *pélog* was more widespread, but from the 1940s to the 1980s, *sléndro* became more common due to the influence of *ludruk*. Coming from Surabaya, where *sléndro* prevailed, this tuning system was used to accompany *ludruk* in Malang, too. Since the 1980s, Djupri continued, there have been more sets with both *pélog* and *sléndro* tunings to accommodate audience requests for a genre of popular central Javanese gamelan music called *langgam* and, since the 1990s, *campur sari*. With more *pélog* sets available, *pélog* was again becoming the preferred tuning for Malangan pieces (p.c., June 22, 2006). Incidentally, commercial cassettes of two different versions of *Beskalan Putri*'s musical accompaniment have further naturalized the use of *pélog* more recently. Released in about 1984 (Joyoboyo) and 2001 (Studio LPK Tari Natya Lakshita and Joyoboyo Studio), both feature *pélog*—perhaps influenced by the belief that this dance was originally performed to the accompaniment of a *pélog* gamelan.

Although much of Djupri's sense of history requires further research, he was doing important ideological work through his explanation. His narrative raises questions about what happened to the *pélog* instruments from the 1940s to the 1980s, the economic factors that allowed for the purchasing of gamelan sets in both tunings, whether a shift in the kinds of materials used for gamelan instruments made purchase of sets in both tunings more affordable, and whether patronage changed. Djupri's history does, however, point to the profound impact that Surabayan and central Javanese repertoires have had on performance in Malang, shedding further light on why many performers were concerned about the disappearance of Malangan styles. Significantly, despite this influence from outside Malang, Djupri told his narrative in a way that reinforced his sense of what constituted Malangan styles—in this case, a predilection for *pélog*.

Rhythmic Features   As with the categorical statements performers made about tuning system, the categorical statements they made about the rhythmic features of *Beskalan Putri* and *Ngremo Putri* reveal important ways performers distinguished *Beskalan* from *Ngremo*—Malang from Surabaya—and thereby identified the particular senses of femaleness they connected to *Beskalan Putri* as a Malangan dance. As in central Java, musicians in Malang use the term *irama* to refer to two aspects of rhythm: what Roger Vetter terms "surface tempo" and "structural tempo" (1981: 208–211; see also Brinner 2008: 40–47). Surface tempo refers to speed while structural tempo refers to the density at which instruments play their melodies in relation to the basic beat. I use the term *irama* to refer to structural tempo, or what could be thought of as structural density, and *tempo* to refer to surface tempo.

To more explicitly distinguish *Beskalan* from *Ngremo*, Kusnadi pointed to specific differences in *irama*. He generalized that *Beskalan*'s music does not have *irama* changes like *Ngremo*'s, likening *Beskalan* to other kinds of Malangan dance by saying that the *irama* of *Beskalan* is steady like that of masked dance. Although he did recognize changes in *irama* and tempo for *Beskalan* when it came down to clarifying the details of performance practice, he consistently specified *irama* for *Ngremo*, conceiving of the basic overall structure of *Ngremo* as alternating between sections in different *irama*. Not only did Kusnadi distinguish the dances by talking about *irama* in different ways, but he also articulated Malangness in contrast to Surabayaness as he linked the steadiness of *irama* to masked dance and *Beskalan*, comparing this steadiness to the changing *irama* of *Ngremo*.

On a deeper level, the steadier *irama* of *Beskalan Putri* implies that it is more refined than *Ngremo Putri*. Following dominant ideologies of Javanese spiritual power in which refinement is taken as a sign of spiritual potency (Anderson 1990a), *Beskalan Putri*'s higher degree of refinement implies that it represents a female persona who is imbued with more spiritual power than the female persona represented in *Ngremo Putri*. In other words, the femaleness symbolized in *Beskalan Putri*, the Malangan dance, represents a more potent female power. A further implication is that dancers have the potential to access and embody a more potent female power by performing *Beskalan Putri* than by performing *Ngremo Putri*. This helps to explain why performers tended to associate *Beskalan Putri* with sacred and/or ceremonial contexts rather than *Ngremo* and tended to find *Beskalan Putri* the more appropriate dance for sacred contexts.

Comparing a Movement and Its Corresponding Drum Pattern Further indicating the refinement performers perceived in *Beskalan Putri* in relation to *Ngremo Putri*, Djupri, Kusnadi, and Supriono pointed to aspects of a movement that Djupri called the "first *mat*." This is significant because the first *mat* is the first main movement in both dances after the dancer's entrance. The articulation of this movement to the drumming reinforces the identity of each dance, which is established initially by the opening sections of music that usually precede the dancer's appearance. When Kusnadi taught me the drum pattern for the first *mat* in *Ngremo*, he pointed out that *Beskalan*'s drumming was like *Ngremo*'s, but reversed. While *Beskalan*'s basic pattern was *tok-dhet-tok-tak*, *Ngremo*'s was *dhet-tok-tak-tok* (see Figure 4.2; p.c., September 2005). He was referring to the placement of the drum strokes *dhet* and *tak*, both stronger sounding to me in this context than *tok*, on the beat in *Beskalan*, and on the weak part of the beat in *Ngremo*. The placement of *dhet* and *tak* on the beat in *Beskalan*, and the correspondence of *tak* with the *gongsèng* (ankle bells) and movement of the head/eyes down and back up, gives the dance a calmness and steadiness. These aspects, along with the slower tempo, contribute to the refined feeling performers associate with *Beskalan Putri*.[19] This contrasts with the energy and tension of *Ngremo* created by *dhet* and *tak* falling on the weak part of the beat, going against the *gongsèng* and head/eye movements (see Figure 4.2). The alternation of the medium stroke *dhung* and low stroke *dong* in the last four beats of *Beskalan*'s pattern is calmer and less sharp than the high-pitched, sparse sounds of *Ngremo*'s *tok* strokes (see

Beskalan Putri (note that *tok* is replaced by the variation *ket tok*)

mm ~ 98

							Head/ eyes down		Head/ eyes up to look straight ahead	[down and up 2x more]	Twist neck to the right and back to center				Twist neck to the left and back to center		
ket tok		dhet		tok		ket tok	. dhung	dhung dhung	tak	[2x more]	dhung dong	. dhung	dong	dang	dhung dong	. dhung	dong	dang
							*		*	[...]				*				*
.						⌒ 6	.		⌒ 5	[...]		.		⌒ 2		.		①

Ngremo Putri

mm ~ 160

							Head/ eyes down		Head/ eyes up to look straight ahead	[down and up 2x more]	Head roll		Chin to the right		Chin to the left		Chin to the right
dhet		tok		tak		tok	dhung	tok	tak	[2x more]	dhung	.	tok	.	tok	.	tok
							*		*	[...]			*		*		*
.						⌒ 6	.		⌒ 5	[...]		.		⌒ 2		.	①

Figure 4.2: First *mat* basic drum patterns for *Beskalan Putri* and *Ngremo Putri*, as taught by Kusnadi. The *gongseng* is marked by an asterisk (*). The tempo markings are taken from field recordings of Djupri playing the drum for *Beskalan Putri* (recorded on March 31, 2006) and Sutanu playing the drum for *Ngremo Putri* (recorded on June 13, 2006).

Figure 4.2). Significantly, Supriono identified the pattern used in *Beskalan Putri* as a distinctive Malangan trait because it is not found in dances from other parts of Java (p.c., January 26, 2007). Whether or not this is true, this is one way he was hearing Malangness in the drumming that accompanied *Beskalan Putri*.

Djupri recognized the similarities between the first *mat* used for *Beskalan Putri* and for *Ngremo Putri* but emphasized their differences. He explained that the first *mat* for *Beskalan Putri* is polite and beautiful. Rather than just beginning to dance, which would be too direct and therefore impolite according to Javanese etiquette, the dancer performs *mat*. Enhancing the politeness and beauty of this movement is the dancer's lowering and raising of the eyes in time to the drumming. *Ngremo* also has a *mat* in which the eyes are lowered and raised, Djupri said, but the dancer moves her or his head more, so the movement is less refined than in *Beskalan Putri* (p.c., February 1, 2006).

I suggest that performers' senses of history affected their perceptions of *Beskalan Putri* in relation to *Ngremo Putri*: they tended to see *Beskalan Putri* as the more refined, spiritually potent dance, in part because they connected it to antiquity and to Malang and were expressing a sense of local pride. Thus as they talked about femaleness, they were also talking about Malangan tradition and identity.

Understanding *Beskalan Lanang* in Relation to *Beskalan Putri*

Skepticism about the Antiquity of Beskalan Lanang

Given that performers talked about *Beskalan Putri*'s performance "in the past" (*dulu*) without hesitation, I was struck that they frequently raised the issue of *Beskalan Lanang*'s existence prior to the early 2000s, when M. Soleh Adi Pramono adapted the dance for a festival. Many seemed to like *Beskalan Lanang* and to enjoy performing it, but they did not believe that it was an old dance or that it constituted "tradition" (*tradisi*). For many performers, it seemed as though *Beskalan*, antiquity, and maleness were not a "natural" fit in the same way that *Beskalan*, antiquity, and femaleness were, which ultimately reinforced conceptual boundaries of femaleness and maleness. *Beskalan* and maleness, many implied, were put together more recently through a conscious creative process of adaptation and experimentation by Djupri and Soleh.

For their parts, both Djupri and M. Soleh Adi Pramono were adamant that *Beskalan Lanang* existed "in the past" and situated the dance's origins in Muskayah's spiritual experiences. As they did in their narratives about *Beskalan Putri*, each man told *Beskalan Lanang*'s history slightly differently. According to Djupri, the illness that overcame Muskayah as a child came in two waves. The first time she fell ill, the spirit of Prabaretna gave her the music and movement for *Beskalan Putri*, as explained earlier. She recovered briefly before falling ill again. During this second bout, she spoke in a man's voice and received the music and movements of *Beskalan Lanang* (p.c., Djupri, August 7, 2006). Muskayah was told that the original dance was *Beskalan Lanang*, but that it could be performed in a female style as well (p.c., Djupri, February 25, 2006; July 6, 2006). By situating *Beskalan Lanang* as the basis for *Beskalan Putri*, Djupri indirectly contradicted dominant assumptions among performers in Malang that *Beskalan Putri* was the older dance and basis for Djupri's and Soleh's invention.

Djupri's narrative about *Beskalan Lanang*'s origins also points to further uses of spiritual beliefs and practices as a means of challenging dominant constructions of gender. One implication is that, in telling this narrative, Djupri connected the senses of female masculinity that Muskayah came to embody as a performer of male style dance to a spiritual experience she had as a child. The image of a little girl speaking in a man's voice suggests another manifestation of female masculinity.

Reinforcing the existence of *Beskalan Lanang*, Djupri provided reasons for its decline and accounted for why so many performers in Malang did not know about it prior to Soleh's adaptation. Djupri said that Muskayah performed either *Beskalan Lanang* or *Beskalan Putri* for events depending on the wishes of the host(s). She was most often asked to perform *Beskalan Putri* because she was so beautiful that people thought that it would be a shame if she performed a male style dance. Because she performed *Beskalan Putri* much more often, women came to her to learn it, but not the male style. For these reasons, *Beskalan Putri* was passed on while *Beskalan Lanang* declined in popularity (p.c., February 25, 2006). Further contributing to its decline was the rising popularity of *Ngremo Lanang*, which essentially replaced *Beskalan Lanang* (p.c., Djupri, November 6, 2005).

While M. Soleh Adi Pramono also attributed the origins of *Beskalan Lanang* to Muskayah's spiritual experiences, he recounted a different creative process. According to Soleh, Muskayah started to go blind later in life. Reflecting on why this eye illness had befallen her, she remembered that she had failed to find Baswara/Jaka Umbaran as instructed by Prabaretna in her dream. She thus created the dance *Tari Umbaran*, which she performed before *Beskalan Putri* to illustrate the object of her and Prabaretna's search. Audiences called the dance *Beskalan Lanang* after the title of one of the compositions that accompanies it—"Gendhing Beskalan"—and because it preceded *Beskalan Putri*.[20] Soleh also attributed its decline and virtual extinction to the popularity of *Ngremo Lanang* (p.c., July 27, 2006).

Although Djupri and Soleh were firm in their beliefs that *Beskalan Lanang* existed in the past, many performers expressed their uncertainty about its antiquity, and in so doing articulated boundaries of gender. Strikingly, neither Muskayah's son Supeno nor her former musician Timan pointed clearly to having seen her or anyone else perform *Beskalan Lanang*. When I asked Supeno whether he had seen Muskayah dance *Beskalan Lanang*, he replied as though he had not heard my question correctly, saying yes, Muskayah taught him not to show off even if he could dance well (p.c., June 28, 2006). During a previous interview, he had said repeatedly that *Beskalan* was a female style dance and that Muskayah danced female style dance. He gave no indication of the existence of *Beskalan* in a male style, but did refer several times to *Ngremo* as a male style dance, contrasting *Beskalan* as a female style dance and *Ngremo* as a male style dance (p.c., March 18, 2006). He, too, talked about *Beskalan* in terms of femaleness and *Ngremo* in terms of maleness.

Timan expressed his unfamiliarity with *Beskalan Lanang* on two occasions, also expressing a sense that *Beskalan* and maleness did not go together. He said that if *Beskalan* were to be performed as a male style dance, it would not be good or appropriate. He said that he never saw *Beskalan Lanang*, but that *Ngremo Lanang*, which was also called *Surabayan Lanang*, existed. Timan insisted that Muskayah could not dance *Surabayan*, just *Beskalan Putri* (p.c., July 4, 2006). A few days later, Timan stopped by Djupri's house during one of my *Beskalan Lanang* lessons. When Djupri told him that I was studying *Beskalan Lanang*, he looked confused and asked whether the dance was *Beskalan Putri*. Djupri said no, it was *Beskalan Lanang*, and referenced Muskayah's stories about the existence of *Beskalan Lanang*. Timan said that he had never seen *Beskalan Lanang*, but that as the times changed, so did dances, implying its recent development (p.c., July 6, 2006). These responses from Supeno and Timan, performers born in 1923 and 1930, respectively, imply the rarity of *Beskalan Lanang* in the past, if it was performed at all.

Many performers who were born in the 1940s or more recently, such as Kusnadi and his musicians, were convinced of the dance's recent origin because they did not remember seeing it in the past or hearing about it from performers older than they (p.c., Kusnadi, February 4, 2006; July 24, 2006; Asbari, June 29, 2006; Achmad Suwarno, April 3, 2006). Musicians' evaluations of *Beskalan Lanang* as a recent invention affected their evaluations of Djupri's dancing. When I organized rehearsals for a video session in order to document Djupri dancing *Beskalan Lanang*, several of the musicians involved critiqued his dancing. In conversations following the rehearsals, some said that his *Beskalan Lanang* was too close to or just like *Ngremo Lanang*. This, too, points to performers' senses of history and gender—that they saw *Beskalan Lanang* in terms of the maleness of *Ngremo Lanang*, rather than vice versa.

Like many of the performers I consulted who associated themselves with eastern styles and areas of the regency, Madya and Sumantri, two musicians my teachers associated with southern Malang styles of music and dance, indicated their unfamiliarity with *Beskalan Lanang* "in the past." In a conversation about *Beskalan* in the 1940s and 1950s, Madya (1930–2007) referred to *Beskalan Topèng*, a male style dance that used *Beskalan Putri*'s music and was danced by a woman. He also talked about *Beskalan Putri*, which he also called *Ngremo Beskalan*, but made no reference to *Beskalan Lanang* (p.c., December 16, 2005). Similarly, Sumantri said that what he understood was that actually there was no *Beskalan Lanang*; there was, however, a masked dance called *Beskalan Topèng* or *Beskalan Patih*, a refined male style dance that opened masked dance performances. He explained that *Beskalan Topèng* was accompanied by music with the same structure as *Beskalan Putri*'s and that the movement was refined, similar to that of *Beskalan Putri*. In highlighting the similarities to *Beskalan Putri* in terms of music and movement as well as Madya's references to female dancers, these two artists evoked senses of femaleness when talking about *Beskalan Topèng*, thereby further linking *Beskalan* to femaleness.

Sumantri referred to *Beskalan Lanang* as a creation (*kreasi*) from Ngadireso (the village in which Djupri lived), implying that it was something newly created or invented, rather than an adaptation or interpretation of a preexisting dance. For Sumantri, too, it seemed that putting *Beskalan* and maleness together was a recent invention. Sumantri said that *kreasi* is fine and a personal or individual right (*hak pribadi*), but that many traditional artists could not accept it (p.c., April 20, 2006). He thus implied that the most conservative musicians and dancers did not accept *Beskalan Lanang* as a Malangan tradition because they believed that it was recently created.

There were, however, some artists whose narratives corroborated Djupri's and Soleh's claims about the existence of *Beskalan Lanang* in the past. Sumi'anah and her husband Sutrisno said that *Ngremo Lanang* developed from a male style dance called *Kiprahan Malangan*, which was like *Beskalan* but used a male style costume. They insisted, though, that there was no *Beskalan Lanang*, just *Kiprahan Malangan*, which resembled what Djupri performed (p.c., April 4, 2006). In saying that *Kiprahan Malangan* was like what Djupri performed, however, they were in effect supporting a history of *Beskalan* in a male style that predated Soleh's adaptation in the early 2000s.

Perhaps they were referring to the name of the dance rather than the content of its choreography. Reinforcing the past existence of *Beskalan Lanang*, one man, a dancer, said that his uncle performed the dance. His uncle (who was already deceased at the time of my fieldwork), was a *ludruk* performer during the *Besut* era (which, following Supriyanto [2001: 11–14] was c. 1915–1920s). He explained that the dance was the same as what Djupri danced (he had seen Djupri perform *Beskalan Lanang* at one of my recording sessions), that Djupri danced "in the old way" (*cara kuna*), and that *Beskalan Lanang* was used in the past for performances of *Besut* (p.c., June 13, 2006).

Furthermore, Henri Supriyanto writes in a photograph caption that *Beskalan Lanang* was used for *lérok* in Malang in the past and that M. Soleh Adi Pramono discovered it and adapted it ("*Lerok Malang tempo doeloe mengenal konvensi Beskalan Lanang. Ragam tari ini digali lagi dan dikemas oleh M. Soleh Adipramono*" [Supriyanto 2001: 21]). His reference to M. Soleh Adi Pramono, as well as the close association between them that I observed, suggest that Soleh may have been a source of this information. Nonetheless, it is noteworthy that Supriyanto, as a *ludruk* scholar, found this information valid and included it in his book as fact.

Making Beskalan *"Male"*

Since M. Soleh Adi Pramono and artists working with him began to adapt *Beskalan Lanang* in about 2000 at the Mangun Dharma Art Center (Padepokan Seni Mangun Dharma or PSMD), it has been simplified and consciously made to be different from *Beskalan Putri*. The efforts to make *Beskalan Lanang* different from *Beskalan Putri* reinforced many performers' senses that *Beskalan Putri* was the older dance—and that, almost as the "embryo" of *Beskalan*, was initially female and had to be made male. Soleh summed the point as he explained that a difference between *Beskalan* and *Ngremo* is that *Ngremo* was a male style dance that was feminized while *Beskalan* was a female style dance that was masculinized (p.c., July 27, 2006). In making *Beskalan* male, performers established boundaries of gender.

The way Djupri performed *Beskalan Lanang* (whether or not performers believed he learned it from Muskayah or created it himself) was very similar to the way he performed *Beskalan Putri* in terms of the overall structure, the movement vocabulary, and the drum patterns. Nonetheless, there were some differences. The movements were performed differently to be appropriate for the male dance style and there were some differences in the music. For one, the dance begins with the piece "Tanjung Sari" and then proceeds to "Gendhing Beskalan" (Figure 4.3).[21] In contrast to the sparser melody that opens *Beskalan Putri*, *Beskalan Lanang* uses a denser melody in a higher

"Tanjung Sari"

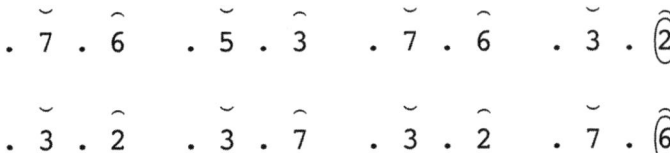

"Gendhing Beskalan"

Figure 4.3: First two compositions used for *Beskalan Lanang*, in the *pélog* tuning system, as taught by Kusnadi.

mode, which gives more momentum and a brighter feel to the music. This and a faster tempo contribute a more dynamic quality to the beginning of the dance that is appropriate to the strong, agile male character being portrayed.

Soleh initially adapted *Beskalan Lanang* for a folk dance festival and competition held in Malang in about 2000. He brought Djupri to PSMD to teach the dance and its music to the dancers and musicians there.[22] Kusnadi learned the drumming by initially playing what he knew from *Beskalan Putri*; Djupri corrected the parts that were different for *Beskalan Lanang*. Adapting *Beskalan Lanang* by starting with *Beskalan Putri* reinforced performers' senses that *Beskalan Putri* was the older dance and had to be modified to create *Beskalan Lanang*. This was also a process by and through which maleness and femaleness were being distinguished and thus defined.

After Djupri introduced *Beskalan Lanang*, Soleh worked with artists at PSMD to adapt the dance—which in its entirety can last as long as about forty minutes to an hour or more—to meet the current expectations of ten- to fifteen-minute choreographies (p.c., Tri Wahyuningtyas, July 3, 2007; Kusnadi, July 24, 2006; M. Soleh Adi Pramono, July 27, 2006). Soleh made a number of changes. For one, he removed the sections in which the dancer stops dancing to sing and gave the vocal part to a male or female vocalist who is seated with the gamelan musicians and sings while the dancers dance (p.c., B. Supriono Hadi Prasetya, June 26, 2006; Kusnadi, July 24, 2006; M. Soleh Adi Pramono, July 27, 2006). This not only shortens the dance, but also makes it easier to perform for dancers who are not trained in singing. Soleh also simplified and clarified some of Djupri's movements and developed a floor plan in order to take advantage of using a group of dancers.[23] These changes "updated" the dance to appeal to contemporary performers and audiences and, intentionally or not, also affected the expression of maleness.

Through his adaptations of the choreography, Soleh drew on his senses of the past and regional identity. Based on his own research, he worked to incorporate influences from different areas of Malang. In addition to movements adapted from Djupri (and by extension from Muskayah) from eastern Malang, he incorporated movements from southern Malang, in effect combining the different origin stories that he had encountered into a single choreography. Similar to what I learned from Madya and Sumantri, Soleh learned that in southern Malang, *Beskalan Lanang* was a strong male style masked dance called *Beskalan Patih*, which he had seen performed. However, given that this was a strong male style dance and what Sumantri described was a refined male style dance, this may have been different from the *Beskalan Topèng* that Madya and Sumantri referenced. To maintain the effect of masked dance, Soleh incorporated movements from southern Malangan strong male style masked dances (p.c., M. Soleh Adi Pramono, July 27, 2006). He was in a sense creating a pan-Malangan representation of masculinity.

Furthermore, Soleh drew on his understanding that *Beskalan Lanang* once existed but died out largely as a result of the popularity of *Ngremo Lanang*. Knowing that *Ngremo* had become popular in part because it was fast and dynamic, Soleh sought to reassert the appeal of a Malangan dance by making *Beskalan Lanang* stronger and more energetic, thereby infusing a Malangan dance with aspects of *Ngremo*'s maleness (p.c., M. Soleh Adi Pramono, July 27, 2006). In making *Beskalan Lanang* more dynamic, Soleh reinforced the idea that maleness should be expressed through energetic strength—quite a contrast to the refinement of *Beskalan Putri*.

The jury's evaluation of *Beskalan Lanang* at the festival was a catalyst for additional transformations of the dance. The jury members deemed that part of the choreography—the second main part of the dance called Ricik-Ricik (after the title of one of the compositions used in this part)—was central Javanese and so disqualified *Beskalan Lanang* from the competition.[24] This was a striking decision because *Beskalan Putri* also had two main parts, the second of which was often called Ricik-Ricik, too (see Figure 4.1). Although the jury members later came to accept that the Ricik-Ricik part was Malangan (p.c., Tri Wahyuningtyas, July 3, 2006), Soleh had already felt the blow of their initial evaluation, and for most performances of *Beskalan Lanang* thereafter, the Ricik-Ricik section was not used. According to Karen Elizabeth Sekararum, the jury's evaluation further motivated Soleh to prove that *Beskalan Lanang* was a Malangan dance (p.c., January 6, 2006). Indeed he was doing so in his conversations with me.

After the competition, *Beskalan Lanang* was further adapted as it was disseminated throughout Malang. One way the dance was circulated was through the recording of its music onto the commercial cassette that PSMD coproduced with the central Javanese dancer Didik Nini Thowok in 2001. The title of the cassette, which may be translated as *A Variety of Malangan Dance Compositions, Volume 2* (*Aneka Gending Tari Malangan, Volume 2*), positions *Beskalan Lanang* as a Malangan dance. According to Tri Wahyuningtyas, *Beskalan Lanang* was further shortened for the cassette so that it would be different from *Beskalan Putri* (p.c., July 3, 2006). (The music for the Ricik-Ricik part is included on the cassette for *Beskalan Putri*.) In about 2002, *Beskalan Lanang* began to be taught in the elementary and junior high schools as part of government sponsored dance education programs (p.c., Karen Elizabeth Sekararum, January 6, 2006; Tri Wahyuningtyas, July 3, 2006). As an aid for dance teachers in the schools, Soleh included *Beskalan Lanang* on a VCD of Malangan dances released by PSMD in 2003, *Tari Tradisional Malangan* (*Traditional Malangan Dance*). Since the video was made as a teaching aid for the schools and the Ricik-Ricik part was not used, it was not included on the VCD (p.c., M. Soleh Adi Pramono, July 27, 2006). Furthermore, the soundtrack from the commercial cassette was used, which did not include the Ricik-Ricik section. *Beskalan Lanang* was effectively institutionalized without this part, and in this way, the male and female styles were institutionalized as different.

For the video, all male dancers were used, further institutionalizing differences between *Beskalan Putri* and *Beskalan Lanang* through the representation of gender. Witanto, one of the dancers in the video, said that since there were only three male dancers at PSMD at the time, including Witanto, Soleh recruited other male dancers to learn the dance. Soleh even requested Supriono, who at that time was away in college in central Java, to come to PSMD in order to participate in the video project, which Supriono did. Strikingly, Soleh did not make a similar effort to recruit male dancers during the initial adaptation process of *Beskalan Lanang* for the festival. Soleh explained that at the time of the festival, there was only one male dancer active at PSMD, and since he needed a group, he selected females (p.c., July 27, 2006). However, by working to recruit men for the video—whereas he did not for the festival—Soleh revealed his preference for the dance to be represented as a male style dance that is performed by males—that is, as a "manly" male same-gender dance rather than a cross-gender dance inflected with female masculinity. He may have been influenced by the Old Order and New Order era ideals of "manly" masculinity with which he had grown up.

Kusnadi revealed his own attitudes toward the performance of gender by speculating that Soleh changed some of the movements to more appropriately articulate maleness. Kusnadi highlighted that Soleh changed the dancer's entrance from stepping into the performance space and tapping the foot while standing in place, as used in *Beskalan Putri* and Djupri's *Beskalan Lanang*, to a fast sideways movement on the toes in a wide demi-plié position (*sirig*). Kusnadi emphasized that the movements of *Beskalan Lanang* and *Beskalan Putri* are actually the same (with the understanding that the movements would be executed in a different manner appropriate for male style dance, such as using a larger movement volume). He speculated that Soleh believed that a *sirig* would be a better way to enter for the male character portrayed. Conveying his own opinion, Kusnadi asserted that the feeling of entering with a tapping of the foot did not fit the male persona, but that "entering with a *sirig* says 'I am a man'" ("*keluarnya sirig kan, 'saya pria'*") (p.c., July 24, 2006). As the maleness of *Beskalan Lanang* was redefined in relation to the femaleness of *Beskalan Putri* and institutionalized through the commercial cassette recording and VCD, differences—boundaries—between maleness and femaleness were also redefined and rearticulated.

Gender, History, and Tradition

Through their senses of history—including what comprised tradition, what has been more recently created, what has its origins in Malang, what has been imported, what was originally in a female style and made into a male style, and what was originally in a male style and made into a female style—performers were contributing to the continuous processes by and through which senses of gender are constructed. In connecting femaleness, *Beskalan Putri*, the past, spiritual power, and Malang, performers were in effect maintaining cultural space for the magnetic power of femaleness and connecting that power to local identity and tradition. The senses of femaleness and its power that performers associated with *Beskalan Putri* shaped ways in which they understood the histories of other dances as they pertain to the expression of gender. They viewed the development of *Ngremo Putri* in terms of influence from *Beskalan Putri*—that *Ngremo Lanang* was feminized in part by incorporating femaleness from *Beskalan Putri*, a femaleness that was closely tied to Malang. In addition, performers understood the creation of *Beskalan Lanang* in relation to *Beskalan Putri*, most seeing *Beskalan Lanang* as the more recent dance and as a masculinization of *Beskalan Putri*.

The importance of *Beskalan Putri* to performers' senses of Malangan tradition provides deeper insight into their concerns about the performance of *Ngremo Tayub* and *Ngremo Putri* "nowadays," as explored in chapters two and three. On some level, performers were seeing both of these dances in terms of a departure from the femaleness represented in *Beskalan Putri* that was so closely connected to their senses of Malangan identity. For *Ngremo Tayub*, performers saw female dancers moving further and further from "tradition" as represented through *Ngremo Lanang*, which they saw as a sort of foil to *Beskalan Putri*. In other words, *Ngremo Lanang* on some level evoked *Beskalan Putri* as its opposite. Thus by departing from *Ngremo Lanang*, dancers were also departing from *Beskalan Putri* as its foil. Furthermore, as women who were taking the representation of gender in their own directions by performing female masculinity, they were moving further and further from the femininity, refinement, and spiritual power many associated with *Beskalan Putri*. *Ngremo Putri* "nowadays," influenced by *Ngremo Tayub*, was also moving further from the influence of *Beskalan Putri*'s femaleness. This reinforced performers' concerns about the preservation of Malangan tradition even as they maintained the power of femaleness in their hearts and minds through their senses of *Beskalan*'s history. *Beskalan Putri* itself, however, has also undergone processes of adaptation—processes that have affected the representation of female power and Malangan tradition through this dance, the topics of the following chapter.

5. Maintaining the Representation of Female Power through *Beskalan Putri*

This chapter examines some of the ways in which artists have maintained cultural space for the representation of female power through *Beskalan Putri* as they have adapted, taught, remembered, learned, performed, and talked about this dance. I focus on representations of female power through *Beskalan Putri* because, building on the senses of history explored in the previous chapter, this dance and the femaleness performers associated with it were critical to their senses of Malangan tradition. This analysis thus further illustrates the selection of tradition and the construction of gender as mutually constitutive cultural processes. Considering artists' concerns with preservation as well as the impact of social, political, and cultural climates on the ways artists represented female power through this dance, I argue that artists represented female power strategically—that is, in a "safe" way in times following trauma.

Changes to *Beskalan Putri* in Times Following Trauma

Beskalan Putri has undergone some striking transformations since the 1960s, including changes in performance contexts. *Andhong* (an itinerant dance tradition featuring one or more female singer-dancers accompanied by a gamelan ensemble) fell out of practice and was thus no longer a context for the performance of *Beskalan Putri*. The dance came to be infrequently used to open *tayub* dance events and *ludruk* theater in part because male and female styles of *Ngremo* replaced *Beskalan* in popularity.

The political events surrounding Soeharto's rise to power in the mid-1960s, discussed in chapter two, also affected the decline in the frequency of the performance of *Beskalan Putri*. Among those with any association, or suspected association, with communist organizations who were imprisoned, exiled, or killed in 1965–1966 were performers, including musicians and dancers (see also Sunardi 2009: 470–471). *Ludruk* performers were targeted because *ludruk* often featured social and political criticism, some performers were associated with communist activity, and some troupes were associated with communist organizations (Peacock 1987: 27–28, 40–41). Following the murder of the generals and lieutenant in 1965, *ludruk* groups were disbanded and performers killed or imprisoned (Peacock 1987: 258). Henri Supriyanto and Wahyudiyanto have described 1965 and the ensuing years (until about 1968) as a "vacuum period" (*masa vakum*) as a result of the political events and performers' fear, suggesting that *ludruk* activity stopped or virtually stopped (Supriyanto 1992: 14, 20; 2001: 18, 26; Wahyudiyanto 2006: 68). Similarly, *ketoprak*, a type of central Javanese theater, ceased for some years in Yogyakarta (Hatley 2008: 30–31), and in Indramayu, a regency in West Java, masked dance and puppet theater were banned through 1969 (Ross 2011: 162). Performers I consulted in Malang noted the fear and suspicion that pervaded their communities; some spoke in hushed tones, indicating that the violence and disorder of this period were etched into their minds.

While some artists did return to the stage when the political situation became less volatile in the late 1960s, others did not. Many were still too traumatized. In places affected by the violence, many lost friends, neighbors, family members, and mentors. As mentioned in chapter two, some artists were banned due to suspicions of association with the Indonesian Communist Party or left-leaning organizations (Larasati 2013: 57, 123). Some artists were prohibited by stigma and/or "[o]fficial policy [that] made it illegal for former political prisoners to work in education, the arts, the media, in the public sector, and many other roles" (translator's note to Rachmadi 2005: 36; see also Sears 1996b: 213).[1] Some artists may have felt that they were too old to perform anyway or had other motives for turning their interests to other activities.

As a newer generation of performers became active in *ludruk* in the late 1960s and early 1970s, they turned to *Ngremo Putri*, a dance that had been gaining in popularity prior to the political disorder. After the 1960s, males came to perform *Beskalan Putri* infrequently, largely because *Ngremo Putri* replaced *Beskalan Putri* as an opening dance for *ludruk*, the primary context in which males performed *Beskalan Putri* (p.c., Asbari, June 29, 2006; Chattam Amat Redjo, April 14, 2006; July 24, 2007; Supriyanto 2001: 24).

The performers who filled the vacancies in the late 1960s and 1970s, including a younger generation of artists, brought with them a more cautious approach to political commentary for a variety of reasons, one of which was governmental surveillance. Some performers in Malang indicated that when performances started again in the late 1960s, some *ludruk* troupes were formed under military sponsorship and supervision, corroborating Supriyanto's findings (1992: 20; 2001: 26). Visiting Surabaya in 1970, James Peacock found that "new troupes had been formed under military control" (1987: 258), and in a 1971 publication, Barbara Hatley observes that "all troupes must have an official government sponsor and many are associated with the military" (1971: 94). In addition to the military, the police also founded *ludruk* groups (Hatley 2008: 31). Such surveillance of performers ensured little overt political criticism (Peacock 1987: 258–259).

The trauma of violence and the increased presence of the military affected the performing arts in other parts of Java as well. Laurie Margot Ross describes a new type of registration card that was issued to performers in the Cirebon region of West Java as "an unapologetic, unsentimental top-down affair with the singular purpose of establishing the parameters of the new military's role" (2011: 166). Similarly, performers in central Java exercised caution. Puppeteers tended to choose subjects for humor that would seem "irrelevant to the government," such as older styles of puppet theater (Sears 1996b: 213). Barbara Hatley found that many *ketoprak* performers in Yogyakarta may have felt too intimidated to resist and/or were grateful for the work opportunity (2008: 37). The same may have been the case among *ludruk* performers in east Java. Given that many performers in different parts of Java were also recovering psychologically from the trauma of violence (and grieving for those they had lost), it is not surprising that they tended to avoid explicit challenges to the state by blatantly resisting New Order ideologies, although some artists did voice opposing views during the New Order era, risking persecution (Sutton 2004: 203).

People responded to pressures from the state in different ways. In some cases, performers demonstrated their abilities to comply with the state's ideals through the ways that they talked about and performed gender. Other artists, however, may have been sincerely attracted to the state's ideas; some may have been indifferent, and some may have overly complied—a strategy of survival, sometimes with subversive effects, that Ariel Heryanto identifies as "hyper-obedience" (2006: 136). Some may have approached performance with all of these feelings and attitudes toward the state at different points in time (Sunardi 2009: 470–471). It was in this New Order context, with the social memory of violence, that *Beskalan Putri* came to be performed primarily by females, and the dance was shortened.

Refining Representations of Femaleness and Its Power?

Chattam Amat Redjo (1943–2013), the dancer, choreographer, and teacher based in the city of Malang referenced in the previous chapter, responded to *Beskalan*'s decreasing popularity by adapting, documenting, and teaching it. Speaking to Chattam's long commitment to *Beskalan Putri*, Sumantri recalled playing the drum for an interpretation of *Beskalan Putri* that Chattam developed in the 1970s (p.c., April 20, 23, 2006). When I interviewed Chattam in 2006, he was working on a project to record musical accompaniment for *Beskalan Putri* of longer and shorter durations as part of his continuing efforts to ensure that the dance did not disappear, noting that the half-hour version would be just for documentation (p.c., April 14, 2006). Devoted to this dance, with the goals of preserving *Beskalan Putri*, keeping it in performed repertoire, and maintaining its integrity, Chattam developed a simplified version of about eight minutes. He aimed to develop an adaptation that was appropriate to teach children and young people and also to make the dance more appropriate for changed times, needs, and audience tastes. This included needs for six- to ten-minute dances in part because class time in schools or arts studios made learning longer dances difficult for students and in part because of audience demand for shorter, livelier dances. He also wanted to produce a cassette so that dancers could perform in situations in which a live gamelan was not available (p.c., April 14, 2006).

The music for this particular shortened version of *Beskalan Putri* was released on the commercial cassette titled *Tari Topèng Bapang* (Jayabaya, n.d.), a project involving the arts organization Kedong Monggo. Chattam recalled the cassette as being from 1984 (p.c., April 14, 2006). Many of the performers I consulted emphasized his role, and, to a certain extent, attributed a certain ownership to him of this adaptation by consistently referring to it as "Chattam's *Beskalan*" ("*Beskalannya Pak Chattam*"). The adaptation captured on the commercial recording provides critical insights into the representation of femaleness and its power in a New Order (1966–1998) context.

What performers termed *Beskalan sing asli*—the "real," "complete," "original," "authentic" *Beskalan*—could last for as long as an hour or more; however, as I explore in chapter six, there were different ideas about what constituted *Beskalan sing asli*.[2] An outline of *Beskalan sing asli* as I learned it from Djupri is presented in Chart 5.1. This version was about half an hour long but could be extended to an hour or more by extending the introductory section of music without dance, lengthening the sections in which the dancer stops dancing to sing, and adding repetition of certain movement sequences (p.c.,

Chart 5.1. Outline of the large-scale structure of *"Beskalan sing asli"* as learned from Djupri, and Chattam Amat Redjo's adaptation. (Note: I have not attempted to indicate relative lengths of each section.)

	"Beskalan sing asli"	Chattam's Adaptation
Part One	Musical introduction without dance (According to Djupri, in some cases, the dancer may sing before appearing.)	Shortened
	Section of dancing	Shortened
	Section in which the dancer stops dancing and sings, standing in place	Removed
	Section of dancing (The dancer may continue to sing while dancing if he or she is able to.)	Shortened
Part Two, or Ricik-Ricik	Section in which the dancer stops dancing and sings, standing in place	Removed
	Section of dancing	

Kusnadi, 2006). By eliminating some of the repetition, removing some of the movements, and removing some of the sections, Chattam worked to shorten the dance while maintaining its essence (see Chart 5.1). Shortening the dance so dramatically involved making many decisions—selections—about what to maintain and what to omit.

As I see it, although it may not have been his conscious intention, through his adaptation, Chattam made the female persona portrayed in the dance closer to the image of ideal womanhood promoted in New Order era ideologies. He was thereby able to preserve this dance in New Order times, while also maintaining a representation of female power, albeit subtly. For example, as I learned through studying the drumming for Chattam's version with Kusnadi, the movements most clearly portraying warriorlike activity—a movement sequence that illustrates the manipulation of a bow and shooting an arrow as well as the second part of the dance, often called Ricik-Ricik— were omitted (Chart 5.1).

The Ricik-Ricik section is "stronger" in character, in part because the overall tempo range is faster and the movement is more martial in feeling (see also Roberts 2001: 8). Budi Utomo taught me to express and embody a sense of physical strength that he associated with maleness by instructing me to use a slightly wider leg stance and slighter larger, wider movements in this section, explaining that the movements were almost the same as the movements of Yogyanese strong male style dance (albeit in a smaller movement volume closer to what one finds in refined male style dance). Utomo noted that one of the difficult aspects about *Beskalan Putri* is that it is a female style dance but also *gagah*—strong in a manly sense. However, he cautioned, one should not be too strong and lose the femininity of the dance (p.c., December 2005).

The removal of the bow and arrow movement and the Ricik-Ricik section in effect makes the female character seem on the surface more like a Sumbadra than a Srikandi (see chapter two). However, the *Beskalan Putri* costume—with its short pants suggesting a female warrior—was retained, thus still implying the martial prowess of the character. In other words, the representation of female power was maintained, even as it was, in a sense, refined.

In Chattam's adaptation, the dancer also does not sing. He removed sections in which the dancer stops dancing to sing, and the dancer does not sing while dancing. (At least, I did not see or hear about performances of Chattam's adaptation in which the dancers sang.) Instead, a female vocalist seated with the gamelan sings while the dancer dances. While the separation of singing and dancing makes *Beskalan Putri* easier to teach dance students, easier for dancers to learn, and shortens the performance, it also has implications related to the representation of female sexuality and its power through the image of the female singer-dancer.

Henry Spiller has underlined that women who sing and dance at the same time in Java are known for their almost overwhelmingly potent sexual appeal (2007; 2010: 97–99), which has contributed to the conflicted position female singer-dancers have long occupied in Javanese society, discussed in chapter two. Societal efforts to control the power of femaleness as manifest through the sexuality of female singer-dancers have been expressed through official and officially sanctioned discourses of respectability, tradition, and art (Hughes-Freeland 1997; 2008b: 144). In some cases, implementing this discourse into practice involved separating the roles of singing and dancing.

As explored by Henry Spiller (2008: 186–195) and Jean Hellwig (1993), West Java saw the creation of the dance form *jaipongan* in the late 1970s, and the artist Gugum Gumbira Tirasondjaja played a large role in its creation and popularization. *Jaipongan* was strongly influenced by *ketuk tilu* (lit. "three *ketuk*"), a type of performance that features female singer-dancers who, accompanied by a small ensemble including three small kettle gongs called *ketuk*, sang and danced with men who requested and paid for songs (Spiller 2008: 162–165). In *jaipongan*, the roles of singing and dancing were separated, and Gugum's dances were intended to be presentational rather than participatory (Spiller 2008: 192–193). As performers who had learned set choreographies and performed in a space separate from viewers, females were reconstituted as respectable, trained artists (or dance students), not singer-dancers associated with prostitution mingling with men for money

(Hellwig 1993: 51; Spiller 2008: 186–189, 192–193). Given that at some events, male guests enter the performance space, request a song as they tip the performers, and dance with the dancers, *jaipongan* is sometimes "reconstituted as a participational dance form" (Spiller 2008: 193–194). Despite what actually happens in some cases, the idea is that "[b]y separating the roles of singer and dancer, women performers circumvent some of the assumptions of low morals associated with ronggeng [female singer-dancers]" (Spiller 2010: 98).

Similarly in central Java, in some cases, the roles of the singer-dancer have been separated (Sutton 1984, 1987; Choy 1984: 65). R. Anderson Sutton has shown that although by the late nineteenth century, and perhaps earlier, there were females who sang but did not dance, the separation of the roles of singer and dancer in courtly and urban gamelan performance contexts was more recent (1984: 124, 126; 1987: 114). Many of the famous older female gamelan vocalists singing at the time of the publication of his essays in the 1980s had been famous singer-dancers in their youth (1984: 127; 1987: 114). Sutton's scholarship and observations suggest that the change from "singer-dancer" to "singer" or "dancer" in courtly and urban contexts was occurring during the course of the twentieth century. The separation of these roles in *Beskalan Putri* since the 1960s, I believe, was part of this trend. Despite discourses of respectability and artistry and some women's specialization in either singing or dancing, female performers nonetheless have had to contend with the negative image of the singer-dancer through New Order times and into the present (Sutton 1984: 127, 131; Cooper 2000: 626–627; Spiller 2007: 46; 2008: 193; Hughes-Freeland 2008c; Larasati 2013: 131–132).

At the same time, the line between female singers and dancers is not always so easy to draw. Many women continue to be competent in both singing and dancing, and a number of traditions featuring women as singer-dancers have continued to be performed throughout the course of the twentieth and into the twenty-first century. *Tayub* with its female singer-dancers was alive in Malang, and females sang and danced in the course of performing *Ngremo Tayub* (see chapter two). Although it was rare for female dancers to sing as they performed *Beskalan Putri*, the practice was not entirely extinct, a point I return to later in this chapter. Other traditions of singing and dancing also exist in Java. Females sing and dance in central Javanese dance-dramas, including *langendriyan* and parts of *wayang wong* (Sutton 1984: 126, n31; 1987: 114). Traditions featuring female singer-dancers have also continued in performances of popular musics, such as *campur sari* and *dangdut*, and the female singer-dancer figure has continued to inspire cultural debate about the public expression of female sexuality (Browne 2000; Spiller 2008: 197; Richter 2008; Daniels 2009: 81–94; Weintraub 2010, 2011; Bader 2011).

In separating the roles of singing and dancing in his adaptation of *Beskalan Putri*, Chattam in effect removed one way of representing female sexuality that was associated with female singer-dancers and had negative connotations. In some senses, this makes *Beskalan Putri* more appropriate for children to learn—that is, girls who are not yet sexually mature and often are expected to exude a certain innocence of childhood when they perform. I have also observed Chattam's adaptation performed by young women, and in those cases, their sexual magnetism was somewhat "contained" by their not singing. As with *jaipongan*, Chattam provided a means for females to perform just as dancers and thereby "circumvent some of the assumptions of low morals associated with ronggeng [female singer-dancers]" (Spiller 2010: 98).

Chattam made his selections to tradition in a complex historical and ideological context. While I do not mean to suggest that Chattam was an unthinking instrument of the New Order regime (which he certainly was not), neither do I wish to underestimate the impact of cultural and political pressures stemming from the state at the time when Chattam was adapting *Beskalan*. Furthermore, Chattam was of a generation living with the social memories of violence against artists in the mid-1960s as well as against women who pushed too hard against state-sanctioned norms, such as members of the progressive women's organization Gerwani (see chapter two). As he worked to preserve the dance and keep it in performed repertoire, he in effect balanced his sense of the essence of the dance with pressures during the New Order era to project ideal constructions of femininity as sweet, demure, and located in the bodies of "respectable" females. In so doing, he maintained a representation of female power through the costume suggesting martial prowess.

Chattam was also working in an atmosphere of concern with cultural preservation. The Indonesian government was officially recognizing the performing arts of East Java in the 1970s, recognition that was manifest in part through the founding of a high-school–level conservatory in Surabaya in 1973 (Sutton 1991: 179). Music and dance experts in east Javanese styles were concerned about the disappearance of local styles and wished to preserve them (ibid. 1991: 179). I view Chattam's work to preserve *Beskalan Putri* as part of artists' and government officials' efforts to identify, preserve, and promote east Javanese traditions—but to preserve these traditions in a way that held currency in New Order times by being shortened and representing gender in ways that were in line with official ideologies.

The representations of femaleness and regional culture in Chattam's adaptation of *Beskalan Putri* as performed by girls and young women continued to carry currency into Reformation era times (1998–present). At the time of my fieldwork, Karen Elizabeth Sekararum explained that *Beskalan Putri* was used at government functions because it is a Malangan dance and considered a "nice female dance" (p.c., January 6, 2006). Girls who were young and pretty had to be used for such events, not males (p.c., Karen Elizabeth Sekararum, November 29, 2005). In other words, a female style dance that was representing Malang and Malangan regional culture at official events had to represent femaleness in a manner that was consistent with official ideologies. In a post-1965 context, girls performing the dance in such contexts can be understood as "replicas" in the sense that Larasati employs the term (2013). She writes, "[r]eplication occurs as new, historically, politically 'clean' dancers are employed to absorb and embody the practices of artists targeted by the state, recreating the image of corporeality in the traditions of those who no longer officially exist" (Larasati 2013: xvi). The performance of *Beskalan Putri* by "replicas"—"new, historically, politically 'clean' dancers"—is yet another manifestation of the impact of social, political, and cultural climates on the ways artists represented female power through this dance.

The remarkable transformation of *Beskalan Putri* since the 1960s from a dance that could last over an hour and was performed by male or female *tandhak*, including itinerant singer-dancers and cross-dressing *ludruk* actors, into a "nice," eight-or-so–minute Malangan dance usually performed by girls and used for government sponsored events, further manifests the close connections between gender and tradition. In this case, too, transformations in the representation of gender and transformations of tradition are mutually constitutive. The eight-minute version, however, was not the only transformation of *Beskalan Putri*.

Recasting the Representation of Female Power through Longer Versions?

Artists' work to remember, learn, and/or perform longer versions of *Beskalan Putri* has maintained some expressions of female power that had been removed in the adaptation by Chattam discussed above, including his own aforementioned efforts to document longer versions. He also maintained cultural space for the representation of the magnetic power of femaleness through his senses of history, explaining *Beskalan Putri*'s use in ceremonial contexts of the past and thus implying the spiritual power of female dancers (see chapter four).

Through the initiative of M. Soleh Adi Pramono and Karen Elizabeth Sekararum, the Mangun Dharma Art Center (Padepokan Seni Mangun Dharma, or PSMD) also undertook projects to learn and perform longer versions of *Beskalan Putri* in the 1990s. Soleh and Karen Elizabeth, who ran PSMD, brought together an elderly drummer and an elderly dancer named Riati (or Riyati; 1920s–1996) who had performed the dance decades earlier (p.c., Karen Elizabeth Sekararum, January 6, 2006; Roberts 2001: 7–8). The drummer and Riati relearned the dance together and performed it at PSMD in 1992. Riati continued to work with the art center, teaching and performing. Among those who studied her interpretation of *Beskalan Putri* were Karen Elizabeth and the English dancer Gillian Roberts, who has also written about Riati's work with PSMD (p.c., Karen Elizabeth, January 6, 2006; Roberts 2001: 7–8). After Riati passed away, Karen Elizabeth explained, the dance became less of a focus at PSMD until Didik Nini Thowok (a renowned central Javanese artist) became interested in it. Emphasizing that *Beskalan Putri* is dynamic, flexible, and continuously changing (as does Roberts in her 2001 article), Karen Elizabeth explained that it became reinvented again when Didik learned the dance (p.c., January 6, 2006).

Didik Nini Thowok and Beskalan Putri

Didik Nini Thowok's work with PSMD in 2001 to learn the dance, sponsoring the commercial recording *Aneka Gending Tari Malangan, Volume 2* featuring *Beskalan Putri*'s music, also affected selections made to the form and content of the dance and provides further insights into males' embodiment of femaleness. He learned *Beskalan Putri* for a performance of cross-gender dance he was invited to give in Japan. He had decided to perform the female style dance *Golek Lambangsari* in the Yogyakarta style, and for his second dance he wished to perform a dance from outside of central Java. He thought about performing *Ngremo Putri* and called M. Soleh Adi Pramono to consult with him. Soleh suggested *Beskalan Putri* and that Didik study it with Rasimoen (or Rasimun; 1921–2004),[3] a respected senior dancer known in Malang for both refined male style masked dance and female style dance. Didik arranged for Rasimoen and Soleh to come to his studio and home in Yogyakarta for a week (p.c., Didik Nini Thowok, July 13, 2006).

Didik explained that before he started lessons, Rasimoen, Soleh, and Didik held a ceremony in which Rasimoen's *ilmu* was "brought down" and given to Didik. This ceremony was a process by and through which Didik came to embody femaleness as he embodied Rasimoen's *ilmu*. Didik identified gendered aspects of Rasimoen's knowledge, referencing the spirit of Muskayah. According to Didik, Soleh said that during the ceremony he saw the figure of Muskayah in a *Beskalan* costume (p.c., July 13, 2006). By referencing Soleh's vision, Didik connected Rasimoen's spiritual knowledge to the figure of a female dancer. On one level, the *ilmu* itself was personified as a female figure—indicating the femaleness that Didik associated with the dance and worked to internalize in his own, male body.

There are further implications in Didik's references to Soleh's vision. One is that Didik received *ilmu* about femaleness from both female (Muskayah) and male (Rasimoen, Soleh) sources. In evoking this synthesis of male and female elements, Didik was further producing male femininity—in effect, speaking to why he had the ability as a male to embody the femaleness of this dance. Furthermore, these "sources" were east Javanese, giving Didik knowledge and ability in the tradition of a different cultural region. Soleh's reference to Muskayah also had a historical dimension as Soleh connected *Beskalan sing asli* (the "real," "authentic," "original" *Beskalan*) to Muskayah, as discussed in the previous chapter. Soleh was thus communicating that Didik was receiving *ilmu* about *Beskalan* from one of its sources of origin, imbuing the *ilmu* with senses of authenticity and authority.

After the ceremony, Didik worked intensively with Rasimoen, practicing with him, interviewing him, and documenting his interpretation of *Beskalan Putri* by photographing him and videotaping him in full costume. Although their encounter was relatively brief, Didik referenced the special bond they formed. After Rasimoen and Soleh returned to Malang, Didik continued to study *Beskalan* by watching the video he had made. While he acknowledged that he watched the video repeatedly in order to memorize the choreography, he indicated that it was the ceremony and his reception of Rasimoen's *ilmu* that had prepared him mentally, spiritually, and physically to learn the dance, and that as he practiced he felt as though he was being guided (p.c., July 13, 2006). Didik thus indicated the value that he placed on spiritual preparation as a means to make himself receptive to knowledge about femaleness.

Reinforcing the paradoxes of his learning process, Didik noted that the strange thing was that he studied in just three days and three nights, recognizing that this was a short amount of time to learn such a long and complicated dance. Didik felt the dance enter him, explaining, "I practiced continuously, watching the video, then it was like being pressed, I was entered, entered, entered, entered, until in the end I danced *Beskalan* without thinking. All of a sudden I knew it by heart, it entered on its own."[4] A dance or piece "entering" a person is a common way of talking about attaining the competence necessary in the arts in Java to perform with *rasa* (feeling; affective power; see chapter one) (Weiss 2003: 26, 32). Didik's reference to the spirit of a woman during the ceremony to bring down Rasimoen's *ilmu* suggests that for him, the spirit of the dance was "female" and entered Didik's male body, giving him the ability to embody the femaleness appropriate for this particular dance. Another implication is that the *ilmu* that Rasimoen embodied was also associated with the female spirit of the dance, making Rasimoen a vessel of *ilmu* that was associated with femaleness as well. As I see it, these spiritual beliefs and practices contributed to Didik's embodiment and expression of male femininity.

Speaking further to the femaleness that Didik learned to embody through this dance, he identified *Beskalan*'s eroticism. Didik explained that he had studied other East Javanese dances before studying *Beskalan Putri*, such as *Ngremo Putri*, *Ngremo Lanang*, and Banyuwangian dance, but had not mastered them. He finally understood how to execute East Javanese neck movements when studying *Beskalan Putri* as well as how to execute coquettish and flirtatious movements. He again referenced male and female sources of this eroticism by talking about the male and female dancers he observed. He talked about the coquettishness of *Beskalan Putri*, and East Javanese dance in general in terms of walking movements, recalling the *tandhak ludruk* (males who specialize in female roles in *ludruk*) that he had seen when he was little. By referring to *tandhak ludruk*, Didik was referring to the male femininity that these dancers embodied. Referring also to female dancers, Didik related that the *tandhak ludruk*'s style of walking was similar to ways of walking in central Javanese dance performed by *lèdhèk* (female singer-dancers). He encountered this way of walking by watching *tayub* dancers, recognizing that walking like this was not easy (p.c., July 13, 2006). Implicit, too, was the magnetic female power that he associated with male *tandhak ludruk* and female *lèdhèk*, manifest in part through their feminine sexual appeal. He thus on one level maintained the controversial sexual power associated with female singer-dancers by imbuing his own performances of *Beskalan Putri* with it.

Although Didik learned a longer version of the dance than Chattam's adaptation, it was still an abbreviated version of *Beskalan sing asli* as my teachers referenced it. Kusnadi, the drummer on the recording, explained that since Didik studied the dance with Rasimoen, the musicians had to be sure to record the music to accompany Rasimoen's interpretation—including the particular movements that Rasimoen used, which were not necessarily the same as what other dancers used—so that Didik would be able to dance to it (p.c., February 4, 2006). The musicians thus practiced with Rasimoen prior to the recording session and Rasimoen danced in the studio to help Kusnadi remember the drumming for Rasimoen's interpretation of the dance (p.c., Kusnadi, July 24, 2006). According to Kusnadi, due to time considerations, certain movement sequences were not repeated. Kusnadi also recalled that Rasimoen told him after the recording that he had forgotten such-and-such movements, which suggests that some of Rasimoen's movements may have been unintentionally omitted. Furthermore, since Didik had not studied the singing, the sections in which the dancer stops dancing to sing were omitted and the singing was performed by a vocalist (who on that recording was Karen Elizabeth Sekararum [*Aneka Gending Tari Malangan, Volume 2*, Studio LPK Tari Natya Lakshita and Joyoboyo Studio, n.d.]).

Nonetheless, the representation of female power was recast. The movement sequence depicting the manipulation of a bow and shooting an arrow as well as the Ricik-Ricik part of the dance were included, thus "reinserting" these expressions of female power through these representations of martial prowess. The cassette that Didik sponsored as well as his performances, however, reinforced *Beskalan Putri* as a tradition in which the dancer does not sing, thus maintaining a separation of singing and dancing roles for this dance. In most of the live performances of *Beskalan Putri* that I observed in Malang, the dancers did not sing either. The exceptions were performances by Karen Elizabeth, a few performances in which I danced (paradoxically performances by American dancers interested in older ways of performing Malangan dances), and a comic routine at a *ludruk* show that featured an old man performing a hilarious parody of *Beskalan Putri* that included one of the singing sections. Similarly, the Ricik-Ricik part was not performed for most of the performances I observed and participated in (in Malang and in other places), including performances given by Didik. While this was often due to time considerations, *Beskalan Putri* was nonetheless usually reinforced as a dance without this more martial section.

Issues of Cultural Authority, Ownership, and Preservation

Didik's embodiment of *ilmu* about *Beskalan Putri* raises some questions related to issues of cultural ownership and authority. On the one hand, *Beskalan Putri* was arguably not Didik's tradition. Didik is from central Java, a cultural region that is related to, but distinct from, the cultural region of east Java. Higher status and prestige has generally been given to central Javanese arts and artists associated with the court cities of Surakarta and Yogyakarta, as explained in chapter one. Didik was based in Yogyakarta, was himself quite wealthy, and was a celebrity in Indonesia from his frequent appearances on television. His status as an urban, wealthy, famous artist based in central Java raises the question of whether he, coming from a position of power and privilege, appropriated a tradition from a marginalized regional culture in order to bolster his career and reap financial benefits. (My own efforts to learn *Beskalan Putri* as an American raise a similar question.) On the other hand, *Beskalan Putri* was arguably part of Didik's tradition as a cross-gender dancer because *Beskalan Putri* has a history of performance by males.

Didik's spiritual connections to *Beskalan Putri* and to his teacher inspired a sense of confidence and permission to perform the dance. By preparing himself spiritually to receive *ilmu* from Rasimoen, Didik prepared himself to become a vessel that could be entered by Rasimoen's spiritual knowledge and the dance. Allowing oneself to become a container or vessel in performance is valued in many parts of Java. Writing about trance dance in West Java, Kathy Foley terms such an approach "the 'empty vessel' school of acting since the actor's central task is to abdicate his own personality and let his body become a vessel for the character he presents" (1985: 36). Writing about transmission in central Javanese performing arts, Sarah Weiss explains, "[t]he piece must 'enter' into the student before the student can perform it with *rasa*; but, in order for the piece to enter the student, the student must be empty—concentrating only on the performance and thus allowing the piece to fill him or her up" (2003: 27).

Like other dancers who allow themselves to become vessels to be filled, Didik was taking a passive role to performance (Foley 1985: 36; Weiss 2003: 42). Taking a passive role in this manner, however, can be a means of demonstrating competence. Sarah Weiss explains that this is one way of achieving a successful performance in Java and that "[i]n both the active seizing of the inner life of a performance and the passive being filled-up by the performance, the performer is described as if she or he were a vessel into and through which energy and potency flow" (2003: 42). In talking about being "entered" by the dance, Didik implied that the dance had a spirit of its own and that the spirit had agency. The spirit of the dance made the decision to enter Didik's body, contributing to his ability and confidence to perform it. This is not to suggest that Didik has taken a passive role in all of his endeavors as an artist, but that for him, when it came to *Beskalan Putri*, allowing himself to be filled by Rasimoen's *ilmu* and the dance was a critical aspect of his learning process.

Didik has felt that *ilmu* about *Beskalan* and the ability to perform it have come to "grow" in his own body, becoming one with him. He explained, "what I received was growing, growing, growing; it developed and became increasingly powerful, became me" (*"kemudian yang saya terima itu kemudian growing, growing, growing, itu berkembang dan menjadi semakin kuat menjadi saya"*) (p.c., Didik Nini Thowok, July 13, 2006). Strikingly, Didik gave particular emphasis to the idea of "growing" by repeating it and using the English word "growing" as he spoke in Indonesian. The image of the dance growing and developing inside Didik evokes the image of an embryo or fetus growing and developing in a woman's womb. On one level, Didik's use of this "growing" imagery connects his experience of learning the dance to pregnancy, a dimension of femaleness connected to motherhood and fertility that he was locating in his male body, in some ways feminizing his body.[5] His description also indicates the oneness of the artist and the work so central to performing with *rasa* (Weiss 2003: 38).

In Didik's case, spiritual knowledge had crossed regional boundaries in addition to boundaries of gender as the knowledge moved from east Javanese performers and spirit(s) to a central Javanese artist. The comments of several performers in Malang attested to the "success" of this transmission across regional boundaries as they recognized Didik's ability as a *Beskalan Putri* dancer. Several said that the only dancer who could perform *Beskalan Putri* like Rasimoen was Didik. One reported that Rasimoen himself, already deceased at the time of my fieldwork, had told him that the only person who could dance *Beskalan* the way he did was Didik.

Didik expressed a sense of responsibility to protect *Beskalan Putri*, along with several other cross-gender dances in his repertoire, thinking of these dances as treasures. "I feel that I present them and I really protect them, like they are something fragile, like I have to be careful," Didik explained. "So I have to present them perfectly, because I respect [these dances] from all aspects, everything about them." (*"[S]aya merasa bahwa saya membawahkan ini dan saya menjaga banget, sepertinya ini something fragile gitu lho, saya harus hati-hati gitu, jadi saya harus menyajikan ini secara perfect gitu lho mbak, itu, karena saya réspék dari everythingnya"*) (p.c., July 13, 2006).

Regarding *Beskalan* as a special dance, Didik has only performed it for particular kinds of events, another means of protecting and preserving it. These events included cultural nights, dinner events, and festivals at venues such as universities, hotels, the court, and theaters, or as he put it, "special places" (*"tempat-tempat yang spesial"*). He performed *Beskalan* for people who were going to appreciate and pay attention to the dance, noting that it was unlikely that he would perform it for a wedding reception, unless the hosts were sponsoring a particularly special occasion featuring traditional dances such as *bedhaya*, a type of court dance (p.c., July 13, 2006). He explained that he does not perform *Beskalan* for entertainment—or simply as entertainment—in part because his audiences in Indonesia expect him to perform comedy routines in such contexts and in part because he does not feel that *Beskalan* is appropriate for entertainment. He feels that *Beskalan* is "too good" (*"terlalu bagus"*); he prefers "serious events" (*"acara yang serius"*) for it. Furthermore, he feels that he must bring a "sacred element" (*"unsur sakralnya"*) to the performance (p.c., Didik Nini Thowok, July 13, 2006).

While the events that Didik listed might not normally or necessarily be considered sacred events by Javanese standards, Didik did note that *Beskalan* can become sacred depending on how it is performed as well as the occasion. Out of respect for the dance, its sacred potential, and his teacher, Didik worked to achieve a state of purity before he performed, in part by praying (p.c., July 13, 2006). Drawn to the energy that he associated with sacred contexts, he explained, "when it is serious and becomes a ceremonial [dance], its energy becomes extraordinary" (*"pada waktu dia serius untuk menjadi sebuah ceremonial itu menjadi, energinya menjadi luar biasa"*) (p.c., Didik Nini Thowok, July 13, 2006). Didik's connection to the sacred in the context of this dance, I posit, was a means by which he worked to embody the magnetic power of its femaleness.

Didik wrote about one such "extraordinary" performance of *Beskalan Putri* through email before this book went into production, referencing female spiritual power in different ways.[6] The performance was held in front of the fourteenth century (Majapahit era) Brahu Temple, a structure located in the area that was once the capital of Majapahit, now the subdistrict of Trowulan in the East Javanese regency of Mojokerto (Holt 1967: 90; Sutton 1991: 123; Kinney 2003: 165, 173, 176). Didik explained that "the energy is still strong" at this temple and that it is "still a very sacred place" because centuries ago it was "used for the cremation of Princess Tri Buwana Tungga Dewi" (wife of the first king of Majapahit, Raden Wijaya) (emails, October 4 and 30, 2013).[7] He also wrote that Gayatri, another wife of Raden Wijaya, was cremated at Brahu Temple and her ashes are interred there (email, Didik Nini Thowok, October 30, 2013), suggesting that this, too, contributed to the temple's energy. Significantly, Didik referenced the cremations of women (and the ashes of one of them), thereby attributing the energy of the temple to power connected with femaleness. One implication is that the spiritual energy of these women had been released into the area and was available for people who were suitable vessels to access and embody.

The night before the performance, Didik "did a ritual meditation around the site of Majapahit including the graveyard of Raden Wijaya [and other places], together with a small group/community of people from Trowulan and the Juru Kunci [graveyard caretaker] who did rituals very often" (email, October 4, 2013). He continued:

> And my feeling told me that I have to fast for one day. What happened? The night of the performance, I start to do my make up and wear the costume of *Beskalan*, and some people including [a woman from Malang who made the costume] said that my face, including my aura was changing very mysteriously. [Another woman] looked at me from top to bottom [and] . . . told me that she saw somebody else, not me anymore. She was a little bit afraid. [The woman who made the costume] also smiled and she understood very well what happened,

what was going on—I was feeling the same thing. When I danced, *Beskalan Putri* was so amazing I couldn't explain, maybe you understand what I mean. (email, Didik Nini Thowok, October 4, 2013)

My understanding, in terms of Javanese spiritual beliefs and practices, is that Didik was able to access and embody the spiritual energy of the locale—energy that was infused with the power of femaleness.

According to Didik, the spiritual energy that went into making the costume affected the performance as well. The costume maker told him that she should fast before making the costume and that she should start making it based on a system of counting used in Javanese spiritual practices. As he wrote, "[t]hat is why the costume itself, when I start to use it and it touches my body, makes me change totally" (email, Didik Nini Thowok, October 4, 2013). That performance, he later realized, was on the same day of the Javanese calendar as when the costume maker started to make his costume. "That is why the power and the energy were so strong that night. Many friends including [the costume maker] told me that I transform, become someone else in spiritual feeling" (email, Didik Ninik Thowok, October 10, 2013). In evoking the spiritual energy that a woman put into making the costume, Didik in effect further referenced female power. As he was transformed physically and spiritually through the spiritual energy of the costume and of the locale—both of which were infused with the energy of women—he was in a sense, "possessed . . . by feminine beauty" (Hughes-Freeland 2008a: 31). This ultimately contributed to a performance of *Beskalan Putri* that was powerful in part because Didik, a male dancer, was able to access and embody the magnetic power of femaleness.

Didik has talked about the particular power that the embodiment and representation of gender through cross-gender performance produces, using the phrase "mystical gender." In an interview with Laurie Margot Ross, he explained:

> When a woman dances the male mask, she is transformed—it is mystical. And when a man dresses up as a woman, in *bedhaya*, we don't always recognize that the dancer is male—it is mystical. He, too, is transformed. I believe a better term [than "transgender"] is "mystical gender." (Didik Nini Thowok, quoted in Ross 2005: 226; see also Hughes-Freeland 2008a: 30)

Didik's discourse about the mystical aspect of cross-gender performance, I believe, is a contemporary manifestation of the centuries-old Hindu and indigenous logics in which androgyny or the combination of male and female elements represents cosmic power and fertility, mentioned in chapter one (Wolbers 1989: 8–11; Sutton 1993: 139; Hughes-Freeland 2008b: 155).

By invoking the sacred and the pure to insist on his respect for *Beskalan Putri* in particular, Didik was showing that he was not using his position of privilege as a central Javanese artist to take advantage of a marginalized east Javanese tradition. On the occasions I was fortunate enough to perform as a master of ceremonies for Didik's shows in 2003 and 2004 in California and in Java, I was struck that when he performed *Beskalan Putri*, he invoked a serious and "sacred" feel by having the stage lights dimmed. He encouraged me and the other masters of ceremonies to highlight *Beskalan*'s uses in both entertainment and ritual contexts in past times. In dimming the lights and performing *Beskalan* with a sense of seriousness—either maintaining a serious, but serene facial expression, or smiling very subtly—he chose to emphasize a sense of sacredness.

Through his work as an artist, Didik has been contributing to the ongoing history and transformations of this dance. Didik's stance that *Beskalan Putri* was not appropriate for entertainment is striking because it contrasted with performance contexts in Malang, where I saw and participated in performances of *Beskalan Putri* for Indonesian Independence Day celebrations and receptions to celebrate life cycle events such as weddings and circumcisions. It is arguable that on one level, Didik was continuing New Order era efforts to "develop" regional traditions into "art" (see, for example, Widodo 1995, Yampolsky 1995, Hughes-Freeland 1997, Wilson 1999, Larasati 2013). I am more inclined, however, to see Didik's work of learning and performing *Beskalan Putri* as a form of social and artistic activism—part of his efforts to make cultural space not only for the expression of male femininity but to also insist that some expressions of male femininity be taken very seriously and respected. Male femininity was not merely about comedy—not just for laughs—but could also be about deep spiritual knowledge, deep connections with a teacher, and the embodiment of a valued regional tradition, one of Java's and Indonesia's cultural treasures. In light of the tendency for *Beskalan Putri* to be performed primarily by females since the 1960s, Didik was also in a sense reclaiming it as a dance that could be performed as a cross-gender dance. The special place this dance and Rasimoen hold in Didik's heart was made particularly clear to me when my husband and I accompanied him to Rasimoen's grave in 2004 so that he could pay his respects to his inspirational teacher.

The Power of Femaleness in Djupri's Narratives

Given the context of *Beskalan Putri*'s transformations since the 1960s, Djupri's narratives about his grandmother's roles in *Beskalan*'s history and her career have captured my interest for what they reveal about the ways an individual (in this case a male) used his sense of the past and his memories to recognize, represent, and thereby maintain the power of femaleness, despite official ideologies that worked to control and subdue it. Djupri (b. 1939), too, lived with social memories from the mid-1960s that linked violence, freethinking women, and female sexuality. I contend that he synthesized personal and social memories, remembering his grandmother strategically. Rather than focusing on the sexual or intellectual aspects of a woman's power as a performer—which could carry potentially dangerous political implications—he focused on his grandmother's spiritual power, recasting the representation of a female singer-dancer (his grandmother) as a spiritually potent healer. It might also have been awkward for a grandson to speak about (or think about) his grandmother's sexuality, another possible motivation for focusing on the spiritual, rather than sexual dimensions of her magnetic female power.

In remembering his grandmother in particular ways, Djupri negotiated multiple ideologies of femininity and womanhood in Java, including those stemming from Javanese spiritual beliefs, national Indonesian discourses, and Islamic perspectives. At the same time, in constructing femaleness to include spiritual and physical strength and in emphasizing women's roles as mothers, healers, and fighters, he contested some dominant constructions of femininity while reinforcing others, all the while making sense of Muskayah's power in a "safe" way. In so doing, he contributed to the preservation of *Beskalan Putri* as a tradition that was steeped in femaleness and female power as he taught me, a foreign researcher who could preserve his narratives through my research projects, such as this book.

Embodying Ilmu *and Spiritual Power*

Appreciating *ilmu* as transferable, "embodiable" packets of knowledge (chapter one) is critical to understanding the implications of Djupri's narratives and, in particular, the process by and through which Muskayah gained *ilmu* about *Beskalan Putri* as a process of embodiment. In his tellings of Muskayah's reception of the dance, Djupri emphasized that Muskayah was not consciously aware of what was happening as a spirit infused her body with knowledge of the movements and musical accompaniment. He explained,

> And it seemed as though someone were making her arms move like a dancer's, going through the sequence of the dance and singing the music. And it was heard as though there was a gamelan performance: there were those playing the music, there was a drummer, too, a complete ensemble. It seemed then like she was taken through the sequence of the dance. It [the spirit] was behind her.

That was called a dream, yes, a dream. But she was not conscious, she did not know where she was, she did not know.[8]

In the context of national discourses about womanhood and social memories of violence associated with Gerwani members, Djupri's emphasis that Muskayah "did not know" as she gained her *ilmu* was a way to safely talk about a woman's knowledge. While he recognized that she became the bearer of this knowledge, he freed her of responsibility for it or potential dangers it could bring. The *ilmu*, after all, was not hers to begin with, but bestowed upon her, transferred to her body. Djupri in effect downplayed her intellectual capacity. However, he also recognized that Muskayah gave *Beskalan Putri* her own additions over the course of her life, thereby acknowledging her personal touches, but without emphasizing her creativity as an intellectual process (p.c., November 12, 2005). The dance suddenly entering the body of a dancer was also similar to the way Didik talked about being "entered," discussed earlier. As with Didik, such sudden abilities to perform a dance imply that beings in the unseen world had selected an individual as the recipient of something special, bestowing them with knowledge, spiritual potency, and cultural authority.

Djupri emphasized that Muskayah did not gain her ability through worldly experience or interaction with other humans because the dance did not exist at the time (p.c., November 12, 2005). He implied that Muskayah revived a dance from hundreds of years ago that had become completely extinct after the fall of Majapahit in 1478 or c. 1520 (see chapter four). She gained knowledge of this dance not through her own experience, intellectual capacity as an artist, or from studying with another person, but through a supernatural encounter. Djupri recalled, "Now I asked [her], 'In the past who taught you, Ma?' 'Who taught me?!'" Djupri said, changing to a higher-pitched, almost defensive tone to indicate Muskayah's voice. "'I got it when I was ill, from when I dreamt. It appeared to me like this and like this.' Like that."[9] He thus reinforced the spiritual nature of her learning process by relaying Muskayah's own insistence that she gained her abilities through her dream.

Although the sociopolitical climate in Indonesia had changed considerably since the mid-1960s, and Muskayah was no longer living when Djupri related these stories about her in 2005–2006, I contend that he was still affected by social memories of violence against women who were considered to be too independently minded like Gerwani members—whose perceived radical nature was linked to their perceived uncontrollable sexuality. Already deceased, Muskayah was not in physical danger, but Djupri was still personally and emotionally invested in remembering her in particular ways.

In de-emphasizing the intellectual aspects of Muskayah's learning process, Djupri underlined the spiritual dimensions and power of her knowledge.

The long-term potency of *ilmu* can be understood in relation to the transmission process by and through which a person gains it. As I have come to understand from my conversations, observations, and experiences in Malang, in terms of a very simple ranking, the most powerful *ilmu* is given in the form of divine inspiration or a divine revelation without the recipient asking. That is, a divine being selects the recipient and bestows the inspiration or revelation upon him or her, as in Prabaretna's selection of Muskayah. Furthermore, that she was a child when she gained her *ilmu* about *Beskalan* implies that she was endowed with a potent inner strength from birth that she did not actively seek. From my conversations with people in Malang, it seems that often those who give up something and receive *ilmu* unintentionally are believed to have more "natural" inner strength than those who consciously pursue it. Consistent with preferences for indirectness in many contexts in Java, such "natural" inner strength is also believed to be more potent. Muskayah's illness was an unintentional sacrifice of health and physical comfort as she received *ilmu*. The second most potent kind of *ilmu* is gained as divine inspiration or a divine revelation that an individual seeks by making the sorts of sacrifices identified in chapter one, such as fasting, giving up sleep, etc. The power of *ilmu* passed through humans ranks still lower, and *ilmu* that is purchased from sorcerers ranks the lowest.[10] While *ilmu* that was bought could be powerful, its efficacy was usually temporary.

I recognize that the potency attributed to *ilmu* is much more complicated than what I have outlined and that there is space for many exceptions. I also recognize that this ranking system outlined above reflects a dominant, male-centered, aristocratic ideology of spiritual power in Java outlined by Benedict Anderson (1990a; see chapter one of this book)—including an ambivalence about money discussed by Suzanne Brenner (1995, 1998) and others (see chapter two of this book). The basic ranking outlined above is nevertheless useful because it elucidates the potency that Djupri implied Muskayah had through a dominant paradigm of spiritual power: Initially the most potent *ilmu* about *Beskalan* was transferred to the body with the most spiritual strength available, which remarkably was the body of a girl. Only then was the *ilmu* passed on slowly and safely to other humans—including men—as they were ready. The spirit of Prabaretna chose Muskayah because no one else was strong enough to receive this *ilmu*. In other words, Muskayah was the most powerful person in her community even as a child. Ward Keeler explains that "Javanese have long assumed that members of the aristocracy necessarily possessed extraordinary potency. . . . In other cases, God is thought to bestow potency for reasons inexplicable, which explains why some rather unlikely people sometimes rise to high position in modern Indonesia" (1987: 41). By relating Muskayah's responsibility to revive and disseminate *Beskalan*, and her activities doing so throughout Malang and in other parts of Java—including for the sultans in Yogyakarta (see chapter four)—Djupri positioned her as one of the most spiritually powerful people on the island. That the spirit of Prabaretna was a woman who selected a girl also attests to the spiritual power that Djupri recognized in a female lineage.

In Banyuwangi at the eastern end of Java, a female lineage can also be understood to be a source of spiritual power as well as a channel by and through which this power is transferred, as Robert Wessing explores in relation to *seblang* (1999). *Seblang* is a type of trance dance that is performed to protect the health, well-being, and fertility of the community's people and crops (Wolbers 1989: 2–3; 1993: 36; Sutton 1993: 138; Wessing 1999: 644–645; Yampolsky 1991a). The dancers who go into trance are also called *seblang* (Wolbers 1989: 2; 1993: 36). In trance, the dancers "are thought to be able to foretell the future and to know the cures for diseases and the like" (Wessing 1999: 646). Wessing observes that the female dancers "belong to a select female line" (1999: 667), and more specifically that they "tend to be descendents of a line of women that ideally goes back to the village founders" (1999: 669). Connecting women's predominance in *seblang* performances to the descent system, he argues that "women can be viewed as the channel through which a descent line's spiritual essence and vitality (that is, fertility) are passed on" (1999: 667). The spiritual power, I suggest, connected to a particular female lineage, is also a manifestation of the power of femaleness.

The image of Muskayah as a girl teaching musicians to accompany her is striking because it challenges power structures within performing ensembles in Java related to gender and age.[11] The idea of a young girl teaching a presumably older man how to drum disrupts cultural norms that put women in a subordinate relationship to men and younger people in a subordinate relationship to those who are older. Assuming that she taught men who were already trained as musicians, she challenged social norms by taking a more authoritative position in relation to those with more performing experience. Whether Muskayah actually did so or not is less important than Djupri's depiction of her doing so, implying that she was given the cultural authority to instruct older males because of the power and prestige that musicians and others in her community attributed to her *ilmu* and to her as the vessel of this *ilmu*.

Djupri reinforced her spiritual potency by relating other ways Muskayah trained musicians. Sometimes when she performed, he divulged, she did not always have enough musicians to play all of the instruments. When this happened, she would look out into the crowd that was amassing to watch her perform, searching for individuals with the potential to play. She called likely candidates over and asked to see their hands. She then knew whether they could play and what instrument they could play, even if they had no prior experience as musicians. She would ask people like this to play particular instruments. They might initially decline, saying, "I can't play yet," but she would tell them to perform anyway, and they could immediately do it. However, the next day, they would no longer be able to do so. As Djupri explained, it was a spiritual being who guided the hands of these people; since Muskayah had the ability to communicate with spirits, a spirit could tell her who had the potential to be guided (p.c., December 1, 2005). Muskayah's inner strength enabled her to possess the spiritual power and *ilmu* necessary to communicate with the spiritual world and to facilitate interaction between spirits and humans. Djupri also implied that spirits were ready to assist Muskayah in her work as a dancer, in effect legitimizing her roles as a dancer and healer by invoking the unseen world.

The magnetic power that she showed in drawing people from centers of political power to the periphery was further evidence of her potency. According to Djupri, Muskayah attracted researchers from the political centers of East Java and Indonesia to the village where she resided. Djupri recalled the arrival of people from Jakarta, the capital of Indonesia, and Surabaya, the capital of the province of East Java, who wished to consult her in 1976 after reading about her in Dutch documents. This was a big event for Djupri because these visitors came in several cars at a time when there were few cars in his village; he remembered the surprise of the other villagers, too (p.c., March 8, 2006). Djupri implied that this special attention and association with cars further attested to her exceptional abilities as a dancer and healer. I wonder, too, if my coming from America to learn about *Beskalan Putri* from him as he learned from her was yet another manifestation of her magnetism, still exerting its pull even after she had passed away.

Healing and Power in a Motherly Capacity

Although dominant Indonesian discourses have portrayed women's motherly roles as subordinate to men's fatherly roles as household heads, motherly roles have also provided opportunities for women to empower themselves and for others to recognize women's power as well as women's contributions to society. Madelon Djajadiningrat-Nieuwenhuis defines Ibuism ("motherism"), which developed in the postcolonial period as an ideology that "sanctions any action provided it is taken as a mother who is looking after her family, a group, a class, a company or the state, without demanding power or prestige in return" (1987: 43–44). Suzanne Brenner has found that many Javanese women who engage in ascetic practices to increase their spiritual power tend to do so in a motherly capacity—that is, "for the benefit of their children and future descendents" rather than working to achieve personal goals, as men tended to do (1995: 36; see also 1998: 182–184). Similarly, Djupri talked about Muskayah's efforts to benefit the people for whom she performed, who became her "family" in a broad, community-oriented sense, thus implying that she was performing in order to help others. On one level, then, as portrayed through Djupri's memories, she exemplified Ibuism, even in times prior to the development of Ibuism as an ideology. Remarkably, she did so through her profession as a singer-dancer, a controversial profession for women, as we have seen. Even in cases where she may have been younger than the people she helped, she nonetheless performed a motherly role to heal and educate by affecting others with her spiritual power.

Djupri emphasized Muskayah's abilities to heal by performing particular movements and singing spiritually potent texts such as mantras in sacred contexts, either during sections of the dance in which the dancer sang or during the introductory section of music before the dancer started to dance. Her potency was so effective, he implied on multiple occasions, that even when she was heavily pregnant and could not dance, she still contributed to healing processes by singing from a seated position. The texts were potent either because they communicated with the unseen world or because they transmitted lessons about life and thereby affected audiences, verbally transmitting *ilmu* and spiritual power.

Understanding singing as a means by and through which *Beskalan Putri* dancers manifested the magnetic power of femaleness provides a deeper understanding of the cultural impact of removing these singing sections from the dance, as in the versions associated with Chattam and Didik. Removing these sections, in addition to affecting the representation of female sexuality, also removes some of the opportunities for the dancer to express his or her power and to transmit his or her *ilmu*. By a similar token, removing these sections can also be understood as a means to make female style dance "safer" as the dancer's power was not directly expressed or represented through the dancer's singing. As a "safer" dance, *Beskalan Putri* was more likely to be preserved in New Order times as a form of regional art. While the power of the texts and melodies were maintained through the singing of a vocalist seated with the gamelan, the representation of the female power of the singer-dancer was altered as the roles of singing and dancing were divided.

Countering this separation, Djupri maintained Muskayah's power as a singer-dancer. At the same time, he did not emphasize her sexual appeal; rather he stressed her motherly role as a healer. He bolstered her motherly image by referencing her activities singing and healing while pregnant, further recasting the image of her as a female singer-dancer in terms of motherhood. While her sexuality was implicit through her pregnancy, it was in terms of bringing forth new life, not in terms of satisfying carnal desires. In talking about Muskayah's power to heal, Djupri both reinforced and challenged dominant gender ideologies stemming from national discourses and orthodox Muslims within his community. Consistent with constructions of women as mothers, Djupri indicated that an ideal woman should contribute to the well-being of her community through a motherly capacity to heal and educate.

Drawing on other aspects of Muskayah's *ilmu*—the dance's philosophical meanings—he reinforced images of an ideal Javanese woman that the dance "teaches." One aspect of Muskayah's *ilmu* was knowledge of the symbolism of the costume, communicated through *jarwa dhosok* (Becker 2000) or *kérta basa* (Beatty 1996: 281) folk etymology, introduced in the previous chapter. For example, the white socks represent "taking the good path" or "doing the right thing" (*lakuné becik*), and being safe and in good health physically and emotionally. The word for one's actions (*lakuné*) stems from the same root as the Javanese word for walk (*mlaku*). The color white represents good (*becik*). Socks, worn on the parts of the body used for walking, symbolize this etymology (p.c., Djupri, February 26, 2006). Developing his point about the costume, Djupri explained that dancers wore white socks to protect their feet from nails and thorns, noting that women in particular had to be careful about "not getting stuck" (p.c., February 26, 2006). This could also be a euphemism for sex outside of marriage. Such behavior is necessary for a woman to be a faithful wife devoted to her husband and to become the mother of his children, an image consistent with dominant Old Order and New Order ideologies.

The dancer educated viewers in other ways, too—as a mother should teach her children—by reinforcing preferred aesthetics for female style dance and senses of womanhood consistent with dominant ideologies. Djupri explained that the character and feel of *Beskalan Putri* should be refined, sweet, and polite, referencing senses of Javanese femininity consistent with images of Kartini- and Sumbadra-like figures. The movements of *Beskalan Putri* overall should illustrate the beauty and sensuality of femaleness—gracefully swaying the hips, gently rolling the shoulders, sinuously moving the head—without being what in a Javanese context is considered to be indecent or overtly sexualized. The restraint, self control, and refinement of *Beskalan*'s movements show audiences how an ideal female should move and physically trains those who study dance to move this way both on and off stage. *Beskalan Putri*, like other forms of dance, thereby "disciplines" bodies (van Orden 2005: 90–91).

Beskalan Putri symbolizes other motherly duties, too, such as protecting children—or the community—through spiritual power. Djupri explained the meaning of one movement as ripping up and throwing away illness, dirt, and/or filth (p.c., Djupri, 2006).[12] Djupri linked another movement to the stirring of ingredients, as in cooking, explaining that this refers to the idea that any ingredient is not so good by itself, but when it is mixed with others, the result is delicious (*énak*). Likewise, all of the movements of the dance are mixed and make for a pleasant (*énak*) whole. The movement also symbolizes harmony between people—the goodness that results when people work together (p.c., Djupri, 2006). This movement thus conveys a motherly responsibility to nurture and feed one's family, and on a deeper level, women's roles in fostering social harmony among a group through their magnetic power. Here I am building again on Nancy Cooper, who shows how female singers foster social harmony by testing men's ability to resist temptation (2000: 617). Both the motherly symbolism of *Beskalan Putri* (as suggested by Djupri) and the sexual appeal of female performers are ways in which the magnetic power of femaleness may be expressed and foster social harmony.

Onlookers did not have to rationally understand such deeper meanings in order to be healed and educated. Muskayah's spiritual power and her *ilmu* would have emanated from her, infusing those who watched as she performed. Judith Becker captures this idea of audiences being affected by the spiritual power that is believed to infuse performances of Javanese arts, writing that "[o]ne of the cultural aspects of Central Javanese gamelan tradition . . . is the fact that hearing any kind of gamelan music bestows upon the listener an aural blessing, even if the listener is not paying attention (!)" (2009: 19–20). This applies to the performance of east Javanese dance, too, such as *Beskalan Putri*, offering a means by and through which the female power of a dancer like Muskayah could affect others.

Strikingly, while Muskayah "mothered" her community and audiences, she did not conform to Old and New Order ideologies of a mother devoted to the home and care of her nuclear family. Djupri recognized that she sacrificed time at home with her own children when they were little because she was so busy with her career (p.c., February 7, 2006). At the same time, as discussed in chapter two, women have long worked outside of the home in Java (Brenner 1998). Djupri thus portrayed his grandmother in complex ways, synthesizing multiple ideologies about femininity and womanhood in Java.

I suggest that as he talked to me about Muskayah and *Beskalan Putri*, Djupri was responding to changes in the performance of the dance, working to ensure the continuity of longer versions of it into current times, and maintaining a space for the representation, embodiment, and accessibility of female power through it. Spiritual and physical power, confidence and perseverance, and social roles of protecting, healing, and educating infused the senses of femaleness that Djupri articulated through his narratives about Muskayah and *Beskalan Putri*. While these articulations were consistent with some models of womanhood projected through stories about legendary heroines, descriptions of women in the courts of the seventeenth to nineteenth centuries, and the activities of female revolutionaries in the twentieth century, they were a far cry from the more demure ideals promoted by the government through national discourses in Old Order (1945–1966) and New Order times (1966–1998). Djupri's portrayal of Muskayah also countered negative representations of female singer-dancers in dominant discourses by drawing attention to her power to heal. At the same time, he was remembering a beloved family member, making his concerns with preservation as well as the issues of cultural authority surrounding these concerns deeply personal.

Djupri's Concerns with Preservation and Issues of Cultural Authority

Djupri seemed to believe that he was given a special duty to preserve and protect his grandmother's *ilmu*—her spiritual knowledge about the dance including its movement, music, history, and symbolism—which he did to the best of his ability. Djupri's relationship with her was deeply meaningful to him and he was personally and emotionally invested in preserving his memories of her. He said that when he remembered her, he was "*bagaimana*," unable to find words; glassy-eyed, he said with the slightest catch in his voice, that of all her grandchildren, he was the closest to her (p.c., February 1, 2006). He also strove to protect what she wished to preserve. According to Djupri, Muskayah, too, was concerned with preservation. Muskayah did not want to teach her daughters, including Djupri's mother, because she did not want them to experience the ridicule and insults that she experienced as a dancer (p.c., November 12, 2005). Times had changed, Djupri explained, and devout Muslims (*santri*) were pressuring women to not study the arts (p.c., November 12, 2005). Muskayah was all too well aware of the conflicted position that female dancers occupied, and yet was also worried that her interpretation of *Beskalan Putri* would disappear if she did not pass it on (p.c., Djupri, February 7, 2006).

For their parts, according to Djupri, Muskayah's daughters were neither interested in learning nor had predilections toward music and dance. Perhaps social pressures discouraging women from pursuing careers as dancers had affected them. Perhaps they did not like to study dance anyway. For a variety of reasons, when it came to her own family, Muskayah decided to transfer her knowledge about the performance practice, history, and meanings of *Beskalan Putri* to Djupri, using his male body as a container for her *ilmu*.

Djupri frequently recalled studying *Beskalan Putri* with Muskayah. He learned this dance, and others, from her as a boy in the early 1950s (p.c., November 6, 12, 2005). He gained *ilmu* from her in their home as she taught him the movements, drumming, singing, and philosophical meanings through practice sessions and spiritual exercises. He related that he learned the drumming after just three lessons with her, but to prepare himself to receive this knowledge so quickly, he fasted and stood for a day and a night with his arms tied up to a beam (p.c., December 1, 2005). Interestingly, both Djupri's and Didik's narratives suggest the importance of the number three in Javanese spiritual beliefs and practices. Djupri also gained her *ilmu* through close personal contact—which implies that her *ilmu* permeated into him. Djupri related how she slept with him when he was little, explaining the symbolism of the dance as he drifted into slumber (p.c., February 1, 2006; June 5, 2006). Such moments must have been magical indeed for a child, and certainly constitutes a process of osmosis. He likely absorbed Muskayah's knowledge as he watched her teach other dancers, too. He recalled dancers, mostly women, coming to their home and studying *Beskalan* with her (p.c., December 1, 2005).

Significantly, Djupri's experiences also point to cultural spaces in which performers subverted dominant norms that linked femaleness to female bodies and maleness to male bodies as *ilmu* moved between females and males. One of these spaces was the home, demonstrating the cultural impact that women's activities in the home—such as Muskayah's teaching—can have in Java (Brenner 1995). In Djupri's experience, the home became a space of cultural resistance and gender negotiation. Sexed performing spaces were no less important as he performed *Beskalan Putri* in the "male" context of *lérok* (an older term for *ludruk*; see chapter three) in the 1950s and in the "female" context of *andhong* from the mid-1950s to the early 1960s (p.c., Djupri, June 15, 2006). Djupri thus subverted boundaries of sex and gender in multiple ways as he learned and performed this dance, thereby preserving Muskayah's *ilmu* and maintaining representations of female power through his own male body.

Djupri stressed that Muskayah chose him as the principal repository of her *ilmu*, explaining that she selected him in part because they had the same *weton*, or Javanese birthday (p.c., November 12, 2005; February 1, 2006). This means that they were born on the same confluence of the seven-day international week and five-day Javanese market week, a particular convergence that occurs every thirty-five days. Many in Java believe that individuals with the same *weton* are similar in character and disposition and have the potential to develop a particularly close relationship because one understands the other so deeply or because they "click" in ways that are otherwise unexplainable.

By invoking frequent contact and the intimacy of the bond with his grandmother, Djupri implied that more of Muskayah's *ilmu* permeated into him than into anyone else, making him a particularly endowed and authoritative repository of her knowledge. Djupri reinforced the frequency of their interactions by recalling that Muskayah had mostly retired from her busy performing career when he was a boy. Since she was at home, he related, she had lots of time to teach him—explaining that she was not able to spend the same amounts of time with her own children when they were little because she was so busy performing (p.c., February 7, 2006). The implication is that although he learned *Beskalan Putri* after just three lessons, he absorbed *ilmu* from her about this dance (and other dances), over the course of many years. Furthermore, according to Djupri, Muskayah taught many dancers, but he implied that she passed her most secret, potent forms of *ilmu*—including her *ilmu* about femaleness (and the power that came with it)—only to him, thus giving him the responsibility and the authority to protect and/or pass on this *ilmu* as he determined appropriate.

Djupri was invested in communicating and preserving his sense of tradition—which included his family's history and his ways of representing femaleness as he interacted with me. He knew that I was consulting other performers about *Beskalan*, including M. Soleh Adi Pramono and performers connected to Soleh and the Mangun Dharma Art Center (which Soleh directed), such as my principal gamelan teacher Kusnadi. Djupri also knew that I was consulting his uncle Supeno (Muskayah's son). Supeno, by his own accounts, learned by watching Muskayah perform and imitating her movements (p.c., March 18, 2006; June 27, 2006). Djupri, however, wanted to be sure that I also learned to dance *Beskalan Putri* from him as he had learned to perform it from Muskayah. Ironically, in referencing, representing, and maintaining femaleness as he learned from Muskayah, Djupri articulated the importance of femaleness to the constitution of his very identity as a male artist and a repository of authoritative cultural knowledge about east

Javanese traditions. In effect he reinforced a complementary relationship between male and female elements central in some Javanese worldviews and undermined the separation of maleness and femaleness promoted in dominant discourses.

Strategic Representations of Female Power

As artists contributed to ongoing transformations of *Beskalan Putri* as a Malangan tradition they represented the magnetic power of femaleness strategically as they adapted, taught, remembered, learned, performed, and talked about this dance. Artists like Chattam, Didik, and Djupri lived with memories of the traumatic times of the mid-1960s and had lived through the reign of the autocratic New Order regime. I have been suggesting that memories of these times, as well as performers' concerns with preservation, affected their approaches to the representation of femaleness through his dance.

The ways in which Didik and Djupri talked about learning *Beskalan Putri* reveals some of the ways in which femaleness was transmitted to and located in male bodies, contributing to males' abilities to express male femininity. Although Didik and Djupri learned *Beskalan Putri* in different time periods, in different places, and from different dancers, both men invoked memories of their teachers and highlighted the spiritual aspects of their learning processes, emphasizing their connections to *ilmu* and to performers of past times.

Didik's and Djupri's experiences learning to embody femaleness as they learned to perform *Beskalan Putri* were clearly both similar and different. In both cases, femaleness in the form of *ilmu* about *Beskalan* was passed to male minds and bodies, making transmission processes a means by and through which performers contested dominant gender norms that mapped femaleness to female bodies. At the same time, Djupri's and Didik's experiences point to different processes of gaining spiritual knowledge and different relationships with teachers. Didik's experience studying for a week with Rasimoen (a man), who did not speak much to Didik and was not a biological member of Didik's family, contrasts with the length and frequency of contact that Djupri had with Muskayah (a woman) over many years, who frequently spoke to him and was his grandmother. However, both men referenced their relationships with their teachers, relationships that have inspired them with a special sense of responsibility toward the dance and *ilmu* about it. Thus the embodiment of male femininity was not only about issues of gender, but also about issues of tradition.

Many performers I consulted had either witnessed or lived through the transformations of *Beskalan Putri* described in this chapter or had heard about such transformations from performers older than they. While they recognized that such transformations were necessary to keep *Beskalan Putri* relevant to current needs, and thus keep it in performed repertoire, they were also concerned about what was being lost. Working with me provided an opportunity and means for some performers to document *Beskalan Putri* (and other dances), in their longer, more complete forms as they understood them. Our documentation efforts, however, raised their own issues of tradition and gender, bringing me to the final chapter of this book.

6. Where Tradition, Power, and Gender Intersect

Performer Interactions

This chapter uses analysis of performer interaction to round off my exploration into gender, power, and tradition, bringing together many of the themes and issues discussed in previous chapters to demonstrate some of the ways that micro-moments of interaction on- and offstage are critical moments of complex cultural and ideological work. Intrigued by what my teachers indicated were the *asli*—the authentic, real, original, complete—forms of *Beskalan*, *Ngremo*, and masked dances, which they talked about reverently but rarely had opportunities to perform, I sponsored rehearsals and recording sessions with the aim of documenting as many of these dances in their entirety as I could. My teachers and the other musicians and dancers I involved expressed their enthusiasm about these opportunities to remember and transmit their senses of the past and tradition through these projects. The prospect of actually seeing and hearing what my teachers had implied were almost-forgotten movements and drumming patterns sent ripples of excitement down my spine.

My bright-eyed optimism was soon replaced by surprise and then concern when disagreements arose between performers as they interacted. Initially I had assumed that they imagined the same choreographies and drum patterns when they referred to the *asli* forms of these dances. I quickly learned, however, that they had their own personal senses of correctness about the movements and movement order that comprised the original, authentic, complete forms of the dances so central to their conceptions of Malangan and east Javanese tradition. I have come to understand and posit here that by resolving their differences of opinion prior to, during, and after any particular performance or rehearsal, musicians and dancers were continuously affecting culture. Specifically, they were negotiating their authority, a manifestation of their spiritual power, as they compromised and cooperated to actively produce tradition, and in so doing, articulated senses of gender (see also Sunardi 2011).

This chapter expands and develops a previously published analysis of performer interaction and gender (Sunardi 2011). My interest in the cultural implications of performer interaction in that article and in this chapter has been most strongly influenced by the work of Benjamin Brinner (1995), whose theory of interaction and attention to performers' competence orient my approach. Building on Brinner's attention to the importance of competence and authority in shaping interactions between performers as well as the ways such interactions affect what is performed, I focus on the relationship between the dancer and the drummer, showing that who actually leads and when depends on a number of factors, including who is more experienced, who is more competent, and who is more assertive (Brinner 1995: 288). Equally pertinent is who makes a mistake at what point in the performance. Tensions between submitting to and resisting authority also affect interaction, particularly given that leadership roles in Javanese performance structures are divided (Brinner 1995: 297; Walton 2007: 37). My research corroborates Henry Spiller's point that the space for the negotiation of authority—the space that exists when it is not always clear who is leading and who is following—allows dancers and drummers to negotiate their senses of gender (2010: 73, 75). I also build on Sarah Weiss's attention to interactions as gendered and the importance of gendered interactions to the continuous production of a performance tradition (2006: 161).

I argue that contradictions between dominant ideologies that privilege the knowledge of a more senior male and a performance structure in which leadership roles are flexible provide spaces for men and women to negotiate their authority and articulate senses of gender in different ways as they negotiate the form and content of a dance. This argument underscores two ways in which interactions between drummers and dancers affect culture: interaction in performance provides spaces for males and females to work out, contest, transform, and/or reaffirm social norms that privilege the authority of older men; and through their interactions, performers generate a particular interpretation of a dance and its music, audibly and visibly contributing to the continuous production and transformation of particular dance traditions. Like Sonja Lynn Downing, who also builds on Brinner (1995), I am interested in how gender, competence, confidence, experience, and age—as well as performers' perceptions of these factors—affect the ways performers negotiate authority and produce particular senses of masculinity and femininity through these negotiations (Downing 2010: 54, 66–68, 71–72). I am also interested in the ways some performers embody the magnetic power of femaleness, thereby maintaining it in Javanese culture.

Relationships between Performers in Terms of Relationships within a Family

In talking about east Javanese presentational dance and its accompanying gamelan music, B. Supriono Hadi Prasetya described the relationship between the drummer and the dancer as one of partnership, explaining that you could call them husband and wife (p.c., November 10, 2005). Supriono's use of this metaphor captures the complexity of the relationship between the drummer and the dancer in Malangan dance, evoking dynamics of power and constructions of gender in a contemporary Javanese context. Complex cultural contradictions underlie the husband-wife metaphor. Like a family, dance performance involves particular roles and relationships between the performers. With these relationships come dynamics of power related to structures of gender and age (Locher-Scholten and Niehof 1987: 9; Errington 1990: 47–48).

On the one hand, the metaphor expresses the complementary nature of male and female elements characteristic of some Javanese worldviews, the powerful position that many women hold within the family as discussed in chapter two (Brenner 1995, 1998), and the give-and-take relationship between the dancer and the drummer. A special and complex relationship exists between the dancer and the drummer in part because the dance movements and drumming patterns are intricately related: the drum patterns express in sound what the dancer performs in movement. As a duo of sorts, the dancer and the drummer shape a particular realization of the dance as they work together. In the context of performers' discourses about interacting in ideal situations, the husband-wife metaphor implies a more-or-less equal, gendered partnership between the drummer and the dancer.

On the other hand, in the context of dominant discourses about family and nation in Indonesia, a husband-wife metaphor also evokes the power and authority given to men as husbands and fathers (Shiraishi 1997; Blackwood 2005; Weiss 2006). Given that most drummers are male and are frequently authoritative members of a group, the husband-wife metaphor implies that dancers should defer to the drummer as women should defer to their husbands and as sons and daughters should defer to their fathers. Also implied is that the musicians should primarily follow the drummer—rather than the dancer—as the dominant "father" figure.

Interestingly, Suradi, Kadam, and Lestari, all men we met in chapter three who had performed as *tandhak ludruk* (*ludruk* artists who specialize in female roles), took a deferential stance to the drummer, placing their trust in him and relying on his guidance. Suradi asserted that east Javanese dance "obeys" (*nurut*) the drum (p.c., May 2, 2006). Kadam and Lestari believed faithfully that drummers would remember the dance. When I asked Kadam about the drummer forgetting, he replied assuredly, "There aren't any that forget, there aren't. They all already know it by heart" ("*Ndak ada yang lupa, ndak ada. O sudah hafal semua*") (p.c., May 23, 2006). Lestari described how the drumming reminded him of movements he might have forgotten on his own (p.c., April 30, 2006). By conceding to and relying on the drummer's authority, even though drummers sometimes do forget (as I discuss below), these men who were specialists in female style dance articulated senses of femininity that were consistent with national constructions in which women are subordinate to men's leadership. They thereby expressed senses of the male femininity they embodied onstage in their offstage conversations with me.

Deference to the drummer did not necessarily suggest "feminine" or "feminized" behavior, however. The degree of competence and confidence among individual men and women was also a factor. The male dancer Witanto (b. 1968), who performed male style dances, said that he frequently waits a brief moment to hear what movement the drumming pattern indicates. Witanto was not necessarily challenging dominant ideas about masculinity by deferring to a more authoritative male. In cases involving an older drummer, he was positioning himself as a "son" in relation to a "father." Because Kusnadi knows Witanto's tendencies, Kusnadi knows that he must lead with his drumming and thereby assume a fatherly role of leading a son (p.c., July 30, 2006).

Furthermore, women were not always deferential, showing that some challenged official ideologies that encouraged them to defer to "fathers" or "husbands," and instead insisted on a more or less equal partnership. At one rehearsal, after running *Ngremo Putri* with a female dancer, the dancer told the male drummer in front of the other musicians and me that he had omitted several movements and that she had just followed his drumming. In so doing, she not only challenged ideals of women deferring to men, she went against a cultural ideal of not pointing out a person's mistakes in front of others. For his part, the drummer sat and listened, smiling. He then told me, and most likely the other performers within earshot, that he shortened the dance because he was tired. A few days later he confessed that he really had forgotten the movements in question and just said that he was tired as an excuse.

These artists negotiated their authority as they interacted during this rehearsal. The male drummer preserved his control without overtly challenging the female dancer by maintaining that he made the decisions about the course of the dance. The dancer's directness in expressing her opinion was probably related to the fact that she was in a similar age group as the drummer. Born in the mid-1950s, she was about ten years his junior (he was born in the mid-1940s), and as a woman in her early fifties in relation to a man in his early sixties, she was more in a "wifely" relationship with him than a "daughterly" relationship. That they knew each other may have also affected their interactions. Her confident personality was certainly no less a factor. Whatever the factors, she challenged dominant constructions of womanhood by refusing to simply concede her authority to a man's. By choosing to follow the drummer's playing despite the omissions of certain movements, and announcing that she did so to the others present, she reaffirmed her knowledge and command of the dance, thereby also manifesting female power in the form of a woman's authority in performing a female style dance.

"Selling and Buying"

Describing ideal situations, many drummers and dancers explained that no one person leads in real-time performance, but that the dancer and the drummer "sell and buy" (*dol-tinuku* in Javanese and *jual-beli* in Indonesian) so that the articulation of the dancer's movements and the drumming patterns precisely match. To "sell" is to initiate an interaction while to "buy" is to follow, or accept what has been "offered." Buying and selling between drummers and dancers is possible because there is room for them to intentionally or unintentionally make decisions in the course of performance (Nettl 1998). The dances that I have discussed in this book—*Beskalan*, *Ngremo*, and masked dance—are memorized, but not entirely fixed. Dancers and drummers usually know or decide upon the movement order or general movement order. Some movement sequences may be repeated, and often the number of repetitions is also decided prior to performance. Sometimes, however, performers intentionally or unintentionally repeat particular sections, omit movements, vary the movement order, and/or adjust the tempo as they realize the dance. The spaces for the drummer and the dancer to lead and to follow each other facilitate the realization of the dance in performance because often little or no rehearsal is involved.

The formulaity of drumming patterns and dance movements as well as the correlation between these patterns and movements allow competent performers to make quick decisions as they listen to and watch each other in action. Similarly, in his study of drummer-dancer interaction in Martinican *bèlè*, Julian Gerstin recognizes that performers can respond to each other quickly because they know which drumming patterns accompany which movements (1998: see especially 152–158). The correlation may become so naturalized for experienced artists in Malang that they feel like they do not have to think. Kusnadi, for one, talked about the drum patterns coming out of the hands on their own after the drumming was learned by heart (p.c., February 4, 2006).

Dancers in Malang sold to and bought from the drummer by tapping the *gongsèng*—the ankle bells—for dances in which the *gongsèng* was used, such as *Beskalan*, *Ngremo*, and the masked dances *Gunung Sari*, *Bapang*, and *Klana*. As I learned from dancers and from my own experience dancing, the dancer can communicate to the drummer by signaling the beginnings and endings of particular sections, adjusting the tempo by tapping the *gongsèng* faster or slower, and using the *gongsèng* to remind the drummer when he has forgotten a movement. The *gongsèng* also provides continuous sonic input to the drummer, giving him a sense of what the dancer is doing, or going to do—and alerting him when the dancer's movements do not match the drumming—even if he is not looking at the dancer. At the same time, the *gongsèng* can sonically confirm that dancers have "bought" from the drummer. Not surprisingly, performers such as Sumantri and Lestari, who believed that the dancer should follow the drummer, did not attribute a leading role to the *gongsèng* (p.c., Sumantri, April 23, 2006; Lestari, April 30, 2006).

The drummer most typically sold to the dancer through drumming patterns. Given that drumming patterns and dance movements do not necessarily correspond in a one-to-one relationship, the dancer's knowledge of the dance affected his or her ability to buy from the drummer. Already having memorized, or at least having some idea of the movements and their order, the dancer could be reminded of a specific movement by the drumming. Sometimes the drummer intentionally used drum patterns to correct a dancer's mistakes or lapses of memory: rather than buying the dancer's error, the drummer reminded the dancer by playing the pattern of the "correct" movement—sometimes slightly louder to gain the dancer's attention.

Strikingly, "forgetting" can also reinforce a performer's influence to determine the course of the dance. Kusnadi admitted to some masked dancers (who were men younger than him) during a rehearsal that he could forget the movement order of some sections and they should know which movements went with which drumming patterns so that they could follow (p.c., May 1, 2006). By telling the dancers that he might forget, Kusnadi indirectly ensured that they pay attention to and buy from him, the more senior man. This was a particularly effective strategy—whether intentional or not—when he and dancers had different opinions about the correct way to perform a dance.

The husband-wife metaphor Supriono used also suggests the roles of the musicians to follow the decisions made by the drummer-dancer duo, similar to an ideal familial structure in which sons and daughters defer to the authority of their parents—a "husband-wife" duo. As the rest of the musicians supporting and following the drummer and the dancer as a duo, they reinforced the drummer-dancer relationship as a more or less equal partnership.

"Taking Care" of Each Other

Dancers and drummers also consistently talked in terms of taking care of each other. Their use of the Javanese words *momong* or *ngemong*—which also refers to taking care of a baby or small child, with the implication of doing so tenderly and patiently—captures a particular sense of trust that ideally exists between drummers and dancers. Ward Keeler writes, "[n]*gemong* means to look after a child, with the understanding that one must indulge and amuse him as well as keep an eye on him" (1983: 154). A drummer may take care of the dancer if he or she is less competent or still a beginner because the drummer expects that the dancer, still in the "childlike" state of learning, will make mistakes. Likewise, dancers may take care of the drummer for the same reasons, "keeping an eye" on the drummer by listening carefully and, in some cases, stealing a quick look at the drummer or giving a little cue with the head. Buying and selling to take care of one another is also a mechanism that reinforces Javanese social norms, such as not embarrassing someone in front of others.

Performers take care of each other by leading or by following. On the one hand, a dancer or drummer may lead the one who does not know the particular dance well or forgets the movement or movement order. On the other hand, a dancer or drummer may have to follow the one who makes a mistake or forgets the movement order that has been agreed upon prior to the performance in order to conceal the other's error. Performers consistently noted that the give-and-take relationship enables the dancer or the drummer to cover the other's mistakes and lapses of memory, exemplifying the interactive network's potential to function as a "safety net" (Brinner 1995: 179). This also reinforces ideas about etiquette in Java about not embarrassing someone in front of others. Kusnadi and Achmad Suwarno explained that the drummer always has to watch the dancer in order to follow him or her if he or she makes a mistake so that the audience will not know (p.c., Kusnadi, February 4, 2006; Achmad Suwarno, February 12, 2006; see Photograph 6.1). Kusnadi explained that he followed me when I forgot to repeat a dance movement during a performance of *Beskalan Putri* and that this was why

Where Tradition, Power, and Gender Intersect 165

Photograph 6.1: A drummer looks toward the stage while playing for *Ngremo Putri* at a *ludruk* performance, likely watching the dancers, 2006.

the drummer should always be watching the dancer—to take care of him or her by concealing his or her errors and helping him or her through the dance as smoothly as possible (p.c., January 19, 2006). He had followed me, too, when I inadvertently omitted a significant portion of a masked dance, instructing the musicians to skip ahead to the change in composition that was necessary to cover my error.

The competence of the dancer also affected the likelihood of Kusnadi's watching him or her closely. He knew by dancers' movements and *gongsèng* when they were confused and so watched them carefully. I observed dancers catch their own mistake and switch back to the movement that they should have performed had they not erred. Kusnadi seemed to read their minds as he followed. He often looked away when he believed that the dancer was clearly in control of the movement and confident in his or her ability to follow his drumming.

The one who follows to conceal the error in effect reinforces his or her competence and authority, particularly when he or she does so unnoticeably. Highlighting his own competence, Suradi said that if the drummer made a mistake, he could follow because he himself could play the drum (p.c., May

2, 2006). An aspect of Kusnadi's competence that impressed other performers was his special ability to take care of dancers in the ways described above (p.c., Stefanus Yacobus Suryantono, January 21, 2006; Budi Utomo, January 2006; Sumi'anah, May 10, 2006; Witanto, July 30, 2006). Significantly, this indicates that assertions of authority and competence are not always about leading.

Motivations to Sell and Buy: Concerns with the Preservation of Tradition

In addition to the social norms and conventions of performance that affected interactions, performers had their own reasons for selling and buying in particular ways. Brinner uses "interactive motivation" as a "rubric" for "the 'why' of interaction, the goals, rewards, pitfalls, and sanctions" (1995: 169). The goals of performing well and the avoidance of a dancer or drummer embarrassing the other in front of the audience were two motivations that I have already identified. Any one individual might have had many motivations for participating, including economic (getting paid) and social (playing with friends).

Correctness was also a key motivation in the realizations of *asli* forms of *Beskalan*, *Ngremo*, and masked dance. Eve Harwood provides insight into why personal ideas of correctness were so important to performers. In her study of African American girls' singing games, she writes, "[w]ithout a written retrieval system, everyone in an oral tradition becomes responsible in some sense for maintaining the authenticity of the repertoire" (Harwood 1998: 114). In the case of *Beskalan*, *Ngremo*, and masked dance, although the basic or skeletal melody—and sometimes the colotomic structure—of the music was notated, the dance movements and much of the musical elaborations were not. Much of the knowledge about these dances and their music thus lay in the realm of oral (and visual) tradition. Ideas of correctness were important to performers because, working without a single, fixed, written, authoritative text, they were striving to maintain authentic Malangan and east Javanese traditions.

As we have seen in this book, many performers were concerned with the maintenance of local tradition and had witnessed the decline in the popularity of *Beskalan Putri* and masked dance over the course of their lifetimes; they feared that these dances as well as Malangan performing arts in general would be completely replaced by more popular styles of music, dance, and theater from central Java and Surabaya (see also Sutton 1991; Sunardi 2010a). Reinforcing this fear of loss is that when *Beskalan Putri* and masked dances are performed, often shortened versions are used, as discussed in chapter five for *Beskalan Putri*. They had also seen *Ngremo Putri* transform dramatically as it came to absorb influences from *Ngremo Tayub* and the popular musics *dangdut* and *campur sari*, discussed in chapter three. In a sense, performers were seeing a loss of Malangan tradition not only through shortened versions of *Beskalan Putri*, but also through the transformations of *Ngremo Putri* that departed from the femaleness, refinement, and power that they associated with *Beskalan Putri*, a point made in chapter four.

Some artists, including my teachers, sought to preserve what they believed were complete, authentic versions of *Beskalan, Ngremo*, and masked dances in performed repertoire and in living memory. They used their opportunities to work with me to export *asli* forms of these dances and to preserve them in the archives of a foreign academic. Different artists, however, had different ideas about what exactly constituted the *asli* forms of dances, leading some to compete in order to establish whose memories of the dance—whose senses of the past—carried the most clout.

Politics of knowledge motivated performers in other ways. Kusnadi's musicians believed in the authority of his knowledge, which contributed to their trust in him as their group leader. For some he was also their teacher or older brother. For these reasons, they seemed unconditionally loyal to him. When disagreements arose between Kusnadi and another performer, the musicians sided with Kusnadi. When Kusnadi gave in to the other's wishes, the musicians followed. The presence of other performers who were not playing or dancing also affected the interactions between those performing: sometimes a performer attempted to assert his or her competence and authority in front of others or was affected by their authority.

My own personal and working relationships with performers was not without ramifications in terms of performers' motivations: before long, I became entangled in local cultural politics surrounding the selection of tradition and thereby implicated in the production of local culture. Kay Kaufman Shelemay rightly emphasizes "that as ethnomusicologists become engaged in research with living musical traditions and the people who carry them, they both intentionally and unwittingly become caught up in the processes and politics of transmission of tradition" (1997: 197). I recognize in retrospect that some performers were motivated to assert their own authority as my teacher when they interacted with each other in front of me. Not realizing that at the time, I may have put them in uncomfortable situations by asking them to perform with each other. Furthermore, different senses of correctness about the performance of Malangan music and dance among the performers I consulted motivated some performers to work with me as a means to document their particular interpretations, which in some cases meant that they were implicitly or explicitly asserting the authority of their knowledge in relation to that of other artists.

Recognizing the flexibility of music and dance in Malang, most performers I consulted did not assume that knowledge about how to perform a particular piece or dance was authoritative simply because it had been institutionalized, such as through publications, commercial cassette recordings, or by being taught in particular ways through particular arts organizations. Instead they evaluated the authority of an individual's knowledge using other criteria, such as the kind of training and experience he or she had. Those considered most authoritative usually came from families of musicians and/or dancers and had learned by performing since their childhoods. Furthermore, because performers, especially dancers, were assumed to have specialties based on what they most frequently performed, some individuals were considered authoritative for one kind of dance but not for others. Memory was another criterion: the further back in the past a performer could remember increased the credibility of his or her knowledge. In most cases this gave more weight to the knowledge of older performers.

At the same time, the exercise of authority was not necessarily synonymous with the insistence on one's own correctness. Often, demonstrating authority meant being in control of making decisions—including choosing to concede to less knowledgeable, less experienced performers. Although paradoxical, conceding in some contexts was consistent with the cultural value placed on indirect manifestations of power in Java as well as performers' efforts to take care of each other as they bought and sold.

A Lesson and a Recording Session

Even brief moments of interaction reveal the many cultural, personal, and aesthetic factors that affect a particular realization of a dance and thereby contribute to the movements and sounds that are selected to comprise tradition. To foreground some of the decision-making processes and cultural factors that underlie specific interactions in particular contexts, I analyze interactions that contributed to particular realizations of *Beskalan Putri*. I draw examples from two instances with which I was most familiar, one of my lessons and one of the video recording sessions I sponsored to document *Beskalan sing asli*. As the participating artists worked to remember *Beskalan sing asli*, they negotiated their personal senses of tradition and their senses of their authority. In so doing, they articulated senses of masculinity and femininity as they interacted within cultural structures and within structures of performance related to gender and age.

A Lesson

Supeno, whom we have met in previous chapters, wished to confirm that I was learning *Beskalan sing asli* correctly and expressed his interest in seeing me dance and hearing me play the drum. Eager for the opportunity to learn from Supeno, and with Kusnadi's approval, I invited him to one of my lessons with Kusnadi. When Supeno arrived, Kusnadi was immediately deferential, asking me to play in order to "check" with Supeno the drumming that Kusnadi had taught me. Supeno graciously confirmed that my drumming was correct. Kusnadi then asked Supeno to play the drum. Taking a modest stance, Supeno said repeatedly that he had forgotten much of the dance (and its drumming) because it had been years since he had performed *Beskalan Putri*. Kusnadi accepted Supeno's conditions, but continued to encourage him gently. Supeno finally agreed to try (Photograph 6.2). I danced along to demonstrate the movements I had learned. He did omit over half of the dance, and at one point slipped into the drumming for *Ngremo*. Kusnadi helped him by singing the drumming for *Beskalan*. Kusnadi then requested to play the drum himself to verify whether his own playing was correct or not.

Afterward, the two men exchanged comments cordially, each verbalizing his respect for the other's knowledge and ability. Supeno praised Kusnadi's drumming, saying that it matched or was precise (*sudah pas*). When Kusnadi pointed out that Supeno had started to play the drum patterns for *Ngremo*, Supeno apologized, saying that it had been years since he had danced or

Photograph 6.2: Supeno at the drum at the Mangun Dharma Art Center, 2006.

played the drum for *Beskalan*. Sympathetic to this error, Kusnadi said that it was easy to slip between the two dances (p.c., June 29, 2006).

Despite Supeno's mistakes and lapses of memory, several factors contributed to Kusnadi's respect for Supeno's knowledge, including Supeno's age. Born in 1923, Supeno was about twenty years older than Kusnadi, who was born in 1944. Kusnadi said frequently that he wanted to learn more from people older than he was because they knew how dances were realized further back in the past. Kusnadi's attitude reinforces Shelly Errington's observations that in island Southeast Asia "[s]eniors—those who are older by absolute age or by generation or by birth order within a generation—are superior to juniors because they are closer to the ancestral source than juniors are" (1990: 47). In other words, Kusnadi valued Supeno's authority because Supeno was closer to *Beskalan*'s ancestors (other older dancers, including those who were deceased) than Kusnadi. Kusnadi also valued the knowledge Supeno had gained from his experience as a *Beskalan Putri* dancer in the past. Kusnadi recognized Supeno's authority in the embodiment of femininity he believed appropriate for this dance, on some level recognizing the magnetic female power Supeno could access and embody (and perhaps still accessed and embodied) despite his maleness. Kusnadi also responded positively to Supeno's modesty and receptiveness of Kusnadi's assistance. Supeno may have acted this way simply because of his personality. Perhaps, too, Supeno knew that he did not have to overtly assert his authority because Kusnadi was so clearly Supeno's junior.

Through their interactions, Kusnadi and Supeno also articulated senses of masculinity as younger and older men as they negotiated their senses of how femaleness should be performed. Interestingly, even though Kusnadi showed his deference to Supeno, as a son would (ideally) show a father, he still "took care" of Supeno by guiding him through the drumming for the dance—much as a son might take care of an elderly parent. Since Kusnadi had been more active as a drummer than Supeno, he remembered *Beskalan* better and was thus in some ways the more knowledgeable performer at the moment of my lesson, even though he was younger and deferential to Supeno's authority.

A Video Recording Session

Interactions that resulted in what participating artists determined to be a less than ideal performance of femaleness insightfully revealed performers' attitudes about gender, ways they believed gender should be represented, and ways they produced it as they negotiated their senses of Malang tradition. I sponsored a video recording session in order to document Budi Utomo's and Kusnadi's interpretations of the first part of *Beskalan sing asli*—although without singing because Utomo did not feel comfortable performing the vocal part. In addition to documenting the particular interpretation of the dance as two of my principal teachers worked together, I also sought to determine whether musicians' senses of the dancer's biological sex affected the ways they played, given that cross-gender dance was not unusual in Malang and that *Beskalan Putri* had a history of being performed by both males and females. I was curious as to whether senses of sex affected articulations of gender. For these reasons, I also invited Wahyu Winarti (b. 1978) to dance, asking Utomo and Wahyu to each take a turn dancing solo. I invited musicians who had worked often with Wahyu, Utomo, Kusnadi, and me to play the other instruments of the gamelan (Photograph 6.3). Despite my goals of documenting *Beskalan sing asli* as they performed it, I have come to view the video I made (as well as my field videos and audio recordings in general) in a similar manner as the Native American artists and producers Beverley Diamond consulted viewed their CDs—that is, "as the 'documentation of a process'" (2005: 123).

Photograph 6.3: Musicians playing during the recording session, including, from left to right, Miskan, Supriadi (rear), Asbari, Komari, Juma'i, and Kusnadi, 2006.

By working with each other, Utomo and Kusnadi produced a particular interpretation of *Beskalan Putri*. Utomo sought to perform the first part of a reconstructed *Beskalan sing asli* as part of his own efforts to preserve Malangan dance traditions. Assuming that he could reconstruct the movements of the complete dance (or at least come closer to it) by making a composite of movements he compiled from older dancers, he worked to combine movement vocabularies he had learned from Riati, Rasimoen, and more recently through my fieldwork, from Djupri. In addition to his memory of their movements and the movements implied by the music on *Aneka Gending Tari Malangan, Volume 2* (n.d.), he also referred to an audio recording he had made with his tape recorder of Riati performing at PSMD (Padepokan Seni Mangun Dharma [Mangun Dharma Art Center]) in the early 1990s.

Prior to the day of the video session I organized, I had relayed to Kusnadi Utomo's goal of incorporating movements from Riati. While Kusnadi readily agreed, he also emphasized the flexibility of this dance as performed by explaining that both Riati and Rasimoen performed *Beskalan* differently depending on what movements they or the drummers remembered during a particular performance. In effect, Kusnadi and Utomo combined their memories of the dancers they had seen perform to generate their own realization of the first part of *Beskalan sing asli*, albeit minus the singing.

I failed, however, to anticipate that Utomo's nervousness would inhibit him from performing as well as he would have liked. I had seen him demonstrate, rehearse, teach, and perform male style masked and nonmasked dances with the entrancing grace, fluidity, strength, and charisma of a master. He had consistently danced *Beskalan Putri* beautifully and confidently during my lessons with him and had spoken about his experiences performing female style masked dance. He had attributed his ability to look like a woman on stage to spontaneity (*spontanitas*), from the movement and demeanor. Recognizing that his competence was not entirely his own, Utomo said that his ability to dance was a gift from God, thus using religiously inspired discourse (he identified as Muslim) to legitimize his expression of contingent male femininity (p.c., January 6, 2006) (Sunardi 2013: 152–153). For these reasons, I did not think that asking him to perform a female style dance was inappropriate or odd.

Also, some months earlier, I had asked him to dance *Beskalan Putri* for a December 2005 performance at PSMD that I had sponsored in part to celebrate my birthday and in part to document Malangan gamelan music. Utomo had declined my invitation to perform *Beskalan Putri*, but he offered to perform a male style masked dance instead as a birthday gift to me (which he did), promising to perform *Beskalan Putri* another time. This led me to believe that if he did not wish to perform *Beskalan Putri* for my recording session, he would have politely refused.

Nonetheless, I unwittingly put Utomo into an uncomfortable situation. I paired him with a drummer who was about twenty years older and a more experienced artist: Utomo was expected to concede his authority as my teacher to another man he knew was also my teacher in front of me. Having him perform *Beskalan Putri* in full costume—something that he had never done before—further affected his level of self-assurance. As I learned, for him, performing female style masked dance and female style nonmasked dance were two different matters. That he had shaved his mustache just for the recording session exacerbated his discomfort with his appearance. It also indicated just how important having me document his interpretation of this dance was to him as well as his commitment to me.

As Clifford Geertz (1957), among others, has shown, much is to be learned through unexpected developments in performance. For Geertz, the unexpected events of a funeral for a child in rural Java—including the refusal of the local religious functionary to officiate, the delayed ceremonial washing and burial of the child's body, and the unusual expressions of emotion by the child's distressed parents—exposed the structures of the ritual's performance and led Geertz to new insights into larger issues of social change related to Islamic modernism (1957). Similarly, although less heart-wrenchingly, Utomo's unexpected nervousness affected his interactions with Kusnadi in some unforeseen ways, exposing the structures of performance and power. The larger issues at hand were the negotiations of authority through articulations of gender—that is, negotiations of authority through the performance of gendered dance styles as well as through the enactment of gendered roles and relationships during the course of the video recording session.

Articulating Senses of Masculinity   Utomo articulated his senses of maleness in terms of authority, sexuality, and gender: He was negotiating his authority as a male artist in a situation where his sexuality and gender as a heterosexual man implicitly became an issue. Supriono, who was helping me to run the recording session, mused that the gamelan musicians may have inadvertently further lowered Utomo's confidence as they likened him to a *tandhak ludruk* (p.c., August 4, 2006). In effect, the musicians' teasing evoked multiple senses of femaleness that they imagined when they saw a male in a *Beskalan Putri* costume, including a history of female impersonation. As covered in chapter four, the costume most frequently used for *Ngremo Putri* is very similar, in some cases nearly identical, to the costume most frequently used for *Beskalan Putri*, which Utomo was wearing. Many aspects of the music and movement of both dances are also similar (Sunardi 2010a, 2010b).

These similarities, plus the historical connections many performers perceived between the two dances, connected female impersonation of the past to that of current times in performers' minds. The musicians' teasing also evoked many *tandhak*'s offstage lives as *waria* (males who dress and live as female), forms of same-sex relationships, and associations with prostitution, further feminizing Utomo.

Utomo, not particularly caring for the manner in which he was being compared to a *tandhak ludruk*, I believe, sought to distance himself from the types of femaleness that many Javanese associate with *tandhak ludruk*. He was ambivalent about the male femininity he was evoking with his own male body when not dancing. For these reasons, he was motivated to reaffirm his masculinity, which he did in several ways, such as maintaining the authority of his knowledge. Neither his authority nor its assertion were necessarily gendered in and of themselves, but by asserting his authority as a knowledgeable dancer who knew *Beskalan sing asli*, Utomo was insisting that he was still Utomo, i.e., an acknowledged dance expert who was a man. However, in so doing, he contradicted social ideals by not always deferring as a younger man to an older man as sons should defer to their fathers. For example, Utomo verbally communicated his wishes to Kusnadi, asserting his particular senses of correctness rather than yielding as a deferential "son" to Kusnadi's ideas without contest.

Utomo also articulated his masculinity through body language. As Kusnadi and Utomo discussed which movements and corresponding drumming patterns to include, Kusnadi sat at the drum while Utomo stood in front of him. At one time, Utomo stood with his legs slightly apart and his hands on his hips. The position of his legs was similar to positions used in some types of male style dance, conveying an air of masculinity that was a striking contrast to the female persona implied through the costume that Utomo was wearing. While such a stance could also be taken to be impolite, I do not believe that Utomo intended to come across as rude; I found him a very polite and sensitive person. However, he did seem to be asserting his authority through a "manly" stance despite, or perhaps because of, factors that feminized him in relation to Kusnadi—the female style costume, the musicians' teasing, and his position as the younger male.

Kusnadi did not always take Utomo's comments about the inclusion or exclusion of particular movements as authoritative—sometimes to Utomo's frustration—because Utomo did not have prior experience performing *Beskalan Putri* as a dancer. Although Utomo knew the dance and taught it, he specialized in masked dance. Kusnadi knew of Utomo's specialization. In contrast, Kusnadi had accompanied a number of *Beskalan Putri* dancers in performance, was the drummer for *Beskalan Putri* on the cassette *Aneka Gending Tari Malangan, Volume 2* (n.d.), and is recognized in Malang for his ability to play the drum for just about any dance. Kusnadi also had more years of experience performing and had seen *Beskalan* performed further back in the past than Utomo (p.c., Kusnadi, 2006). As the clearly older, more experienced man, Kusnadi had the cultural authority given to father figures, which put Utomo into the position of a "son" in terms of age and experience. Kusnadi's assertions of authority may have exacerbated Utomo's nervousness. One result was a performance that satisfied neither man.

Utomo's nervousness and articulations of masculinity contributed to a tempo that he and Kusnadi found to be too fast. Utomo said that the musicians kept pushing the tempo, particularly toward the end, which affected the feel (p.c., August 5, 2006). Kusnadi admitted that he played at a relatively faster tempo, providing several reasons. One was that he found Utomo's expression to be manly, even though he was dancing female style dance (p.c., August 7, 2006). In other words, the femaleness evoked by the dance and the costume did not trump the maleness that Kusnadi perceived in Utomo's movement and demeanor. He recognized that Utomo did not perform femaleness as convincingly as possible because Utomo was nervous and inexperienced performing this dance, and not simply because he was a male. Other reasons Kusnadi provided included Utomo's tendency to rush and Utomo's memory lapses—which Kusnadi also attributed to Utomo's nerves. Kusnadi said that he played the drum at a faster tempo because he was working to follow (p.c., August 5 and 7, 2006). One implication is that he could not relax and simply play. In short, both men pointed to the faster tempo as a factor that contributed to a less than ideal performance of *Beskalan Putri* and the femaleness that it represented.

By helping Utomo in performance (and by specifying the ways he helped), Kusnadi articulated a fatherly sense of masculinity and reinforced his own authoritative knowledge. For example, in one sequence, a slow walking movement is followed by a transitional movement pattern. After this transitional pattern the slow walk may be repeated or a fast walk may be performed. Whether or not the slow walk is repeated at this point is a decision that the dancer and drummer typically make prior to the performance. Kusnadi and Utomo had decided to repeat the slow walk to perform the dance consistently with their ideas of *Beskalan sing asli*. However, Utomo forgot to repeat the slow walk during his take. Kusnadi followed, buying the fast walking movement that Utomo sold.

Strikingly, in this instance it was the older, more experienced man who followed the younger man of lesser experience. Yet, in Java, those who follow by buying do not necessarily concede their authority, but in some cases prove both their authority and their competence. In "taking care" of Utomo, Kusnadi effectively demonstrated to the other performers present that he had greater command of the dance, delicately balancing his motivations to maintain authenticity and to assert a fatherly sense of authority by deciding when to follow and when to lead.

Kusnadi's work to take care of Utomo also complicates ideas about power and relationships between males in Java. On one level, manifesting authority subtly in performance is consistent with the value that many Javanese place on indirect expressions of power. As discussed in this book, according to dominant, male-centered Javanese aristocratic ideals, refined behavior manifests an individual's power and is thus often highly valued in many contexts, particularly in interactions between males (Anderson 1990a; Keeler 1987; Djajadiningrat-Nieuwenhuis 1987; Brenner 1995, 1998; Weiss 2006; Sears 2007). Refined, indirect expressions of authority are also preferred in interactions between musicians in the performance of central Javanese gamelan (Brinner 1995) and between the puppeteer and musicians in the performance of central Javanese shadow puppet theater (Keeler 1987: 180–183), also contexts involving predominantly male performers. It is also important to bear in mind, as Karen Elizabeth Schrieber shows through her analysis of Malangan hobbyhorse dancing and masked dance drama, that not all Javanese aspire to refinement and that performers also negotiate power and authority through more unrefined means (1991).

Following dominant notions of power in Java, ideal expressions of authority are those that are refined and indirect because powerful individuals should not have to visibly exercise their authority by raising their voices or giving direct orders; a sign of their power is that they need only to make suggestions or requests (Anderson 1990a: 54). In addition to manifesting power, indirect and refined expressions of authority imply the high amount of knowledge that an individual has because one way to gain power is through knowledge (Anderson 1990a: 54–58), also seen in this book. In other words, the more knowledge one has, the more power he or she can acquire and/or access. If one were to directly and overtly insist on his or her authority, he or she would be showing that he or she has a lesser amount of power and is therefore less knowledgeable. By taking care of Utomo, Kusnadi was indirectly asserting his authority and thereby manifesting his power and his knowledge as a masculine, fatherly figure through a dominant, male-centered paradigm of power.

On another level, Kusnadi's decision to follow Utomo adds another dimension to the expression and negotiation of power in Java. It may seem that

Kusnadi's decision to follow either contradicts the idea that others follow the lead of a powerful person or indicates that Kusnadi was not that powerful. However, Kusnadi was not conceding his authority to Utomo, but working to help Utomo and was thereby expressing his command of the situation. Kusnadi was the person in control of making decisions, including the decision to concede to a less knowledgeable artist for the sake of a smoother performance, a move that can also be understood by the Javanese word *ngalah*. As Ward Keeler explains, *ngalah* "expresses the decision on the part of a stronger or more righteous party to yield voluntarily to another" and "is an ability much praised in Java" (1983: 156). By indirectly cementing his leadership and the authority of his knowledge, Kusnadi reinforced cultural constructions of an older, more knowledgeable, more powerful, fatherly male who has a social responsibility to take care of a younger, less experienced man.

Performing Femaleness   Wahyu performed well, and the success of her performance was linked to her embodiment of femaleness. Kusnadi determined the feel of her take to be pleasant. He explained that he was influenced by what he found was convincingly "female" movement execution, specifying that by dancing slowly, Wahyu was able to realize the character of the dance (p.c., August 5 and 7, 2006). Speaking to the impact of her biological sex, Kusnadi emphasized that he restrained the tempo because Wahyu was a woman (p.c., August 5, 2006). Through his concern that Wahyu would not be able to keep up with a fast tempo or would need to overly exert herself, Kusnadi reinforced the constructions of femaleness performed through the dance and articulated a fatherly responsibility to take care of a daughter. Kusnadi's prior knowledge of her ability as well as his recognition of her authority as a dancer may have predisposed him to perceiving her femaleness, too. Before the session, he had spoken highly of her abilities as a female style dancer.

Wahyu articulated senses of femaleness not only by dancing but also by acknowledging Kusnadi's authority and deferring to his lead. As seen earlier, not all female dancers deferred as easily to the drummer; I observed women of different ages, in addition to the *Ngremo Putri* dancer discussed earlier, instruct Kusnadi as they danced and as they talked to him, sometimes contributing to tensions in the performance or rehearsal. Wahyu, however, was receptive to Kusnadi's verbal instruction from the very beginning of the session. Prior to her take, she did not try to tell Kusnadi how to play the drum or how the dance should go; instead, as a younger woman in the position of a "deferential daughter," she did as asked and followed the decisions that he made. For example, before she danced, Kusnadi told her to exit by walking in a particular way. She tried it, asking him if that was what he wanted. He said yes. As she danced, for the most part, she followed his lead by executing the movements and repetitions he indicated through his drumming. That Wahyu was obedient affected the way that Kusnadi drummed for her.

Through her compliance, Wahyu also negotiated Kusnadi's and Utomo's authority and asserted her own—reinforcing the point that asserting authority is not always about leading. This was particularly evident during one moment in which she received conflicting signals from Utomo, who was cueing her visually from offstage in an effort to help her, and Kusnadi. Wahyu was thus balancing the instructions she was receiving from Utomo—someone who had taught her and was in some senses a sort of "older brother"—and from Kusnadi—the more senior artist and in some senses a sort of "father." For the most part, she followed Kusnadi's drumming, even as she heeded Utomo's signals by watching him. In one instance, however, she did follow Utomo's cue even though it contradicted Kusnadi's drumming. Her ability to shift between the drumming and Utomo without losing her flow ultimately displayed her command of the dance.

Wahyu effectively used her articulation of femaleness—her performance of a female style dance as well as her acknowledgement of older men's authority—to men's benefit. By following the drumming for the most part, she helped Kusnadi to relax and play smoothly. As indicated above, she also allowed Utomo space to express his authority, even as she maintained hers. In so doing, she was instrumental in facilitating what the participating artists determined to be a good take. Wahyu's role in facilitating performance through her interaction with men is similar to the role that female *gendèr* (a type of metallophone) musicians play through their interactions with male puppet masters in old-style shadow puppet theater, analyzed by Sarah Weiss (2006). She writes, "[l]ike Javanese wives in traditional households, . . . [the female *gendèr* player] is the unobtrusive force that makes everything flow appropriately, seemingly without effort on the part of anyone" (Weiss 2006: 98).

Three particularly pertinent implications emerge from Weiss's point, and they are corroborated through my research. First is the value that many Javanese place on indirect expressions of power. The *gendèr* player exudes an "unobtrusive force," a power that is not overt. This power comes from her command of the tradition, thereby revealing her knowledge and competence. Second, the power of the *gendèr* player enables the puppet master and the musicians to perform smoothly. Third, that Weiss compares the *gendèr* player to wives evokes the complementary aspects of femaleness and maleness in some Javanese worldviews, as did Supriono's use of the husband-wife metaphor introduced earlier in this chapter. This metaphor is particularly appropriate in the case of old-style shadow puppet theater because, in many cases, the *gendèr* player was the puppeteer's wife (Weiss 2006). Like female *gendèr* players, Wahyu enabled Kusnadi to play smoothly by exuding "an unobtrusive force" in performance. This power—a manifestation of her magnetic female power—stemmed from her knowledge and command of the dance. Furthermore, the femaleness she articulated by enacting the female persona of the dance and as she interacted with Kusnadi complemented the maleness that Kusnadi was articulating as a drummer and as a more senior artist. The direction of deference between the dancer and the drummer was, for the most part, consistent with cultural expectations based on power structures of age and gender—that is, as a younger female, Wahyu would defer to Kusnadi, the older male—contributing to Kusnadi's positive evaluation of Wahyu's performance.

Returning to Nancy Cooper's ideas about women's power, I contend that Wahyu exercised her magnetic female power to men's benefit and to foster social harmony (Cooper 2000: 617). Supriono reported that the musicians teased her as they teased Utomo, noting that one of the musicians compared Wahyu's breasts to Utomo's, in part because they were in the same female style costume (p.c., August 4, 2006). The joking and its sexual innuendo indicated that the magnetic attracting power of female sexuality drew the musicians to both Wahyu and Utomo. Whereas such joking exacerbated Utomo's discomfort, Wahyu used the joking and her own female power as a young woman to foster a comfortable atmosphere—a type of social harmony. She laughed, smiled, and jested in return, on one level "deferring" to the joking by accepting it, and on another level using it to her benefit. The pleasant relationship she fostered with the musicians facilitated her performance, contributing to participating artists' positive evaluation of her take and recognition of her ability as a dancer. In effect, she used her female power to negotiate her authority.

Wahyu was also careful to articulate a sense of "proper" and "respectable" womanhood. She thereby challenged the licentious reputations that have haunted female artists throughout the twentieth century and into the present, discussed in chapters two and five (Cooper 2000: 626–628; Sutton 1987: 116–119; Spiller 2008; Hughes-Freeland 2008c). Many of the women I consulted were aware of these negative stereotypes and countered them by explicitly expressing their propriety and respectability through their verbal discourse, comportment, and behavior, as have female performers in central Java (Cooper 2000: 626–627; Sutton 1987: 118–119) and West Java (Spiller 2008: 189). Wahyu countered negative reputations by embodying an ideal Javanese female persona—one who is polite, smiling, friendly, and beautiful, but not overtly sexy—as she performed the dance. She also behaved consistently with dominant constructions of an ideal young woman—polite, smiling, friendly, beautiful, and respectful of older men.

In the course of making selections to tradition, performers produced senses of maleness and femaleness both as the performed personas portrayed in the dance and as their own selves. Strikingly, critical to what my teachers deemed "successful" performances of gender were aspects that reinforced dominant ideals characteristic of Old and New Order times, which were being carried forth and also contested in the Reformation era.

Interactions and Individuals

Through their interactions with each other, musicians and dancers intentionally and unintentionally made selections to produce tradition, negotiate knowledge, and articulate senses of gender. That the agents involved were predominately men demonstrates the importance of maleness in producing femaleness. Selling and buying, performers put forth their personal ideas of correctness, yet doing so did not necessarily mean that a performer insisted on his or her correctness during performance. Performers often manifested their authority by maintaining the control to make decisions—whether to sell or to buy.

Performers in Malang negotiated authority and articulated different senses of gender as they interacted in some seemingly paradoxical, ironic, and subtle ways. Kusnadi reinforced the model of an authoritative father figure consistent with dominant constructions about manhood by following Utomo. In the course of performing female style dance, Utomo negotiated his authority as a younger man in relation to an older man, Kusnadi. Through her articulations of femaleness, including deference as a younger woman, Wahyu reinforced the authority of her own knowledge, allowed Kusnadi to reinforce his, and fostered a comfortable atmosphere among the musicians, all of whom were male. Yet, Kusnadi's, Utomo's, and Wahyu's interactions were not so unusual in a cultural context where female style dance may be performed by males or females, where the expression of authority may be manifest by following the lead of another, and where the power of femaleness is important to performers' senses of local tradition and identity.

My guilty conscience for putting my teachers into awkward situations, as well as insights from scholars such as Shelemay (1997), has driven me to include some reflection on my own role as a foreign researcher in fostering many of the situations and interactions that have been the subjects of my analyses. Some of the dynamics affecting the recording sessions I sponsored, my lessons, rehearsals I sponsored and/or participated in, and performances in which I participated were products of specific cultural contexts and historical moments that involved my presence in Malang as a foreign researcher, my particular relationships with musicians and dancers, and their motivations to assert their senses of the past through performance. My teachers were invested in their cultural authority in the context of my recording sessions because they felt responsible as my teachers and because they sought to preserve their particular interpretations of Malangan and east Javanese dances that they believed were disappearing and not being represented satisfactorily in other forums. The performances that I have documented, however, are neither realizations of completely fixed dances and music nor authoritatively authentic renditions of a single original but, like most performances documented or not, interpretations that come from negotiations between individuals.

Particular realizations of Malangan dances have now become a part of the specific archive that I have assembled. My archive, like any, is the product of decisions—and mistakes—that performers and I made, the cultural politics that affected those decisions, and the politics of the documentation processes. These performances are neither realizations of fixed texts nor "authentic" renditions of a single, "authoritative," "original" *Beskalan, Ngremo*, or masked dance because such dances no longer exist, if they ever did. As Kusnadi put it, what is drummed for a particular performance is what the dance becomes (p.c., April 24, 2006). A dancer might add that what is danced for a particular performance is what the dance becomes.

Afterword

In exploring dance performance as a dynamic site of cultural negotiation and change, this book has argued that through the continuous transformations performers have made to tradition, they have been negotiating culturally constructed boundaries of gender and sex—sometimes reinforcing these boundaries, sometimes transgressing them, sometimes doing both simultaneously. I have approached the cultural production of tradition and gender as mutually constitutive processes, examining how dancers and musicians have pushed at the gender dualism characteristic of dominant ideologies to articulate complex senses of gender—including senses of female masculinity and male femininity (Halberstam 1998; Boellstorff 2004b, 2005b, 2007)—in particular ways in specific contexts. In effect performers were creating cultural space for the expression of gender pluralism (Peletz 2006). They were also showing the expression of gender to often be contingent or situational (Oetomo 2000; Boellstorff 2007; Blackwood 2010).

As we have seen, individual artists developed personal strategies for situating themselves within the constantly evolving constellations of personal, local, national, and global values that surround the negotiation of masculinity and femininity. Such strategies have included theatrical approaches (e.g., makeup, costuming, movements), musical approaches (e.g., ways of singing, ways of playing the drum), and spiritual approaches (e.g., negotiating Islamic beliefs and practices, using *ilmu* and/or mantras, interacting with spirits). Some individuals have taken gender transgression offstage in various ways, from living as a woman who knows she is not slow or relaxed, to living as a woman with the controversial occupation of singer-dancer, to living as a man who recognizes the femaleness in himself, to living as a *waria*. These have not always been comfortable processes for individuals, and living with the social consequences of their decisions and/or activities as artists has not always been easy.

I have been particularly interested in the ways performers maintain and make cultural space for the magnetic power of femaleness through their hearts, minds, and bodies despite a variety of cultural pressures that work to contain, control, and suppress it. We have seen this power expressed in various ways, including sexually, economically, spiritually, martially, through leading roles—as in leading the direction of artistic innovation—and through following. We have also seen different ways male and female performers have accessed, embodied, and enabled female power through cross-gender dance, through same-gender dance, through their senses of history, and through their senses of local tradition. Indic senses of *shakti*—spiritual power or cosmic energy gendered female—present in Java since medieval times, are not only still present but are a critical aspect of Javanese culture (Becker 1988, 1991, 1993; Hughes-Freeland 1995). In Malang, female power is essential to performers' senses of local tradition, particularly as represented in *Beskalan Putri*.

In spite of performers' concerns about the future of local tradition—or perhaps because these concerns were so strong—I remain optimistic and excited about the future of the performing arts in Malang. On visits following the period of my fieldwork, I have seen younger dancers coming into their own as artists and new drummers in the making. The news my husband and I have received from friends in Malang through text messages and Facebook, as well as the videos we have found posted to YouTube, suggest that musicians and dancers are continuing to actively engage with the arts. I was pleasantly surprised when my husband showed me a photograph on Facebook of one our friends, a young male dancer we had known for his strong male style masked dancing, in a *Beskalan Putri* costume. I do not have the sense that Malangan arts are dying; I have a sense that they are very much alive and will continue to transform—sometimes subtly and sometimes dramatically, sometimes intentionally and sometimes unintentionally—as artists continue to make music and dance relevant and meaningful within their communities, as well as critical sites of cultural and ideological work in the twenty-first century.

Notes

Note on Conventions

1. As an administrative division of a province in Indonesia, a *kabupaten* is analogous to a county in the United States. *Kabupaten* is also frequently translated as "district."

Preface

1. Since the time of my fieldwork, PSMD has undergone some changes in management.
2. Mujiati gives 1986 (2004: 39, 130). Karen Elizabeth Schrieber (1991: 2) and Ki Soleh Adi Pramono (2004: 67) give 1989.
3. Muliono also spelled his name Mulyono and Muliyono.
4. For one of his scholarly projects, see Wahyudi and Simatupang (2005).
5. Chapter one of Hayes's book is titled "Diary of a Mad Black Woman Festigoer," a nod to Tyler Perry's *Diary of a Mad Black Woman* (2010: 9).

Chapter 1. Aims and Approaches

1. I thank Sarah Weiss for directing my attention to *shakti* and reminding me of Judith Becker's work during a conversation at the 2011 Society for Ethnomusicology Meeting (p.c., November 2011).
2. Here I follow the centuries that Becker (1993) specifies when writing about medieval Java.
3. In that instance, the other musician "did not make it back from Paris in time" (Benamou 2010: 116).
4. Other terms are also used for the role of the female singer-dancer in Java, including *talèdhèk* or *lèdhèk*, *lènggèr*, and *ronggèng* (see Sutton 1984: 120). Which terms

people use vary by region, generation, and performing context (Sutton 1984: 120–121 n5). For example, I did not hear these other terms used to talk about male *tandhak* in *ludruk*. Because of the licentious reputation terms such as *tandhak* carry, many artists who performed as female singer-dancers that I met called themselves by the more culturally sensitive term *waranggana* (heavenly nymph, goddess, or angel) (Sutton 1984: 132; Cooper 2000: 614; Brinner 2008: 74). Some referred to themselves as *seniwati*, a feminized form of the Indonesian word *seniman*.

5. This is not to suggest that adult women did not play gamelan. During my fieldwork a few women reminisced about playing in women's gamelan groups in the past, and during a visit to Malang during the summer of 2011, I practiced drumming with a women's gamelan group in Tulusbesar.

6. My sources on the institutionalization of the performing arts through government cultural policies designed to promote ideals of the Indonesian nation include Judith Becker (1980), R. Anderson Sutton (1991, 2002), John Pemberton (1994), Amrih Widodo (1995), Philip Yampolsky (1995), Felicia Hughes-Freeland (1997), Nancy Cooper (2000), René Lysloff (2001/2002), Benjamin Brinner (2008), and Rachmi Diyah Larasati (2013).

Chapter 2. Maintaining Female Power through Male Style Dance

1. Srikandi is a character from the Mahabharata epic, which has its origins in India and was imported to Java centuries ago—by the eighth and ninth centuries (Sears 1984: 1, 13). Despite these Indian origins, the character of Srikandi has come to be localized, symbolizing particular senses of Javanese and Indonesian femininity. For other models of warrior women in Javanese story cycles, see Carey and Houben (1987: 13), Kumar (1980: 6), and Pausacker (1991: 291).

2. Like Srikandi, Sumbadra is a character from the Mahabharata epic. Here again, despite the Indian origins of this story cycle, Sumbadra has come to symbolize particular senses of Javanese and Indonesian femininity.

3. P.c., Karen Elizabeth Sekararum, January 6, 2006; Sri Handayani, March 29, 2006; Sri Utami, August 3, 2006.

4. P.c., Karen Elizabeth Sekararum, November 29, 2005; Madya, December 17, 2005; Cuci Indrawati, December 21, 2005; Kusnadi, 2005–2006.

5. Robert Hefner, conducting field research in rural East Java in the 1970s and 1980s (in the regencies of Malang, Pasuruan, Probolinggo, and Lumajang) was also struck by the *Ngremo* dancer's womanly beauty despite the male transvestism in the *tayuban* he observed (1987b: 76 n3, 79).

6. This musician did not seem to be using "prima donna" (*primadona*) in a negative sense as might be suggested in English, but in a positive sense to indicate Sri Utami's celebrity, charisma, and impact as a performer, even as he expressed his ambivalence about that impact. This musician's usage of the word *primadona* was typical of the way I heard this word used during my fieldwork.

7. P.c., Kusnadi, November 17, 2005; Anik Nurdjanah, February 9, 2006; February 21, 2006; Achmad Suwarno, April 3, 2006; Asbari, June 29, 2006; Sri Utami, August 3, 2006; Ngatmuji, August 12, 2006. Some performers called *Ngremo* performed with

a tipping section *Ngremo Tembel* or *Ngremo Tembelan*. Some referred to *Ngremo Tayub* as *Ngremo Tembel* as well.

8. "*Ngendhang ya teges, ya enak, kalau ngendhang. Ya, seperti orang laki. 'O aku kudu gaya wong lanang.' Harus seperti orang laki-laki, ya opo carané. Ya memang kalau ngetaké ya seperti orang laki-laki. Sama aja. Itu anehnya, tapi memang ada, kalau boleh dikatakan sakral, ilmu*" (p.c., Djupri, January 6, 2006).

9. "*Mungkin karakter juga, ya, karakter dari gerak itu yang lebih keras, kemudian lebih lebar dan lebih terbuka begitu, saya lebih enak membawakannya itu lho . . . . Kalau saya mikirnya putri, itu lebih kecil, lebih anuh harus—aduh, wis! Saya pikir lebih rumit gitu lho, daripada gerak putra yang lebih bebas dan punya kekuatan gitu lho*" (p.c., Tri Wahyuningtyas, July 1, 2006).

10. "*Nggak, kita kan ya 'is, perkerjaan itu, mbak. Kenapa harus opo ya, malu, kenapa? Kita kan, kerja kan, kerja to, untuk makan? Kalau, kalau urusan agama kita ya sama yang di atas gini. Ya, jadi nggak boleh dicampur aduk. Yang penting kita benar gitu aja, ya? Kerjaé halal gitu*" (p.c., Sri Handayani, March 29, 2006).

Chapter 3. Negotiating Pressures in Terms of Gender

1. Muliono recognized that a male character could enter a female dancer as well (p.c., January 3, 2006). Spiritual aspects of dance could thus be a strategy of articulating female masculinity, too.

2. He was not sure of the exact year of his marriage, but based on his children's ages and how old he believed he was when he married, we figured that it was in the mid-1990s.

3. Since Muliono's wife did not formally participate in my research, I have used a pseudonym for her name.

4. Some older performers used the term *lérok* (or *lerok*), which they said was what *ludruk* used to be called (p.c., Supatman, December 6, 2005; March 26, 2006; Djupri, June 15, 2006; Supeno, March 18, 2006). Djupri explained that after the early 1960s *lérok* came to be called *ludruk* (p.c., June 15, 2006). Supriyanto also recognizes *lerok* as another name for *ludruk* (2001: 10) and uses *lerok* to name earlier periods of *ludruk*'s history spanning from 1907 to the 1920s (2001: 11–12). *Lerok* (or *lerog*) may refer to other traditions of folk dance in east Java, too (see Brandon 1967: 48, and Peacock 1987: 55).

5. For an account of another *tandhak ludruk* in Malang who lives as a *waria*, Mama Chandra, see Pawestri (2006: 102–109).

6. I use the feminine pronoun because Mama Samsu lived as a *waria*.

7. Similarly, Ben Murtagh's *waria* interlocutors in Surabaya said that *waria* had to be brave to live openly as such (2011: 407).

8. Here I follow Boellstorff's practice of italicizing "*gay*" to indicate that the Indonesian concept is not exactly the same as the English-language concept "gay" (Boellstorff 2005a: 575; 2005b: 8; 2007: 8).

9. Djupri's use of *ilmu* was not particular to cross-gender dance. He also described using *ilmu* when performing male style dance, such as *ilmu* from the god Arjuna for *Ngremo Lanang*, to look handsome and attractive to women.

10. He also said that there was a male body suit if a woman wanted to become a man (p.c., June 15, 2006).

11. For more on Lestari's fascinating life and career, see Pawestri (2006: 94–100).

12. A similar continuum of male femininity was indicated by *waria* Ben Murtagh consulted in Surabaya in 2008 as they identified *waria, gay* feminine, and *gay* identities (2011: 393, 407).

13. See Pawestri (2006: 76 n36) for more of Kadam's discourse on gender identity in terms of percentage of male and female "elements" (*unsur*). For more on Kadam's remarkable life and career, see Pawestri (2006: 79–94).

14. I thank an anonymous reviewer for *Bijdragen tot de Taal-, Land- en Volkenkunde* for helping me to develop this analysis of Kadam's language (Sunardi 2009: 466 n20).

Chapter 4. Constructing Gender and Tradition through Senses of History

1. Marc Perlman also explores the connections that central Javanese musicians make between female and rural styles, noting too that urban musicians usually denigrate musical practices associated with village culture (1998).

2. P.c., Kusnadi, November 17, 2005; Supatman, December 6, 2005; Madya, December 17, 2005; Tri Wahyuningtyas, December 17, 2005; Djupri, June 15, 2006; Chattam Amat Redjo, April 14, 2006; Panoto, May 16, 2006; Asbari, June 29, 2006; Sutanu, June 7, 2006; Timan, July 4, 2006; and Satupah, July 7, 2006. Clifford Geertz also observed such groups in the 1950s; he referred to the dancers as *klèdhèk* or *tandhak*, reporting that such groups could include as many as three dancers (1960: 296).

3. I have added information about the dates of the kingdoms that Djupri included in his narrative, drawing from Holt (1967: 66), Koentjaraningrat (1985: 44), Kinney (2003: 81–87, 155–163) and Ricklefs (2008: 21, 39).

4. It is not unusual in Java for people to change or alter their names to mark a change in status or the beginning of a new stage in their lives.

5. Thinking back many decades into the past, Timan (b. 1930), a musician who used to accompany Muskayah when he was a boy, thought that by about 1945 she was no longer dancing. He also thought that she was about seventy in 1945 and over 100 when she died (p.c., July 4, 2006). This would place her birth around 1875.

6. Other artists offered different interpretations about what the dance portrayed. Supriono explained that in another version of this story, *Beskalan Putri* illustrates Jaka Umbaran dressed as a woman searching for Prabaretna (p.c., March 30, 2007). Kusnadi maintained that *Beskalan* does not illustrate a story; it is just an opening dance (p.c., May 22, 2007). On other occasions, Kusnadi recognized that the dance portrays a female warrior and an ideal female persona, just not a particular character from a story.

7. On one occasion, Djupri explained that Jaka Umbaran was from Singosari and Prabaretna was the daughter of the head (*kangjeng bupati*) of Malang, which was part of Singosari at that time (p.c., February 7, 2006). On another occasion, Djupri explained that Prabaretna was the daughter of the king of Singosari while Jaka Umbaran was the son of one of the king's advisors (p.c., August 7, 2006).

8. However, this is not the only costume that dancers are remembered to have worn for *Beskalan Putri*. For example, on one occasion, Kusnadi mentioned that *andhong* in the past wore a long cloth (*kain*)—I assume he meant batik—wrapped around the lower body and a Javanese blouse (*kebaya*) (p.c., July 23, 2006). During the time of my fieldwork, the dancers I saw all wore the "knightly" costume.

9. I am assuming that when Djupri referred to the white shirt, he was referring to the white robe.

10. "*Orangnya tran lalu tahu-tahu memegang, yang tahu itu ya orang-orang biasa yang waras: 'Iho, arèk iki olèh nendi nyekel ginian? Nyekel buku iku.' Gitu*" (p.c., Djupri, November 12, 2005).

11. As mentioned in chapter one, prior to that in the nineteenth century, *gandrung* had been performed by males (Wolbers 1986: 79; 1989: 8; 1993: 35; Yampolsky 1991a; Sutton 1993: 136).

12. This photograph is reproduced in Supriyanto (1992: 21) and Supriyanto (2001: 16).

13. Following Timan's narratives that suggest Muskayah was born around 1875, she could have started dancing as early as the 1880s.

14. Durga is recognized in central Java, too, where rulers have made offerings to her involving buffalo sacrifice (Carey and Houben 1987: 17; Brakel 1997; Headley 2000: 19–20; 2004, esp. photographs on 287–290).

15. For example, Kusnadi identified influences from Malangan masked dance and Malangan *jaranan* (p.c., February 2007; July 26, 2007).

16. An anonymous reviewer for *Asian Music* productively pointed out that "Ganggong's" melody is the same as the central Javanese *lancaran mlaku* "Tropongan," and that compositions named "Ricik-Ricik" also exist in central Javanese repertoires as a Yogyanese *ladrang* and a Solonese *lancaran*. The central Javanese compositions named "Ricik-Ricik," the reviewer noted, bear no resemblance to the "Ricik-Ricik" used for *Beskalan Putri* (Sunardi 2010a: 121 n18).

17. Kusnadi taught me to use different colotomic structures for "Ganggong" for *Ngremo Putri* and for *Beskalan Putri*. I understand the use of these different structures as a means to differentiate the feel of each dance. The *kempul* stroke on every beat for "Ganggong" as used for *Ngremo Putri* gives the music a more driving momentum than the sparser use of the *kempul* for "Ganggong" in *Beskalan Putri*, contributing to an energy and tension in *Ngremo* that contrasts with the overall calmer feel of *Beskalan*. I return to the energy and tension of *Ngremo* versus the calmer feel of *Beskalan* later in this chapter.

18. These performers included Kusnadi (p.c., February 4, 2006; February 28, 2006; June 24, 2006), Djupri (p.c., February 5, 2006; June 22, 2006), Asbari (p.c., June 2006), Timan (p.c., July 4, 2006), and Satupah (p.c., July 7, 2006).

19. I am indebted to the drummer Dennis Suwarno for directing my attention to the impact of the sounds of the drum strokes on the feeling of the drum patterns and the dance.

20. Djupri, however, did not talk about *Beskalan Lanang* as a dance that preceded *Beskalan Putri*. For more on *Beskalan Lanang* see Wibowo (1996).

21. During my fieldwork, Kusnadi consistently referred to "Tanjung Sari" as "Ijo-Ijo." Subsequently, however, he recalled that the title of this piece is "Tanjung Sari" and instructed me to use this title.

22. P.c., Djupri, 2006; Tri Wahyuningtyas, July 3, 2006; Kusnadi, July 24, 2006; M. Soleh Adi Pramono, July 27, 2006.

23. P.c., Warananingtyas Palupi, November 15, 2005; Tri Wahyuningtyas, July 3, 2006; M. Soleh Adi Pramono, July 27, 2006; Witanto, July 30, 2006; Mujiati (2004: 73).

24. P.c., Karen Elizabeth Sekararum, January 6, 2006; B. Supriono Hadi Prasetya, June 26, 2006; Kusnadi, July 24, 2006; Tri Wahyuningtyas, July 3, 2006; M. Soleh Adi Pramono, July 27, 2006; Witanto, July 30, 2006.

Chapter 5. Maintaining the Representation of Female Power through Beskalan Putri

1. See Rachmadi (2005) for an account by a central Javanese puppeteer of his experiences as a prisoner from 1965–1979 and the ban from performing he faced for twenty years following his release.

2. P.c., Supeno, February 26, 2006; March 18, 2006; Djupri, February 26, 2006; March 7, 2006; Chattam Amat Redjo, April 14, 2006; Timan, July 4, 2006; Asbari, June 29, 2006; Satupah, July 7, 2006; Kusnadi, 2006. For the phrase "*Beskalan sing asli*," I leave "*sing asli*" in lowercase letters because these words are not part of the dance's name. This is analogous to "the real *Beskalan*" versus "The Real *Beskalan*" (see also Sunardi 2011: 52 n8).

3. The date of Rasimoen's birth is from Roberts (2001: 6).

4. "*[S]aya kan latihan terus sambil melihat videonya, terus kemudian seperti pres, saya itu dimasuk, masuk, masuk, masuk itu sampai akhirnya saya menari Beskalan itu sudah nggak pakai mikir itu. Tiba-tiba hafal itu masuk dengan sendirinya gitu, mbak*" (p.c., Didik Nini Thowok, July 13, 2006).

5. Many thanks go to Luis-Manuel Garcia for helping me at the 2010 Meeting for the Society for Ethnomusicology to develop my analysis by directing my attention to the ways Didik's verbal discourse feminized his body (p.c., November 14, 2010).

6. The material quoted from Didik's emails was written in English. I have edited the text and punctuation into standard English and altered his spelling of Mojopahit to Majapahit to maintain stylistic consistency in this book.

7. I have supplemented Didik's account with information about Raden Wijaya from Kinney (2003: 157) and Ricklefs (2008: 20). Raden Wijaya's royal name was Kertarajasa Jayawardhana and he ruled from 1294–1309 (Kinney 2003: 157; Ricklefs 2008: 20).

8. "*Dan kelihatannya Mak Mus ada yang nyandhak tangané nyuruti jogèd, nyuruti dan pakai gendhing cangkem, dan kedengaran itu ya juga ada seperti, seperti ada gelaran gamelan, ada yang ngendhingi, orangnya itu, ada panjak kendhang juga, ya komplet. Kelihatan, lalu duruti jogèd. Ada di belakangé. Itu ya dikatakan mimpi, ya*

mimpi. Tapi orangnya itu apa ya, nggak éling-éling, nggak tahu sayanya ada di mana nggak tahu" (p.c., Djupri, November 12, 2005).

9. *"Sekarang saya tanya, 'Biyèn sing muridi sopo, mak?' 'Sopo muridi? O aku olèh aku lara, olèh aku mimpi. Kétokku géné géné géné géné.' Gitu."* (p.c., Djupri, November 12, 2005).

10. Ward Keeler found a similar hesitation about obtaining *ilmu* from sorcerers among puppet masters in central Java, reflecting a belief that a puppet master should have *ilmu* on his own accord (1987: 236). He also found that "[i]t is always more flattering to his [a puppeteer's] status to have gotten his ngèlmu [*ilmu*] from non-human sources" (ibid.).

11. I thank Laurel Sercombe for helping me, at the 2009 Society for Ethnomusicology Northwest Chapter Meeting, to develop this analysis by drawing my attention to the remarkable image of a little girl teaching mostly male musicians (p.c., February 21, 2009).

12. Clara Brakel-Papenhuyzen's (1995) attention to the terminology used in central Javanese classical dance inspired me to ask about the names and meanings of the dances I studied in Malang.

Glossary

asli: original, authentic, real
Beskalan: the name of a Malangan presentational dance
Beskalan Lanang: *Beskalan* in the male style
Beskalan Putri: *Beskalan* in the female style
Beskalan sing asli: the "original," "real," "authentic" *Beskalan*
gamelan: a type of ensemble that in Java is usually comprised mostly of gongs, metal-keyed percussion instruments, and drum(s)
gongsèng: a set of small spherical bells that dancers wear on their right ankles for some dances
ilmu: knowledge; science; or a particular type of knowledge that is of a secret, spiritual nature; see *ngèlmu*
kidungan: a type of east Javanese singing
ludruk (or *ludrug*): a form of east Javanese popular theater
Malangan: of or pertaining to Malang, in Malang style
ngèlmu/èlmu: knowledge, often of a secret, spiritual nature; see *ilmu*
Ngremo: the name of an east Javanese presentational dance
Ngremo Lanang: *Ngremo* in the male style
Ngremo Putri: *Ngremo* in the female style
Ngremo Tayub: a sub-style of *Ngremo Lanang*
PSMD: Padepokan Seni Mangun Dharma (Mangun Dharma Art Center)
tandhak: female singer-dancer or a male performer who performs as a female singer-dancer
tandhak ludruk: artist who plays female roles in *ludruk*; in Malang most *tandhak ludruk* are male
tayub: event in which professional female dancers sing and dance with guests for tips; also called *tayuban*
waria: a male who dresses and lives as female

Works Cited

Andaya, Barbara Watson. 2007. "Studying Women and Gender in Southeast Asia." *International Journal of Asian Studies* 4/1: 113–136.
Anderson, Benedict R. O'G. 1965. *Mythology and the Tolerance of the Javanese.* Ithaca: Modern Indonesia Project, Southeast Asia Program, Department of Asian Studies, Cornell University.
———. 1990a. "The Idea of Power in Javanese Culture." In *Language and Power: Exploring Political Cultures in Indonesia*, 17–77. Ithaca: Cornell University Press.
———. 1990b. "Further Adventures of Charisma." In *Language and Power: Exploring Political Cultures in Indonesia*, 78–93. Ithaca: Cornell University Press.
———. 1996. "'Bullshit!' S/he Said: The Happy, Modern, Sexy, Indonesian Married Woman as Transsexual." In *Fantasizing the Feminine in Indonesia.* Ed. Laurie J. Sears, 270–294. Durham: Duke University Press.
Babiracki, Carol M. 1997. "What's the Difference? Reflections on Gender and Research in Village India." In *Shadows in the Field: New Perspectives for Fieldwork in Ethnomusicology.* Ed. Gregory F. Barz and Timothy J. Cooley, 121–136. New York: Oxford University Press.
Bader, Sandra. 2011. "Dancing Bodies on Stage: Negotiating *Nyawer* Encounters at *Dangdut* and *Tarling Dangdut* Performances in West Java." *Indonesia and the Malay World* 39/115: 333–355.
Bakan, Michael B. 1999. *Music of Death and New Creation: Experiences in the World of Balinese Gamelan Beleganjur.* Chicago: The University of Chicago Press.
Barz, Gregory F., and Timothy J. Cooley, eds. 1997. *Shadows in the Field: New Perspectives for Fieldwork in Ethnomusicology.* New York: Oxford University Press.
Beatty, Andrew. 1996. "Adam and Eve and Vishnu: Syncretism in the Javanese Slametan." *Journal of the Royal Anthropological Institute* 2/2: 271–288.
———. 1999. *Varieties of Javanese Religion: An Anthropological Account.* Cambridge: Cambridge University Press.

Beaudry, Nicole. 1997. "The Challenges of Human Relations in Ethnographic Enquiry: Examples from Arctic and Subarctic Fieldwork." In *Shadows in the Field: New Perspectives for Fieldwork in Ethnomusicology*. Ed. Gregory F. Barz and Timothy J. Cooley, 63–83. New York: Oxford University Press.

Becker, Alton. 2000. "Text Building, Epistemology, and Aesthetics in Javanese Shadow Theater." In *Beyond Translation: Essays toward a Modern Philology*, 23–70. Ann Arbor: The University of Michigan Press.

Becker, Judith. 1979. "Time and Tune in Java." In *The Imagination of Reality: Essays in Southeast Asian Coherence Systems*. Ed. A. L. Becker and Aram A. Yengoyan, 197–210. Norwood: Ablex Publishing Corporation.

———. 1980. *Traditional Music in Modern Java: Gamelan in a Changing Society*. Honolulu: The University Press of Hawaii.

———. 1988. "Earth, Fire, *Sakti*, and the Javanese Gamelan." *Ethnomusicology* 32/3: 385–391.

———. 1991. "The Javanese Court Bedhaya Dance as a Tantric Analogy." In *Metaphor: A Musical Dimension*. Ed. Jamie C. Kassler, 109–120. Sydney: Currency Press.

———. 1993. *Gamelan Stories: Tantrism, Islam, and Aesthetics in Central Java*. Program for Southeast Asian Studies, Arizona State University.

———. 2009. Liner notes. In *That Bright World: Music for Javanese Gamelan*. Compositions by Jody Diamond. New York: New World Records. 80698-2.

Becker, Judith, and Alton Becker. 1981. "A Musical Icon: Power and Meaning in Javanese Gamelan Music." In *The Sign in Music and Literature*. Ed. Wendy Steiner, 203–215. Austin: University of Texas Press.

Benamou, Marc. 2002. "Wayang Character Types, Musical Categories, and a Reconsideration of the Alus-Kasar Dichotomy." In *Puppet Theater in Contemporary Indonesia: New Approaches to Performance Events*. Ed. Jan Mrázek, 271–283. Ann Arbor: Centers for South and Southeast Asian Studies, University of Michigan.

———. 2010. *Rasa: Affect and Intuition in Javanese Musical Aesthetics*. Oxford: Oxford University Press.

Biddle, Ian, and Freya Jarman-Ivens. 2007. "Introduction: Oh Boy! Making Masculinity in Popular Music." In *Oh Boy! Masculinities and Popular Music*. Ed. Freya Jarman-Ivens, 1–17. New York: Routledge.

Blackburn, Susan. 2008. "Indonesian Women and Political Islam." *Journal of Southeast Asian Studies* 39/1: 83–105.

Blackburn, Susan, Bianca J. Smith, and Siti Syamsiyatun. 2008. Introduction. In *Indonesian Islam in a New Era: How Women Negotiate Their Muslim Identities*. Ed. Susan Blackburn, Bianca J. Smith, and Siti Syamsiyatun, 1–21. Clayton, Victoria [Australia]: Monash University Press.

Blackwood, Evelyn. 2005. "Gender Transgression in Colonial and Postcolonial Indonesia." *Journal of Asian Studies* 64/4: 849–879.

———. 2007. "Transnational Sexualities in One Place: Indonesian Readings." In *Women's Sexualities and Masculinities in a Globalizing Asia*. Ed. Saskia E. Wieringa, Evelyn Blackwood, and Abha Bhaiya, 181–199. New York: Palgrave Macmillan.

———. 2010. *Falling Into the Lesbi World: Desire and Difference in Indonesia*. Honolulu: University of Hawai'i Press.

Blackwood, Evelyn, and Saskia E. Wieringa. 2007. "Globalization, Sexuality, and Silences: Women's Sexualities and Masculinities in an Asian Context." In *Women's Sexualities and Masculinities in a Globalizing Asia*. Ed. Saskia E. Wieringa, Evelyn Blackwood, and Abha Bhaiya, 1–20. New York: Palgrave Macmillan.

Boellstorff, Tom. 2004a. "The Emergence of Political Homophobia in Indonesia: Masculinity and National Belonging." *Ethnos* 69/4: 465–486.

———. 2004b. "Playing Back the Nation: *Waria*, Indonesian Transvestites." *Cultural Anthropology* 19/2: 159–195.

———. 2005a. "Between Religion and Desire: Being Muslim and *Gay* in Indonesia." *American Anthropologist* 107/4: 575–585.

———. 2005b. *The Gay Archipelago: Sexuality and Nation in Indonesia*. Princeton: Princeton University Press.

———. 2007. *A Coincidence of Desires: Anthropology, Queer Studies, Indonesia*. Durham: Duke University Press.

Brakel, Clara. 1993. "Character Types and Movement Styles in Traditional Javanese Theatre." In *Performance in Java and Bali: Studies of Narrative, Theatre, Music, and Dance*. Ed. Bernard Arps, 59–71. London: School of Oriental and African Studies, University of London.

———. 1997. "*Sandhang-pangan* for the Goddess: Offerings to Sang Hyang Bathari Durga and Nyai Lara Kidul." *Asian Folklore Studies* 56/2: 253–283.

Brakel-Papenhuijzen, Clara. 1992. *The Bedhaya Court Dances of Central Java*. Leiden: E. J. Brill.

———. 1995. *Classical Javanese Dance: The Surakarta Tradition and Its Terminology*. Leiden: KITLV Press.

Brandon, James R. 1967. *Theatre in Southeast Asia*. Cambridge: Harvard University Press.

Brenner, Suzanne A. 1995. "Why Women Rule the Roost: Rethinking Javanese Ideologies of Gender and Self-Control." In *Bewitching Women, Pious Men: Gender and Body Politics in Southeast Asia*. Ed. Aihwa Ong and Michael G. Peletz, 19–50. Berkeley: University of California Press.

———. 1996. "Reconstructing Self and Society: Javanese Muslim Women and 'The Veil.'" *American Ethnologist* 23/4: 673–697.

———. 1998. *The Domestication of Desire: Women, Wealth, and Modernity in Java*. Princeton: Princeton University Press.

Brinner, Benjamin. 1995. *Knowing Music, Making Music: Javanese* Gamelan *and the Theory of Musical Competence and Interaction*. Chicago: The University of Chicago Press.

———. 2008. *Music in Central Java: Experiencing Music, Expressing Culture*. New York: Oxford University Press.

———. 2009. *Playing across a Divide: Israeli-Palestinian Musical Encounters*. Oxford: Oxford University Press.

Browne, Susan. 2000. "The Gender Implications of Dangdut Kampungan: Indonesian 'Low-Class' Popular Music." Centre of Southeast Asian Studies Working Paper 109. Clayton, Victoria [Australia]: Monash Asia Institute, Monash University.

Buckland, Theresa Jill. 2006. "Dance, History, and Ethnography: Frameworks, Sources, and Identities of Past and Present." In *Dancing from Past to Present: Nation, Culture, Identities*. Ed. Theresa Jill Buckland, 3–24. Madison: The University of Wisconsin Press.

Butler, Judith. 1990. "Performative Acts and Gender Constitution: An Essay in Phenomenology and Feminist Theory." In *Performing Feminisms: Feminist Critical Theory and Theatre*. Ed. Sue-Ellen Case, 270–282. Baltimore: The Johns Hopkins University Press.

———. 1993. *Bodies That Matter: On the Discursive Limits of "Sex."* New York: Routledge.

———. 1999. *Gender Trouble: Feminism and the Subversion of Identity*. New York: Routledge.

Carey, Peter, and Vincent Houben. 1987. "Spirited Srikandhis and Sly Sumbadras: The Social, Political and Economic Role of Women at the Central Javanese Courts in the 18th and Early 19th Centuries." In *Indonesian Women in Focus: Past and Present Notions*. Ed. Elsbeth Locher-Scholten and Anke Niehof, 12–42. Dordrecht: Foris Publications.

Choy, Peggy. 1984. "Texts through Time: The Golèk Dance of Java." In *Aesthetic Tradition and Cultural Transition in Java and Bali*. Ed. Stephanie Morgan and Laurie Jo Sears, 51–81. Madison: Center for Southeast Asian Studies, University of Wisconsin.

Clara van Groenendael, Victoria M. 2008. *Jaranan: The Horse Dance and Trance in East Java*. Trans. Maria J. L. van Yperen. Leiden: KITLV Press.

Clifford, James. 1997. "Spatial Practices: Fieldwork, Travel, and the Disciplining of Anthropology." In *Anthropological Locations: Boundaries and Grounds of a Field Science*. Ed. Akhil Gupta and James Ferguson, 185–222. Berkeley: University of California Press.

Collins, Elizabeth Fuller, and Ernaldi Bahar. 2000. "To Know Shame: *Malu* and Its Uses in Malay Societies." *Crossroads: An Interdisciplinary Journal of Southeast Asian Studies* 14/1: 35–69.

Connerton, Paul. 1989. *How Societies Remember*. Cambridge: Cambridge University Press.

Cooley, Timothy J. 1997. "Casting Shadows in the Field: An Introduction." In *Shadows in the Field: New Perspectives for Fieldwork in Ethnomusicology*. Ed. Gregory F. Barz and Timothy J. Cooley, 3–19. New York: Oxford University Press.

Cooper, Nancy I. 2000. "Singing and Silences: Transformations of Power through Javanese Seduction Scenarios." *American Ethnologist* 27/3: 609–644.

Coplan, David B. 1993. "Ethnomusicology and the Meaning of Tradition." In *Ethnomusicology and Modern Music History*. Ed. Stephen Blum, Philip V. Bohlman, and Daniel M. Neuman, 35–48. Urbana: University of Illinois Press.

Cowan, Jane K. 1990. "Introduction: Entering the Dance." In *Dance and the Body Politic in Northern Greece*, 3–27. Princeton: Princeton University Press.

Crawford, Michael. 2001. "East Java." *The New Grove Dictionary of Music and Musicians*. Vol. 12. Ed. Stanley Sadie; executive editor John Tyrrell, 329–335. New York: Grove.

Daniels, Timothy. 2009. *Islamic Spectrum in Java*. Burlington, Vt.: Ashgate Publishing Company.

———, ed. 2013. *Performance, Popular Culture, and Piety in Muslim Southeast Asia*. New York: Palgrave Macmillan.

Day, Tony. 2002. "Wayang Kulit and 'Internal Otherness' in East Java." In *Puppet Theater in Contemporary Indonesia: New Approaches to Performance Events*. Ed. Jan Mrázek, 189–198. Ann Arbor: Centers for South and Southeast Asian Studies, University of Michigan.

Diamond, Beverley. 2005. "Media as Social Action: Native American Musicians in the Recording Studio." In *Wired for Sound: Engineering and Technologies in Sonic Cultures*. Ed. Paul D. Greene and Thomas Porcello, 118–137. Middletown: Wesleyan University Press.

Diamond, Catherine. 2008. "Fire in the Banana's Belly: Bali's Female Performers Essay the Masculine Arts." *Asian Theatre Journal* 25/2: 231–271.

Djajadiningrat-Nieuwenhuis, Madelon. 1987. "Ibuism and Priyayization: Path to Power?" In *Indonesian Women in Focus: Past and Present Notions*. Ed. Elsbeth Locher-Scholten and Anke Niehof, 43–51. Dordrecht: Foris Publications.

Downing, Sonja Lynn. 2010. "Agency, Leadership, and Gender Negotiation in Balinese Girls' Gamelans." *Ethnomusicology* 54/1: 54–80.

Errington, Shelly. 1990. "Recasting Sex, Gender, and Power: A Theoretical and Regional Overview." In *Power and Difference: Gender in Island Southeast Asia*. Ed. Jane Monnig Atkinson and Shelly Errington, 1–58. Stanford: Stanford University Press.

Foley, Kathy. 1985. "The Dancer and the Danced: Trance Dance and Theatrical Performance in West Java." *Asian Theatre Journal* 2/1: 28–49.

Foster, Susan Leigh. 1986. *Reading Dancing: Bodies and Subjects in Contemporary American Dance*. Berkeley: University of California Press.

———. 1995. "Choreographing History." In *Choreographing History*. Ed. Susan Leigh Foster, 3–21. Bloomington: Indiana University Press.

Franko, Mark. 1993. *Dance as Text: Ideologies of the Baroque Body*. Cambridge: Cambridge University Press.

Frederick, William H. 1982. "Rhoma Irama and the Dangdut Style: Aspects of Contemporary Indonesian Popular Culture." *Indonesia* 34: 102–130.

Garber, Marjorie. 1992. *Vested Interests: Cross-Dressing and Cultural Anxiety*. New York: Routledge.

Geertz, Clifford. 1957. "Ritual and Social Change: A Javanese Example." *American Anthropologist* 59/1: 32–54.

———. 1960. *The Religion of Java*. Chicago: The University of Chicago Press.

Geertz, Hildred. 1961. *The Javanese Family: A Study of Kinship and Socialization.* New York: The Free Press of Glencoe, Inc.

Gerstin, Julian. 1998. "Interaction and Improvisation between Dancers and Drummers in Martinican Bèlè." *Black Music Research Journal* 18/1–2: 121–165.

Gold, Lisa. 1998. *The Gender Wayang Repertoire in Theater and Ritual: A Study of Balinese Musical Meaning.* PhD dissertation. University of California, Berkeley.

Gupta, Akhil, and James Ferguson, eds. 1997. *Anthropological Locations: Boundaries and Grounds of a Field Science.* Berkeley: University of California Press.

Hahn, Tomie. 2004. "Shifting Selves: Embodied Metaphors in *Nihon Buyo*." In *Women's Voices across Musical Worlds.* Ed. Jane A. Bernstein, 308–325. Boston: Northeastern University Press.

———. 2007. *Sensational Knowledge: Embodying Culture through Japanese Dance.* Middletown: Wesleyan University Press.

Halberstam, Judith. 1998. *Female Masculinity.* Durham: Duke University Press.

Hamera, Judith. 2002. "An Answerability of Memory: 'Saving' Khmer Classical Dance." *Drama Review* 46/4: 65–85.

Harnish, David D., and Anne K. Rasmussen. 2011. "Introduction: The World of Islam in the Music of Indonesia." In *Divine Inspirations: Music and Islam in Indonesia.* Ed. David D. Harnish and Anne K. Rasmussen, 5–41. Oxford: Oxford University Press.

Harwood, Eve. 1998. "Go On Girl! Improvisation in African-American Girls' Singing Games." In *In the Course of Performance: Studies in the World of Musical Improvisation.* Ed. Bruno Nettl with Melinda Russell, 113–125. Chicago: The University of Chicago Press.

Hatley, Barbara. 1971. "Wayang and Ludruk: Polarities in Java." *Drama Review* 15/2: 88–101.

———. 1990. "Theatrical Imagery and Gender Ideology in Java." In *Power and Difference: Gender in Island Southeast Asia.* Ed. Jane Monnig Atkinson and Shelly Errington, 177–207. Stanford: Stanford University Press.

———. 2007. "Subverting the Stereotypes: Women Performers Contest Gender Images, Old and New." *Review of Indonesian and Malaysian Affairs* 41/2: 173–204.

———. 2008. *Javanese Performances on an Indonesian Stage: Contesting Culture, Embracing Change.* Singapore: NUS Press; Honolulu: University of Hawai'i Press.

Hayes, Eileen M. 2010. *Songs in Black and Lavender: Race, Sexual Politics, and Women's Music.* Urbana: University of Illinois Press.

Headley, Stephen C. 2000. *From Cosmogony to Exorcism in a Javanese Genesis: The Spilt Seed.* Oxford: Oxford University Press.

———. 2004. *Durga's Mosque: Cosmology, Conversion and Community in Central Javanese Islam.* Singapore: Institute of Southeast Asian Studies.

Hefner, Robert W. 1985. *Hindu Javanese: Tengger Tradition and Islam.* Princeton: Princeton University Press.

———. 1987a. "Islamizing Java? Religion and Politics in Rural East Java." *Journal of Asian Studies* 46/3: 533–554.

———. 1987b. "The Politics of Popular Art: *Tayuban* Dance and Culture Change in East Java." *Indonesia* 43: 75–94.

———. 1997. "Islam in an Era of Nation-States: Politics and Religious Renewal in Muslim Southeast Asia." In *Islam in an Era of Nation-States: Politics and Religious Renewal in Muslim Southeast Asia.* Ed. Robert W. Hefner and Patricia Horvatich, 3–40. Honolulu: University of Hawai'i Press.

———. 2008. "A Conservative Turn in Indonesian Islam? Genesis and Future." In *Muslim Politics and Democratisation in Indonesia,* 33–50. Clayton, Victoria [Australia]: Monash Asia Institute, Monash University Press.

Hellwig, Jean. 1993. "*Jaipongan*: The Making of a New Tradition." In *Performance in Java and Bali: Studies of Narrative, Theatre, Music, and Dance.* Ed. Bernard Arps, 47–58. London: School of Oriental and African Studies, University of London.

Heryanto, Ariel. 2006. *State Terrorism and Political Identity in Indonesia: Fatally Belonging.* London: Routledge.

———. 2008a. "Citizenship and Indonesian Ethnic Chinese in Post-1998 Films." In *Popular Culture in Indonesia: Fluid Identities in Post-Authoritarian Politics.* Ed. Ariel Heryanto, 70–92. London: Routledge.

———. 2008b. "Pop Culture and Competing Identities." In *Popular Culture in Indonesia: Fluid Identities in Post-Authoritarian Politics.* Ed. Ariel Heryanto, 1–36. London: Routledge.

Hidajat, Robby. 2006. "Tafsir Struktur Tari Remo dan Tari Beskalan." ["Comparison of the Structure of Ngremo and Beskalan."] In *Cakrawala: Seni Pertunjukan Indonesia.* Ed. Robby Hidajat, 173–211. Malang: Jurusan Seni dan Desain, Fakultas Sastra, Universitas Negeri Malang.

Hobsbawm, Eric. 1983. "Introduction: Inventing Traditions." In *The Invention of Tradition.* Ed. Eric Hobsbawm and Terence Ranger, 1–14. Cambridge: Cambridge University Press.

Holt, Claire. 1967. *Art in Indonesia: Continuities and Change.* Ithaca: Cornell University Press.

Houben, Vincent J. H. 2003. "Southeast Asia and Islam." *Annals of the American Academy of Political and Social Science* 588: 149–170.

Hughes-Freeland, Felicia. 1991. "Javanese Visual Performance and the Indian Mystique." In *The Art and Culture of South-East Asia.* Ed. Lokesh Chandra, 125–150. New Delhi: International Academy of Indian Culture and Aditya Prakashan.

———. 1993. "*Golék Ménak* and *Tayuban*: Patronage and Professionalism in Two Spheres of Central Javanese Culture." In *Performance in Java and Bali: Studies of Narrative, Theatre, Music, and Dance.* Ed. Bernard Arps, 88–120. London: School of Oriental and African Studies, University of London.

———. 1995. "Performance and Gender in Javanese Palace Tradition." In *'Male' and 'Female' in Developing Southeast Asia.* Ed. Wazir Jahan Karim, 181–206. Oxford: Berg Publishers.

———. 1997. "Art and Politics: From Javanese Court Dance to Indonesian Art." *Journal of the Royal Anthropological Institute* 3/3: 473–495.

———. 2006. "Constructing a Classical Tradition: Javanese Court Dance in Indonesia." In *Dancing from Past to Present: Nation, Culture, Identities.* Ed. Theresa Jill Buckland, 52–74. Madison: The University of Wisconsin Press.

———. 2007. "Charisma and Celebrity in Indonesian Politics." *Anthropological Theory* 7/2: 177–200.

———. 2008a. "Cross-Dressing across Cultures: Genre and Gender in the Dances of *Didik Nini Thowok*." Asia Research Institute Working Paper Series No. 108. Singapore: Asia Research Institute, National University of Singapore. http://www.ari.nus.edu.sg/publication_details.asp?pubtypeid=WP&pubid=1264 [accessed July 18, 2014].

———. 2008b. *Embodied Communities: Dance Traditions and Change in Java*. New York: Berghahn Books.

———. 2008c. "Gender, Representation, Experience: The Case of Village Performers in Java." *Dance Research* 26/2: 140–167.

Janarto, Herry Gendut. 2005. *Didik Nini Thowok: Menari Sampai Lahir Kembali*. [*Didik Nini Thowok: Dancing until Reborn*.] Malang: Sava Media; Yogyakarta: LPK Tari Natya Lakshita.

Kartomi, Margaret J. 1973. "Music and Trance in Central Java." *Ethnomusicology* 17/2: 163–208.

———. 1976. "Performance, Music and Meaning of Réyog Ponorogo." *Indonesia* 22: 84–130.

Keeler, Ward. 1983. "Shame and Stage Fright in Java." *Ethos* 11/3: 152–165.

———. 1987. *Javanese Shadow Plays, Javanese Selves*. Princeton: Princeton University Press.

———. 1990. "Speaking of Gender in Java." In *Power and Difference: Gender in Island Southeast Asia*. Ed. Jane Monnig Atkinson and Shelly Errington, 127–152. Stanford: Stanford University Press.

Kinney, Ann R., with Marijke J. Klokke and Lydia Kieven. Photographs by Rio Helmi. 2003. *Worshipping Siva and Buddha: The Temple Art of East Java*. Honolulu: University of Hawai'i Press.

Kisliuk, Michelle. 2000. "Performance and Modernity among BaAka Pygmies: A Closer Look at the Mystique of Egalitarian Foragers in the Rain Forest." In *Music and Gender*. Ed. Pirkko Moisala and Beverley Diamond, 25–50. Urbana: University of Illinois Press.

Koentjaraningrat. 1980. "Javanese Terms for God and Supernatural Beings and the Idea of Power." In *Man, Meaning and History: Essays in Honour of H. G. Schulte Nordholt*. Ed. R. Schefold, J. W. Schoorl, and J. Tennekes, 127–139. The Hague: Martinus Nijhoff.

———. 1985. *Javanese Culture*. Singapore: Oxford University Press.

Kumar, Ann. 1980. "Javanese Court Society and Politics in the Late Eighteenth Century: The Record of a Lady Soldier. Part I: The Religious, Social, and Economic Life of the Court." *Indonesia* 29: 1–46.

Kunst, Jaap. 1949. *Music in Java: Its History, Its Theory and Its Technique*. Vols. 1 & 2. The Hague: Martinus Nijhoff.

Larasati, Rachmi Diyah. 2013. *The Dance That Makes You Vanish: Cultural Reconstruction in Post-Genocide Indonesia*. Minneapolis: University of Minnesota Press.

Li, Siu Leung. 2003. *Cross-Dressing in Chinese Opera*. Hong Kong: Hong Kong University Press.

Locher-Scholten, Elsbeth, and Anke Niehof. 1987. Introduction. In *Indonesian Women in Focus: Past and Present Notions*. Ed. Elsbeth Locher-Scholten and Anke Niehof, 1–11. Dordrecht: Foris Publications.

Lysloff, René T. A. 2001/2002. "Rural Javanese 'Tradition' and Erotic Subversion: Female Dance Performance in Banyumas (Central Java)." *Asian Music* 33/1: 1–24.

Manuel, Peter. 1988. *Popular Musics of the Non-Western World: An Introductory Survey*. New York: Oxford University Press.

Morris, Rosalind C. 1995. "All Made Up: Performance Theory and the New Anthropology of Sex and Gender." *Annual Review of Anthropology* 24: 567–592.

Mrázek, Jan. 2000. "Javanese *Wayang Kulit* in the Times of Comedy: Clown Scenes, Innovation, and the Performance's Being in the Present World: Part Two." *Indonesia* 69: 107–172.

———. 2005. "Masks and Selves in Contemporary Java: The Dances of Didik Nini Thowok." *Journal of Southeast Asian Studies* 36/2: 249–279.

Mujiati. 2004. "Tari Beskalan Lanang: Karya Mohamad Soleh Adi Pramana Di Padepokan Seni Mangun Dharmo Desa Tulus Besar Kecamatan Tumpang Kabupaten Malang." ["Beskalan Lanang Dance: A Work of Mohamad Soleh Adi Pramana at the Mangun Dharmo Art Center in the Village of Tulus Besar, Subdistrict of Tumpang, Regency of Malang."] Skripsi S-1. Surakarta: Sekolah Tinggi Seni Indonesia.

Mulder, Niels. 2005. *Mysticism in Java: Ideology in Indonesia*. Yogyakarta: Kanisius Publishing House.

Murtagh, Ben. 2011. "*Gay, Lesbi* and *Waria* Audiences in Indonesia: Watching Homosexuality on Screen." *Indonesia and the Malay World* 39/115: 391–415.

Nettl, Bruno. 1998. "Introduction: An Art Neglected in Scholarship." In *In the Course of Performance: Studies in the World of Musical Improvisation*. Ed. Bruno Nettl with Melinda Russell, 1–23. Chicago: The University of Chicago Press.

Neuman, Daniel M. 1993. "Epilogue: Paradigms and Stories." In *Ethnomusicology and Modern Music History*. Ed. Stephen Blum, Philip V. Bohlman, and Daniel M. Neuman, 268–277. Urbana: University of Illinois Press.

Oetomo, Dédé. 1996. "Gender and Sexual Orientation in Indonesia." In *Fantasizing the Feminine in Indonesia*. Ed. Laurie J. Sears, 259–269. Durham: Duke University Press.

———. 2000. "Masculinity in Indonesia: Genders, Sexualities, and Identities in a Changing Society." In *Framing the Sexual Subject: The Politics of Gender, Sexuality, and Power*. Ed. Richard Parker, Regina Maria Barbosa, and Peter Aggleton, 46–59. Berkeley: University of California Press.

Onghokham. 1972. "The Wayang Topèng World of Malang." *Indonesia* 14: 110–124.

Pausacker, Helen. 1991. "Srikandhi and Sumbadra: Stereotyped Role Models or Complex Personalities?" In *The Art and Culture of South-East Asia*. Ed. Lokesh Chandra, 271–297. New Delhi: International Academy of Indian Culture and Aditya Prakashan.

Pawestri, Tjundomanik Tjatur. 2006. Transvesti *Pada Seni Pertunjukan Ludruk Malang*. [*Female Impersonators in Malang Ludruk Performances.*] Skripsi Sarjana Antropologi Tari. Institut Kesenian Jakarta.

Peacock, James L. 1978. "Symbolic Reversal and Social History: Transvestites and Clowns of Java." In *The Reversible World: Symbolic Inversion in Art and Society*. Ed. Barbara A. Babcock, 209–224. Ithaca: Cornell University Press.

———. 1987. *Rites of Modernization: Symbolic and Social Aspects of Indonesian Proletarian Drama*. Chicago: The University of Chicago Press.

Peletz, Michael G. 2006. "Transgenderism and Gender Pluralism in Southeast Asia since Early Modern Times." *Current Anthropology* 47/2: 309–340.

Pemberton, John. 1994. *On the Subject of "Java."* Ithaca: Cornell University Press.

Perlman, Marc. 1998. "The Social Meanings of Modal Practices: Status, Gender, History, and *Pathet* in Central Javanese Music." *Ethnomusicology* 42/1: 45–80.

Pigeaud, Th. 1938. *Javaanse Volksvertoningen: Bijdrage tot de Beschrijving van Land en Volk*. Batavia: Volkslectuur.

Ponder, H. W. 1990. *Javanese Panorama: More Impressions of the 1930s*. Singapore: Oxford University Press.

Pramono, Ki Soleh Adi. 2004. *Naskah Pedhalangan Wayang Topeng Malang: Paseban Cikal-Bakalipun Kitha Malang*. [*Script of a Dhalang's Narration for a Malang Masked Dance Play: The Meeting of the Malang City Founder.*] Malang: Sava Media and Padhepokan Seni Mangun Dharma.

Rachmadi, Ki Tristuti. 2005. "My Life as a Shadow Master under Suharto." In *Beginning to Remember: The Past in the Indonesian Present*. Ed. Mary S. Zurbuchen, 38–46. Singapore: Singapore University Press in association with Seattle: University of Washington Press.

———. 2005. "Translator's Note: My Life as a Shadow Master under Suharto." In *Beginning to Remember: The Past in the Indonesian Present*. Ed. Mary S. Zurbuchen, 35–37. Singapore: Singapore University Press in association with Seattle: University of Washington Press.

Raffles, Thomas Stamford. 1988. *The History of Java*. Vol. I. Singapore: Oxford University Press.

Rasmussen, Anne K. 2010. *Women, the Recited Qur'an, and Islamic Music in Indonesia*. Berkeley: University of California Press.

Retsikas, Konstantinos. 2007a. "Being and Place: Movement, Ancestors, and Personhood in East Java, Indonesia." *Journal of the Royal Anthropological Institute (N.S.)* 13: 969–986.

———. 2007b. "The Power of the Senses: Ethnicity, History and Embodiment in East Java, Indonesia." *Indonesia and the Malay World* 35/102: 183–210.

Richter, Max M. 2008. "Musical Sexualisation and the Gendered Habitus in Yogyakarta." *Indonesia and the Malay World* 36/104: 21–45.

Ricklefs, M. C. 2008. *A History of Modern Indonesia since c. 1200*. Stanford: Stanford University Press.

Roberts, Gillian. 2001. "Connecting with the Spirit: A Personal Perspective on Dancing in East Java." *Contemporary Theatre Review* 11/2: 1–12.

Roosa, John. 2006. *Pretext for Mass Murder: The September 30th Movement and Suharto's Coup d'État in Indonesia*. Madison: The University of Wisconsin Press.

Ross, Laurie Margot. 2005. "Mask, Gender, and Performance in Indonesia: An Interview with Didik Nini Thowok." *Asian Theatre Journal* 22/2: 214–226.

———. 2011. "The Artist Registry: Tracking Itinerant Artists before and after Suharto's 1965 Coup D'État in the Cirebon Region, West Java." *Indonesia and the Malay World* 39/114: 145–169.

———. 2013. "Performing Piety from the Inside Out: Fashioning Gender and Public Space in a Mask 'Tradition' from Java's Northwest Coast." In *Performance, Popular Culture, and Piety in Muslim Southeast Asia*. Ed. Timothy P. Daniels, 13–43. New York: Palgrave Macmillan.

Ruckert, George E. 2004. *Music in North India: Experiencing Music, Expressing Culture*. New York: Oxford University Press.

Schrieber, Karen Elizabeth. 1991. *Power in the East Javanese Jaranan and Wayang Topeng*. MA thesis. University of Virginia, Charlottesville.

Sears, Laurie Jo. 1984. "Epic Voyages: The Transmission of the *Ramayana* and *Mahabharata* from India to Java." In *Aesthetic Tradition and Cultural Transition in Java and Bali*. Ed. Stephanie Morgan and Laurie Jo Sears, 1–30. Madison: Center for Southeast Asian Studies, University of Wisconsin.

———. 1996a. "Introduction: Fragile Identities: Deconstructing Women and Indonesia." In *Fantasizing the Feminine in Indonesia*. Ed. Laurie J. Sears, 1–44. Durham: Duke University Press.

———. 1996b. *Shadows of Empire: Colonial Discourse and Javanese Tales*. Durham: Duke University Press.

———. 2007. "Postcolonial Identities, Feminist Criticism, and Southeast Asian Studies." In *Knowing Southeast Asian Subjects*. Ed. Laurie J. Sears, 35–74. Seattle: University of Washington Press in association with Singapore: NUS Press.

Sears, Laurie J., and Joyce Burkhalter Flueckiger. 1991. Introduction. In *Boundaries of the Text: Epic Performances in South and Southeast Asia*. Ed. Joyce Burkhalter Flueckiger and Laurie J. Sears, 1–16. Ann Arbor: Center for South and Southeast Asian Studies, University of Michigan.

Seeger, Anthony. 2004. *Why Suyá Sing: A Musical Anthropology of an Amazonian People*. Urbana: University of Illinois Press.

Shaw, Alison. 2005. "Changing Sex and Bending Gender: An Introduction." In *Changing Sex and Bending Gender*. Ed. Alison Shaw and Shirley Ardener, 1–19. New York: Berghahn Books.

Shelemay, Kay Kaufman. 1997. "The Ethnomusicologist, Ethnographic Method, and the Transmission of Tradition." In *Shadows in the Field: New Perspectives for Fieldwork in Ethnomusicology*. Ed. Gregory F. Barz and Timothy J. Cooley, 189–204. New York: Oxford University Press.

Shiraishi, Saya S. 1997. *Young Heroes: The Indonesian Family in Politics*. Ithaca: Southeast Asia Program, Cornell University.

Siegel, James. 2006. *Naming the Witch*. Stanford: Stanford University Press.

Smith, Bianca J. 2008. "*Kejawen* Islam as Gendered Praxis in Javanese Village Religiosity." In *Indonesian Islam in a New Era: How Women Negotiate Their Muslim Identities*. Ed. Susan Blackburn, Bianca J. Smith, and Siti Syamsiyatun, 97–118. Clayton, Victoria [Australia]: Monash University Press.

Spiller, Henry. 2007. "Negotiating Masculinity in an Indonesian Pop Song: Doel Sumbang's 'Ronggeng.'" In *Oh Boy! Masculinities and Popular Music*. Ed. Freya Jarman-Ivens, 39–57. New York: Routledge.

———. 2008. *Focus: Gamelan Music of Indonesia*. New York: Routledge.

———. 2010. *Erotic Triangles: Sundanese Dance and Masculinity in West Java*. Chicago: The University of Chicago Press.

Steinberg, David Joel, ed. 1987. *In Search of Southeast Asia: A Modern History*. Honolulu: University of Hawaii Press.

Stoler, Ann Laura, with Karen Strassler. 2002. "Memory-Work in Java: A Cautionary Tale." In Ann Laura Stoler, *Carnal Knowledge and Imperial Power: Race and the Intimate in Colonial Rule*, 162–203. Berkeley: University of California Press.

Sumarsam. 1995. *Gamelan: Cultural Interaction and Musical Development in Central Java*. Chicago: The University of Chicago Press.

———. 2008. "Islam, Colonialism, and Javanese Performing Arts: The Lost Gamelan of Gresik." Society for Asian Music Keynote Lecture given at the Society for Ethnomusicology Annual Meeting. Middletown, U.S. October 26.

———. 2011. "Past and Present Issues of Islam within the Central Javanese Gamelan and *Wayang Kulit*." In *Divine Inspirations: Music and Islam in Indonesia*. Ed. David D. Harnish and Anne K. Rasmussen, 45–79. Oxford: Oxford University Press.

Sunardi, Christina. 2007. *Gendered Dance Modes in Malang, East Java: Music, Movement and the Production of Local Senses of Identity*. PhD dissertation. University of California, Berkeley.

———. 2009. "Pushing at the Boundaries of the Body: Cultural Politics and Cross-Gender Dance in East Java." *Bijdragen tot de Taal-, Land- en Volkenkunde* 165/4: 459–492.

———. 2010a. "Making Sense and Senses of Locale through Perceptions of Music and Dance in Malang, East Java." *Asian Music* 41/1: 89–126.

———. 2010b. "Errata, Asian Music 41:1." *Asian Music* 41/2: 227–232.

———. 2011. "Negotiating Authority and Articulating Gender: Performer Interaction in Malang, East Java." *Ethnomusicology* 55/1: 31–54.

———. 2012. "Islam in Java: A Powerful Presence." *Seattle Times* (The *Seattle Times* Newspapers in Education Series), May 31.

———. 2013. "Complicating Senses of Masculinity, Femininity, and Islam through the Performing Arts in Malang, East Java." In *Performance, Popular Culture, and Piety in Muslim Southeast Asia*. Ed. Timothy P. Daniels, 135–160. New York: Palgrave Macmillan.

Sunindyo, Saraswati. 1996. "Murder, Gender, and the Media: Sexualizing Politics and Violence." In *Fantasizing the Feminine in Indonesia*. Ed. Laurie J. Sears, 120–139. Durham: Duke University Press.

Supanggah, Rahayu. 2003. "Campur Sari: A Reflection." *Asian Music* 34/2: 1–20.

Supriyanto, Henri. 1992. *Lakon Ludruk Jawa Timur.* [*East Javanese Ludruk Stories.*] Jakarta: Penerbit PT Gramedia Widiasarana Indonesia.

———. 2001. *Ludruk Jawa Timur: Pemaparan Sejarah, Tonel Direksi, Manajemen dan Himpunan Lakon.* [*East Javanese Ludruk: Historical Analysis, Directors, Management, and Collection of Stories.*] Surabaya: Dinas P dan K Propinsi Jawa Timur.

Suryakusuma, Julia I. 1996. "The State and Sexuality in New Order Indonesia." In *Fantasizing the Feminine in Indonesia*. Ed. Laurie J. Sears, 92–119. Durham: Duke University Press.

Suthrell, Charlotte. 2004. *Unzipping Gender: Sex, Cross-Dressing and Culture.* Oxford: Berg.

Sutton, R. Anderson. 1984. "Who Is the *Pesindhèn*? Notes on the Female Singing Tradition in Java." *Indonesia* 37: 118–133.

———. 1987. "Identity and Individuality in an Ensemble Tradition: The Female Vocalist in Java." In *Women and Music in Cross-Cultural Perspective*. Ed. Ellen Koskoff, 111–130. New York: Greenwood Press.

———. 1991. *Traditions of Gamelan Music in Java: Musical Pluralism and Regional Identity.* Cambridge: Cambridge University Press.

———. 1993. "*Semang* and *Seblang*: Thoughts on Music, Dance, and the Sacred in Central and East Java." In *Performance in Java and Bali: Studies of Narrative, Theatre, Music, and Dance.* Ed. Bernard Arps, 121–143. London: School of Oriental and African Studies, University of London.

———. 2002. *Calling Back the Spirit: Music, Dance, and Cultural Politics in Lowland South Sulawesi.* Oxford: Oxford University Press.

———. 2004. "'Reform Arts'? Performance Live and Mediated in Post-Soeharto Indonesia." *Ethnomusicology* 48/2: 203–228.

Taylor, Diana. 2003. "Acts of Transfer." In *The Archive and the Repertoire: Performing Cultural Memory in the Americas*, 1–52. Durham: Duke University Press.

Thomas, Helen, and Jamilah Ahmed. 2004. Introduction. *Cultural Bodies: Ethnography and Theory*. Ed. Helen Thomas and Jamilah Ahmed, 1–24. Oxford: Blackwell Publishing.

Tiwon, Sylvia. 1996. "Models and Maniacs: Articulating the Female in Indonesia." In *Fantasizing the Feminine in Indonesia*. Ed. Laurie J. Sears, 47–70. Durham: Duke University Press.

———. 2005. "Crossing the Line: Cross Gender Acts as Contemplation." In *Cross Gender*. Idea of Didik Nini Thowok and Yohanes Sigit Supradah. Ed. Setiyono Wahyudi and G. R. Lono Lastoro Simatupang, 109–113. Malang: Sava Media; Yogyakarta: LPK Tari Natya Lakshita.

Turino, Thomas. 2008. *Music as Social Life: The Politics of Participation.* Chicago: The University of Chicago Press.

van Doorn-Harder, Pieternella. 2006. *Women Shaping Islam: Reading the Qur'an in Indonesia*. Urbana: University of Illinois Press.

van Orden, Kate. 2005. "Violence, Dance, and *Ballet de Cour*." In *Music, Discipline, and Arms in Early Modern France*, 81–124. Chicago: The University of Chicago Press.

Vetter, Roger. 1981. "Flexibility in the Performance Practice of Central Javanese Music." *Ethnomusicology* 25/2: 199–214.

Wahyudi, Setiyono, and G. R. Lono Lastoro Simatupang, eds. 2005. *Cross Gender. Idea of Didik Nini Thowok and Yohanes Sigit Supradah*. Malang: Sava Media; Yogyakarta: LPK Tari Natya Lakshita.

Wahyudiyanto. 2006. "Ketika Ngremo Melompat Pagar." ["When Ngremo Jumps the Fence."] In *Cakrawala: Seni Pertunjukan Indonesia*. Ed. Robby Hidajat, 59–78. Malang: Jurusan Seni dan Desain, Fakultas Sastra, Universitas Negeri Malang.

Walton, Susan Pratt. 1996. *Heavenly Nymphs and Earthly Delights: Javanese Female Singers, Their Music and Their Lives*. PhD dissertation. University of Michigan, Ann Arbor.

———. 2007. "Aesthetic and Spiritual Correlations in Javanese Gamelan Music." *Journal of Aesthetics and Art Criticism* 65/1: 31–41.

Weintraub, Andrew N. 2004a. "The 'Crisis of the *Sinden*': Gender, Politics, and Memory in the Performing Arts of West Java, 1959–1964." *Indonesia* 77: 57–78.

———. 2004b. *Power Plays: Wayang Golek Puppet Theater of West Java*. Athens: Ohio University Press; Singapore: Institute of Southeast Asian Studies.

———. 2010. *Dangdut Stories: A Social and Musical History of Indonesia's Most Popular Music*. Oxford: Oxford University Press.

———. 2011. "Morality and Its (Dis)contents: *Dangdut* and Islam in Indonesia." In *Divine Inspirations: Music and Islam in Indonesia*. Ed. David D. Harnish and Anne K. Rasmussen, 318–336. Oxford: Oxford University Press.

Weiss, Sarah. 2002. "Gender(ed) Aesthetics: Domains of Knowledge and 'Inherent' Dichotomies in Central Javanese Wayang Accompaniment." In *Puppet Theater in Contemporary Indonesia: New Approaches to Performance Events*. Ed. Jan Mrázek, 296–314. Ann Arbor: Centers for South and Southeast Asian Studies, University of Michigan.

———. 2003. "*Kothong Nanging Kebak*, Empty yet Full: Some Thoughts on Embodiment and Aesthetics in Javanese Performance." *Asian Music* 34/2: 21–49.

———. 2006. *Listening to an Earlier Java: Aesthetics, Gender, and the Music of Wayang in Central Java*. Leiden: KITLV Press.

Wessing, Robert. 1999. "A Dance of Life: The *Seblang* of Banyuwangi, Indonesia." *Bijdragen tot de Taal-, Land- en Volkenkunde* 155/4: 644–682.

———. 2006. "*Homo Narrans* in East Java: Regional Myths and Local Concerns." *Asian Folklore Studies* 65/1: 45–68.

Wibowo, Susnania Widaryanti. 1996. "Analisis Bentuk Dan Gaya Penyajian Tari Beskalan Lanang Di Desa Ngadireso, Kecamatan Poncokusumo Kabupaten Malang." [Analysis of the Form and Presentation Style of Beskalan Lanang in the Village of Ngadireso, Subdistrict of Poncokusumo, Regency of Malang.] Skripsi Sarjana Pendidikan. Surabaya: Institut Keguruan Dan Ilmu Pendidikan.

Widodo, Amrih. 1995. "The Stages of the State: Arts of the People and Rites of Hegemonization." *RIMA* 29/1 & 2: 1–35.
Wieringa, Saskia. 2002. *Sexual Politics in Indonesia*. New York: Palgrave Macmillan.
Wieringa, Saskia E., and Evelyn Blackwood. 1999. Introduction. In *Female Desires: Same-Sex Relations and Transgender Practices across Cultures*. Ed. Evelyn Blackwood and Saskia E. Wieringa, 1–38. New York: Columbia University Press.
Williams, Raymond. 1977. "Traditions, Institutions, and Formations." In *Marxism and Literature*, 115–120. Oxford: Oxford University Press.
Williams, Sean. 1998. "Constructing Gender in Sundanese Music." *Yearbook for Traditional Music* 30: 74–84.
———. 2001. *The Sound of the Ancestral Ship: Highland Music of West Java*. Oxford: Oxford University Press.
Wilson, Ian Douglas. 1999. "*Reog Ponorogo*: Spirituality, Sexuality, and Power in a Javanese Performance Tradition." *Intersections: Gender and Sexuality in Asia and the Pacific*, Issue 2. http://intersections.anu.edu.au/issue2/Warok.html [accessed July 18, 2014].
Wolbers, Paul Arthur. 1986. "Gandrung and Angklung from Banyuwangi: Remnants of a Past Shared with Bali." *Asian Music* 18/1: 71–90.
———. 1989. "Transvestism, Eroticism, and Religion: In Search of a Contextual Background for the Gandrung and Seblang Traditions of Banyuwangi, East Java." *Progress Reports in Ethnomusicology* 2/6: 1–21.
———. 1993. "The *Seblang* and Its Music: Aspects of an East Javanese Fertility Rite." In *Performance in Java and Bali: Studies of Narrative, Theatre, Music, and Dance*. Ed. Bernard Arps, 34–46. London: School of Oriental and African Studies, University of London.
Wong, Deborah. 2004. *Speak It Louder: Asian Americans Making Music*. New York: Routledge.
Yampolsky, Philip. 1991a. "Songs before Dawn." Liner notes to *Music of Indonesia 1: Songs before Dawn: Gandrung Banyuwangi*. Smithsonian/Folkways Recordings CD SF40055.
———. 1991b. "Indonesian Popular Music." Liner notes to *Music of Indonesia 2: Indonesian Popular Music: Kroncong, Dangdut, and Langgam Jawa*. Smithsonian/Folkways Recordings CD SF40056.
———. 1995. "Forces for Change in the Regional Performing Arts of Indonesia." *Bijdragen tot de Taal-, Land- en Volkenkunde* 151/4: 700–725.
Zurbuchen, Mary S. 2005. "Historical Memory in Contemporary Indonesia." In *Beginning to Remember: The Past in the Indonesian Present*. Ed. Mary S. Zurbuchen, 3–32. Singapore: Singapore University Press in association with Seattle: University of Washington Press.

Discography

Aneka Gending Tari Malangan, Volume 2. n.d. Yogyakarta: Studio LPK Tari Natya Lakshita and Malang: Joyoboyo Studio. Audio cassette.
Tari Topèng Bapang. n.d. Jayabaya. Audio cassette.

Videography

Tari Tradisional Malangan. 2003. Padepokan Seni Mangun Dharma. VCD.
Tyler Perry's Diary of a Mad Black Woman. 2005. Dir. Darren Grant. Santa Monica: Artisan Home Entertainment: Distributed by Lions Gate Home Entertainment. DVD.

Index

Note: Page numbers in italics indicate illustrations.

Andaya, Barbara, 35–36
Anderson, Benedict, 2–3, 4, 37, 64
andhong (itinerant performance), 96–97, 101, 105, 127, 154, 189n8
Asbari, 108
author dance lesson, 169–170

Bahar, Ernaldi, 70
Bapang (male-style masked dance), 15, 17, 22, 60, 112, 130, 163
Becker, Judith, 3, 152
bedhaya (court dance), 34
Benamou, Marc, 7, 56, 185n3
Beskalan (Malangan presentational dance), 13–15, 22–25. See also *Beskalan Lanang* (*Beskalan* in the male style); *Beskalan Putri* (*Beskalan* in the female style); *Beskalan sing asli* (authentic *Beskalan*); *ludruk* (a form of east Javanese popular theater)
Beskalan Lanang (*Beskalan* in the male style), 12, 122; antiquity speculations, 117–121; *Beskalan Putri* (*Beskalan* in the female style) relationship, 117–125; choreographic adaptations, 125; differentiation from *Beskalan Putri* (*Beskalan* in the female style), 121–125; Djupri interpretation, 121–122, 190n21; history and tradition overview, 125–126; Malangan evolution, 124; "maleness" development, 120–125; movement, 43–46; musical differentiation, 121–122; other forms, 120; overview, 13–15; performance contexts, 15–17; tempo adaptation, 123; tuning system, *122*
Beskalan Putri (*Beskalan* in the female style), 12; antiquity, 97, 189n13; *Beskalan Lanang* (*Beskalan* in the male style) relationship, 117–125; *Beskalan sing asli* (authentic *Beskalan*) relationship, 138; boundary transcendance, 141; changes over time, 102; Chattam, 130–135; costumes, 99, 143, 151; court culture tradition, 97–98, 104, 130–140; cross-gender performance reclamation, 144; cultural authority issues, 139–144; cultural preservation concerns, 134–135; dancing/singing separation, 139; dancing/singing traditions, 133–134; Djupri narratives, 96–102; drumming, 115–117, *116*; Dutch colonial era, 104; eroticism, 138; female power, 102–105, 116, 130–135; fertility connection, 104; Hindu-Buddhism element, 99; history and tradition, 125–126, 140; *ilmu* (spiritual knowledge), 98, 136–138, 140–144, 146, 190n10; interpretation variations, 97–98, 150, 188n6; Islam relationship, 100–102; length variations, 127–144; Malangan culture and tradition, 96–99, 102–103, 114, 116–117; male dancer expectations, 88–93; musical compositions, 109–112, *110*; mystical aspect, 143–144;

Beskalan Putri (continued): New Order (Soeharto) relationship, 127–135, 156, 190n1; *Ngremo Lanang* (*Ngremo* in the male style) relationship, 105–106; *Ngremo Putri* (*Ngremo* in the female style) relationship, 106–117; ongoing transformations, 105, 156–157; overviews, 13–15, 127, 156–157; performance contexts, 15–17; performance venue specifications, 141–143, 144, 190n7; philosophical meaning, 151–153; political turmoil and violence impact, 127–129, 190n1; preservation methods, 139–144; rhythm features, 115–116; singing/dancing separation, 132–134, 139; singing/dancing traditions, 133–134; Soleh, 102–103; spiritual inspiration, 136–138; tradition preservation, 156; tuning system, 112–114; video recording session, 171–180; water buffalo, 104. *See also* Muskayah (formerly Sukanthi); *specific performers*

Beskalan sing asli (authentic *Beskalan*): author lesson, 168–170; *Beskalan Putri* (*Beskalan* in the female style) relationship, 138; Chattam adaptations/New Order relationship, 130–132; Didik version, 138; explained, 130, 190n2; Muskayah (formerly Sukanthi) connection, 137; structural outline, *131*; Utomo interpretations, 131–132; video recording session, 171–180

Blackburn, Susan, 60

Blackwood, Evelyn, 10, 11, 74

Boellstorff, Tom, 10–11, 66, 73

Brenner, Suzanne, 36–37, 74, 147, 150

Brinner, Benjamin, 28–29, 159

Browne, Susan, 55

Buckland, Theresa, 27

Butler, Judith, 8, 9, 14

campur sari (popular music style): audience tastes, 83; dancing/singing boundaries, 133; described, 24; drumming, 57; instruments, 57; New Order (Soeharto) effect, 40–41; ongoing audience demand, 31; performers, 48; singing/dancing traditions, 133; tradition preservation concerns, 167; tuning system, 113–114

Chattam, 150–151; *Beskalan Putri* (*Beskalan* in the female style), 56, 104, 130–135, 138, 150–151; Muskayah (formerly Sukanthi), 103; *Ngremo Putri* (*Ngremo* in the female style) and *Beskalan Putri* (*Beskalan* in the female style) and female representations, 107, 109

Clara van Groenendael, Victoria M., 97

Collins, Elizabeth Fuller, 70

Connerton, Paul, 28

Cooper, Nancy, 3, 4, 34–35, 179

court culture, 23–24, 97–98, 104, 130–140. *See also* tradition, history and gender construction

cross-gender dance, 14–15, 20–21. *See also specific dances*

dangdut (popular music style): audience tastes, 24, 31; explained, 24; female economic power, 55, 56; female sexuality issue, 42, 133; Islam, 61; *Ngremo* influence, 83–84, 167; *Ngremo Tayub* (a sub-style of *Ngremo Lanang*), 55; notation, 56–57, *56*; onstage v. offstage gender negotiations, 61; restraint and spiritual power, 35; singing/dancing traditions, 133

Daratista, Inul, 61

Day, Tony, 24, 31

Dharma Wanita (national association of civil servants' wives), 40

Dhedes, 34

Diamond, Beverley, 171

Didik (Didik Nini Thowok): *Beskalan Lanang* (*Beskalan* in the male style) adaptation, 124; *Beskalan Putri* (*Beskalan* in the female style), 136–144, 150–151, 190n5, 190n7; *ilmu* (spiritual knowledge), 136–144, 146, 190n5, 190n7; Old Order (Soekarno) v. New Order (Soeharto), 156

Djadjadiningrat-Nieuwenhuis, Madelon, 149–150

Djupri: audience infatuation and escapism, 77–81; *Beskalan Lanang* (*Beskalan* in the male style), 117–122, 190n21; *Beskalan Putri* (*Beskalan* in the female style), 96–102; female dancers of the past as influence, 44–45; history and the past, 100–101; *ilmu* (spiritual knowledge) protection, 7; *kidungan* (east Javanese singing type), 52; makeup and costuming, 79; Malangan tradition, 113–114; memory synthesization, 144–145; motherhood and spirituality, 149–153; performance expectations, 88; onstage v. offstage gender elements, 80–81; tuning system shifts, 113–114. *See also* Muskayah (formerly Sukanthi)

Downing, Sonja Lynn, 159–160

drumming, *56, 116, 165, 169, 171*; *Beskalan Putri* (*Beskalan* in the female style), 115–117, 130; dancing relationship, 160–162; *Ngremo Lanang* (*Ngremo* in the male

style), 57; *Ngremo Putri* (*Ngremo* in the female style), 83–84, 109, 115–117; *Ngremo Tayub* (a sub-style of *Ngremo Lanang*), 57; patterns, 163. See also *gamelan* (Javanese musical ensemble: gongs, metal-keyed percussion instruments, drums); musicians; notation article on pp. x–xi; *pélog* (tuning system); *sléndro* (tuning system); *specific dance type notation diagrams*
Durga, 104, 189n14

èlmu. See *ilmu*
Errington, Shelly, 170

Female Desires: Same-Sex Relations and Transgender Practices across Cultures (Wieringa and Blackwood), 10
female-style dance by men: dancers' narratives, 67–75; gender expression expectations, 75–93; gender pressures and redefinition, 93; history, 63–67; Islamic ideologies reinforcing traditional masculinity tradition, 64; male dancer narratives, 67–75; maleness ideologies background, 75–93; New Order gender differentiation, 65; Old Order masculine model, 64–65; overviews, 63, 93. See also *Beskalan Putri* (*Beskalan* in the female style); *Ngremo Putri* (*Ngremo* in the female style); *waria* (males who dress and live as female); *specific performers*
female warrior spirit. See Muskayah (formerly Sukanthi); Prabaretna
Foley, Kathy, 140

gamelan (Javanese musical ensemble: gongs, metal-keyed percussion instruments, drums), 19; *andhong* (a type of itinerant performance), 127; *campur sari* (popular music style), 24, 31, 57; *dangdut* (popular music style), 24, 57; female singers, 34, 38, 133, 150, 173; history, 101; leadership, 18; musicians, 186n5; *Ngremo Tayub* (a sub-style of *Ngremo Lanang*), 87; notation systems, 112–114; in performance, 48, 122, 132, 145, 150, 152; performance structure and roles, 18–20; protocol, 15; versatility, 18–19, 130. See also drumming; musicians; *pélog* (tuning system); *sléndro* (tuning system); *specific notation diagrams*
gamelan sekaten (gamelan in court culture tradition), 101
gandrung (social dance type), 20, 102, 189n11

"Ganggong," 110, 111, 189n16, 189n17
Garber, Marjorie, 14
Gatotkaca (legendary masculine hero), 64
Geertz, Clifford, 77, 173
gender and sex: the body, 9–11; boundaries, 7–9; dancers, 17–18; gender differentiation ideologies, 64–67; gendered dance styles, 11–15; gender expression expectations, 75–77, 93; instability, 7–9; musicians, 18–20; performance contexts, 15–17; performance structure and roles, 17–20; relationship, 7–9. See also cross-gender dance; *specific dances*
Gerstein, Julian, 162–163
Gerwani (progressive women's organization), 39, 108, 146
Gold, Lisa, 27
gongsèng (spherical ankle bells for dances), 17–20, 163
Gunung Sari (male-style masked dance), 17, 68, 99, 163

Hahn, Tomie, 8, 28
Halberstam, Judith, 43, 44, 50
Handayani, Sri, *47*, 47–48, *49*, 60–61
Hatley, Barbara, 129
Hefner, Robert, 29–32, 60–61
Hellwig, Jean, 132
Herawati, Luluk Ratna, 44
Heryanto, Ariel, 129
Hidajat, Robby, 104
history. See "Old Order" (Soekarno) v. "New Order" (Soeharto) eras; tradition, history and gender construction
Hughes-Freeland, Felicia, 3, 25, 28, 29, 40

Ibuism, 149–150
"The Idea of Power in Javanese Culture" (Anderson), 2–3, 4
ilmu (spiritual knowledge), 4–7, 79–80, 144–149, 147, 187n9. See also *specific dances*; *specific performers*
Indonesian Communist Party, 39, 40, 128
Indonesian National Army, 37
interactions of performers. See performer interactions
irama (rhythm term), 114–116
Islam, 29–32, 60–61, 73–75, 100–102, 173, 187n8

jaipongan, 132–133, 134
Jaka Umbaran, 98–99, 188n7
jaranan (hobby horse), 97–98, 106

Kadam, 90, 91–93, 161
Kangjeng Ratu Kidul (goddess of the South Sea), 34
Kartini, Raden Adjeng (Javanese noblewoman), 38
Keeler, Ward, 69, 147–148, 177
ketoprak (central Javanese popular theater type), 42, 70, 128, 129
kidungan (east Javanese singing type), 51–55, *51*, *52*, *53*, 81–82, *82*
Klana (male-style masked dance), 17, 56, 67, 69, 163
Kusnadi: author dance lesson, 169–170; *Beskalan Lanang* (*Beskalan* in the male style) choreographic adaptations, 125; *Beskalan Lanang* (*Beskalan* in the male style) recent origin, 119–120; *Beskalan Putri* (*Beskalan* in the female style) - *Ngremo Putri* (*Ngremo* in the female style) movement and drumming relationship, 115–117; drumming, 18, 41, 56; "Ganggong," 189n17; *Ngremo Putri* (*Ngremo* in the female style) and *Beskalan Putri* (*Beskalan* in the female style), 109–112, 189n17; performers' mutual caretaking, 164–165; tempos, 111–112; video recording session, 171–180

langendriyan, 21, 133
Larasati, Rachmi Diyah, 40
lérok (old form of *ludruk*), 70, 71, 154, 187n4. See also *ludruk* (a form of east Javanese popular theater); Supatman
Lestari, 89–90, 161
Li, Siu Leung, 14
ludruk (a form of east Javanese popular theater), 16, 19, 48; explained, 15, 187n4; makeup and costuming, 46–47; musical compositions, 109–112; musicians, *19*; New Order (Soeharto) relationship, 127–129; *Ngremo Lanang* (*Ngremo* in the male style) relationship, 105–106; performance contexts, 15–17; political turmoil and violence impact, 127–129. See also *specific dances*; *tandhak ludruk* (artist who plays female *ludruk* roles; in Malang, most are male); *waria* (males who dress and live as female)
Lysloff, René, 25

Madya, 120, 123
Majapahit (kingdom of the past), 23, 96, 100, 104, 142, 146, 190n6
Malangan (Malang-style), 13–15. See also *specific dances*; *specific performers*
male dancer narratives, 67–75
male-style dance by females, 33–35, 37, 38–42; ambivalence, 33–42; beauty v. handsomeness, 186n5; body appearance boundaries, 43–51; *dangdut* performances, 35; female power variations, 35–42; gender boundaries beyond performance, 58–61; gender boundary negotiation, 43–58; gender negotiation on- and offstage, 58–61; "ideal woman" imagery, 38, 61; Islam, 60–61; makeup and costuming, 46–51; male-female juxtaposition, 46–47; male-female separation efforts, 41–42; movement, 43–46; "Old Order" v. "New Order" eras, 39; overviews, 33, 61–62; performer dance preferences, 58–59; singing, 51–55, *51*, *53*; sonic boundary negotiation, 51–57; violence against women, 40; women in leadership roles, 42; working women tradition, 35–37. See also *specific dances*; *specific performers*
Mama Samsu/Samsuarto: biographical/experiential narrative, 72–75; feminine refinement expectation, 91; generational differences regarding gender ideology, 91; Islam negotiation, 73–75; Reformation era (1998–present), 66–67; *waria* (males who dress and live as female) identity, 66–67, 72, 187n6, 187n7
Mangun Dharma Art Center (PSMD/Padepokan Seni Mangun Dharma), 69, 121, 135–136, 172
masked dance, 13–15. See also *Bapang* (male-style masked dance); *Gunung Sari* (male-style masked dance); *Klana* (male-style masked dance); *specific dances*
Mataram dynasty, 34
Mrázek, Jan, 42
Muliono, *99*; biographical/experiential narrative, 67–70; experiential and performing narrative, 67–70; gender redefinitions, 93, 187n1; *Gunung Sari* (male-style masked dance), 68, *99*; male-female spirituality, 187n1; male-style dance by females, 45–46; marriage, 187n2; name(s), 93, 185n3; wife, 187n3
musical notation, *51*, *53*, *56*. See also drumming; *gamelan*; notation article on pp. x–xi
musicians, *171*. See also drumming; gamelan *sekaten*; musical notation; *specific instruments*; *specific performers*

Muskayah (formerly Sukanthi): audience impact, 152–153; *Beskalan Putri* (*Beskalan* in the female style) and *ilmu* (spiritual knowledge) embodiment, 144–149; birth and death date suppositions, 188n5, 189n13; childhood illness and recovery, 96, 118; dance preferences, 58; ethos preservation, 153–156; femaleness relationship to singing and dancing, 151; healing, 100, 149–150; *Ibuism*, 150; Malang connection, 102–103; martial arts, 58; motherhood and spirituality, 149–153; musician training, 148–149, 190n11; name(s), 188n4; power and knowledge, 100–101, 153–156; Prabaretna link, 98; spiritual potency, 96–97, 98, 101–102, 144–149. See also *Beskalan Putri* (*Beskalan* in the female style); Djupri

"New Order" v. "Old Order" eras. *See* "Old Order" v. "New Order" eras
ngèlmu. *See ilmu*
Ngremo (east Javanese presentational dance), 13–15, 22–25. See also *Ngremo Lanang* (*Ngremo* in the male style); *Ngremo Putri* (*Ngremo* in the female style); *Ngremo Tayub* (a sub-style of *Ngremo* Lanang)
Ngremo Lanang (*Ngremo* in the male style), 48; *Beskalan Putri* (*Beskalan* in the female style) relationship, 105–106; drumming, 56, 57; history and tradition, 125–126; movement, 43–46; musical accompaniment, 55–57, 56; overviews, 13–15, 125–126; performance contexts, 15–17; refinement, 44; singing, 51–55, *51, 53*; Supatman, 70, 71
Ngremo Putri (*Ngremo* in the female style), 76, 111, 165; audience tastes, 83–84; *Beskalan Putri* (*Beskalan* in the female style) relationship, 106–117; costumes, 107–108; *dangdut* (popular music style), 83–84; drumming, 56, 83–84, 109, 115–117, *116, 165*; femaleness and *Beskalan Putri* (*Beskalan* in the female style) influence, 108; female power representations, 116; feminine aspects, 44; *kidungan* (a type of east Javanese singing), 81–82; Malangan culture, 114, 116–117; male dancer expectations, 88–93; movement-drum pattern relationship, 115–117; musical accompaniment, 55–57, 56; musical compositions, 109–112, *110*; "New Order" (Soeharto) developments, 108–109; overviews, 13–15; performance contexts, 15–17; performance expectations by other performers, 84–87; performer ambivalence about *waria* (males who dress and live as female), 86–87; rhythm features, 115–116; singing, 51–55, *51, 53*, 81–82; Supatman, 70, 71; tuning system, 112–114
Ngremo Tayub (a sub-style of *Ngremo* Lanang), 49; drumming, 56, 57; female emphasis in makeup and costume, 46–47; female masculinity, 47–50; feminine look, 44; gender subversion, 45–46; history and tradition, 55–56, 125–126; as Malangan, 52; male-female juxtaposition, 45–46; musical accompaniment, 55–57, 56; overviews, 13–15, 125–126; performance contexts, 15–17; primadonna ambiance, 52; singing, 51–55, *51, 53*; tipping, 50, 53, 55–56, 186–187n7
notation. *See* musical notation; notation article on pp. x-xi; notation diagrams for specific dances

Oetomo, Dédé, 78, 86–87
"Old Order" (Soekarno) v. "New Order" (Soeharto) eras, 37, 44–45, 64–67, 91–93, 108, 109
Onghokham, 65

Padepokan Seni Mangun Dharma (PSMD/ Mangun Dharma Art Center), 69, 121, 135–136, 172
Palupi, Warananingtyas, 58–59, 85
Panji legend, 97
Pawestri, Tjundomanik Tjatur, 67
Peacock, James, 64, 65–66, 77, 78, 92, 129
pélog (tuning system), 112–114, 122
performer dance preferences, 58–59
performer interactions, 156; author experience, 158–160, 167–168, 169–180, 180–181; author lesson, 169–171; dancer-drummer relationship, 160–162; drumming patterns, 163; family member interaction comparison, 160–166; "forgetting" technique, 163–164; mutual caretaking, 164–166; overviews, 158–160, 180–181; performance quality concerns, 166–168; politics, 167–168; recording session, 170–180; selling-buying analogy, 162–164; tradition preservation concerns, 166–168
performer relationships. *See* performer interactions
politics. *See* "Old Order" (Soekarno) v. "New Order" (Soeharto) eras

Prabaretna, 97–99, 100, 102, 118–119, 147, 188n7
Pramono, M. Soleh Adi. *See* Soleh
Prasetya, B. Supriono. *See* Supriono
PSMD (Padepokan Seni Mangun Dharma/Mangun Dharma Art Center), 69, 121, 135–136, 172
puppet, 6, 20, 42, 48, 95, 128–129
puppeteer, 31, 38, 42, 176, 178–179, 191n10

Rao, V. Narayana, 27
rasa (feeling, mood, and/or taste), 5
Rasimoen, 136–144, 156, 172, 190n3
Rasmussen, Anne, 29–32
Redjo, Chattam Amat. *See* Chattam
Reformation era (1998–present), 41–42, 66–67
Riati (Riyati), 136, 172
Ricklefs, M.C., 100
Ross, Laurie Margot, 129, 143

same-gender dance, 14–15
Samsuarto. *See* Mama Samsu/Samsuarto
Schrieber, Karen Elizabeth, 68
seblang (ritual dance type), 20, 148
Sekararum, Karen Elizabeth, 45, 46–47, 54, 123–124, 135–136, 139
sex and gender. *See* gender and sex
Shelemay, Kay Kaufman, 167
Shiraishi, Saya, 38, 64
Singosari (kingdom of the past), 23, 34, 96–97, 100, 103, 188n7
sléndro (tuning system), 51, 53, 112–114
Soeharto, 39. *See also* "Old Order" (Soekarno) v. "New Order" (Soeharto) eras
Soekarno, 39, 64–65. *See also* "Old Order" (Soekarno) v. "New Order" (Soeharto) eras
Soleh: *Beskalan Lanang* (*Beskalan* in the male style), 117–124; *Beskalan Putri* (*Beskalan* in the female style), 102–103, 104, 135–144, 190n5, 190n7; Malang gamelan sets, 112; Muskayah and *Beskalan Lanang* (*Beskalan* in the male style), 118–119; video recording session, 124
Spiller, Henry, 9, 35, 50, 69, 104, 132, 159
spiritual power, 2–7. *See also ilmu* (spiritual knowledge); *specific dancers*; *specific dances*
Srikandi (strong female character in Javanese theater), 37–38, 186n1
Stoler, Ann, 27

Strassler, Karen, 27
Sukanthi. *See* Muskayah (formerly Sukanthi)
Sultan Agung, 34
Sumantri, 104, 107, 109, 130
Sumbadra (refined female character in Javanese theater), 38–40, 61, 186n2
Sumi'anah, 51, 52, 53, 107, 120–121
Supatman, 70–71, 93, 101, 187n4
Supeno, 169; *Beskalan Lanang* (*Beskalan* in the male style), 119; *Beskalan Putri* (*Beskalan* in the female style), 95, 155; *Beskalan sing asli* (authentic *Beskalan*), 169–170; costumes, 79; *ilmu* (spiritual knowledge), 80; *kidungan* (a type of east Javanese singing), 51; Muskayah (formerly Sukanthi), 103, 119, 155; tuning system, 113
Suprapto, Totok. *See* Totok
Supriono: *Beskalan Putri* (*Beskalan* in the female style), 188n6; *Beskalan Putri* (*Beskalan* in the female style) - *Ngremo Putri* (*Ngremo* in the female style) movement and drumming relationship, 115–117; costumes, 108; drumming-dancing relationship, 115, 117; female-style dance by men, 85; *gamelan* (Javanese musical ensemble: gongs, metal-keyed percussion instruments, drums), 173; *kidungan* (a type of east Javanese singing), 81–82; performer interactions, 160–161, 164, 173, 178–180; *tandhak ludruk* (artist who plays female *ludruk* roles; in Malang, most are male), 85; video recording session, 124, 173
Supriyanto, Henri, 107–108, 121, 128
Surabaya Radio Republik Indonesia group, 85
Suradi, 90, 161, 165–166
Surakarta, 34
Suryantono, Stefanus Yacobus, 45, 51, 186n5
Suthrell, Charlotte, 14
Sutrisno, 107, 120–121
Sutton, R. Anderson, 23, 133
Suwarno, Achmad, 56, 164–165
Suwarno, Dennis, 85

tak (sharp, loud drumstroke), 58, 115
tandhak (female singer-dancer or male performer who performs as a female singer-dancer), 17–18, 75, 77–87, 89–91, 135, 174. *See also tandhak ludruk* (artist who plays female *ludruk* roles; in Malang, most are male)

tandhak ludruk (artist who plays female *ludruk* roles; in Malang, most are male), 76, 82; audience tastes and expectations, 77–84, 91; backstage behavior, 90–91; body suit, 80–81, 188n10; comedy, 82; costumes, 80–81, 188n10; *dangdut* (popular music style), 83–84; described, 75–77; drumming, 83–84; gender confusion, 78–79; gender expression expectations, 75–77; generational differences, 91; *ilmu* (spiritual knowledge), 79–80; infatuation and escapism, 77–79; Islam, 78, 89–90; *kidungan* (a type of east Javanese singing), 81–82, *82*; Mama Samsu/Samsuarto, 187n7; "New Order" (Soeharto) gender differentiation effect, 65–66; offstage behavior, 91; passing as women, 85–86; performance expectations by other performers, 84–87; performance structure and roles, 17–20; sexual fantasy of male femininity, 79; singing, 81–82, *82*; spatial boundaries, 90–91; onstage v. offstage gender elements, 80–81; "super-womanliness," 78–79; *waria* (males who dress and live as female) ambivalence, 86–87

Tantric philosophy, 3

tayub (event in which professional female dancers sing and dance with guests for tips), 15, 17, 20, 31, 40–41, 54–55, 57

tayuban. See *tayub* (event in which professional female dancers sing and dance with guests for tips)

tembel/nembel (tipping), 50, 52–53, 55–56, 186–187n7

tembelan. See *tembel/nembel* (tipping)

Thowok, Didik Nini. *See* Didik

Timan, 103, 113, 119, 188n5, 189n13

Totok, 66–67, 72, 73, 74

tradition, history and gender construction: *Beskalan Lanang* (*Beskalan* in the male style), 117–125; *Beskalan Putri* (*Beskalan* in the female style), 96–106; complexity, 24–25, 27–29; courtly culture, 23–24; cultural institutionalization, 23; economic aspects, 24–25; foreign influences, 24; interpretation variations, 26–27; memory and senses of the past, 25–29; *Ngremo Putri* (*Ngremo* in the female style), 106–117; ongoing changes and developments, 27–29; overviews, 94–95, 125–126; "recorded" v. "received" texts, 27; regional culture presentation, 22–25; status and prestige, 24–25. See also *Beskalan sing asli* (authentic *Beskalan*); court culture

Utami, Sri, 52, 54
Utomo, Budi, 131, 171–180, *172*

Vetter, Roger, 114
video recording session, 171–180
violence against women, 40

Wahyu (name of a dancer, see Winarti, Wahyu), *12*, *76*, 171, 177–180
Wahyudiyanto, 128
Wahyuningtyas, Tri, *12*, *46*, 58–59, 124
Walton, Susan, 5
waria (males who dress and live as female): ambivalence toward, 86–87; community acceptance, 88–89; defined, 4; gender expression expectations, 75–77; generational differences, 91–93; Islam negotiation, 73–75, 187n8; Reformation era (1998–present), 66–67. See also *specific waria*
wayang wong (form of dance theater), 20, 133
Weintraub, Andrew, 38, 42
Weiss, Sarah, 5, 95, 140, 159
Wieringa, Saskia, 10, 39
Williams, Raymond, 28
Williams, Sean, 8, 9, 35
Wilson, Ian, 25, 65
Winarti, Wahyu, *12*, *76*, 171, 177–180
Witanto, 124, 161

Yampolsky, Philip, 25

Zurbuchen, Mary, 27

CHRISTINA SUNARDI is an associate professor of music at the University of Washington, Seattle.

New Perspectives on Gender in Music

In Her Own Words: Conversations with Composers
 in the United States   *Jennifer Kelly*
Roll Over Tchaikovsky! Russian Popular Music
 and Post-Soviet Homosexuality   *Stephen Amico*
A Feminist Ethnomusicology: Writings
 on Music and Gender   *Ellen Koskoff*
Stunning Males and Powerful Females: Gender
 and Tradition in East Javanese Dance   *Christina Sunardi*

The University of Illinois Press
is a founding member of the
Association of American University Presses.

Composed in 10.5/13 Adobe Minion Pro
at the University of Illinois Press
Manufactured by Sheridan Books, Inc.

University of Illinois Press
1325 South Oak Street
Champaign, IL 61820-6903
www.press.uillinois.edu